THE POWER OF THE STORY:
Fiction and Political Change

▼ ▼ ▼

THE POWER OF THE STORY:
Fiction and Political Change

▼ ▼ ▼

Michael Hanne

Berghahn Books
Providence • Oxford

Published in 1994 by

Berghahn Books
Editorial offices:
165 Taber Avenue, Providence, RI 02906, U.S.A.
Bush House, Merewood Avenue, Oxford OX3 8EF, UK

© Michael Hanne
All rights reserved.
No part of this publication may be reproduced
in any form or by any means without the permission
of Berghahn Books.

Library of Congress Cataloging-in-Publication Data
Hanne, Michael.
    The power of the story : fiction and political change / Michael Hanne.
        p.   cm.
    Includes bibliographical references and index.
    Contents: Narrative and power -- Ivan Turgenev : A sportsman's notebook (1852) -- Harriet Beecher Stowe : Uncle Tom's cabin (1852) -- Ignazio Silone : Fontamara (1933) -- Alexander Solzhenitsyn : One day in the life of Ivan Denisovich (1962) -- Salman Rushdie : The satanic verses (1988).
    ISBN 1-57181-019-6
    1. Fiction--19th century--History and criticism. 2. Fiction--20th century--History and criticism. 3. Political fiction--History and criticism. I. Title.
PN3499.H28   1994   94-36032
809.3'9358--dc20   CIP

British Library Cataloguing in Publication Data
A CIP catalog record for this book is available from
the British Library.

Printed in the United States.

*To my parents, and to Marija,
who, in their different ways,
made this book possible*

CONTENTS

▼ ▼ ▼

ACKNOWLEDGMENTS	iv
1. NARRATIVE AND POWER	1
2. IVAN TURGENEV: *A Sportsman's Notebook* (1852)	43
3. HARRIET BEECHER STOWE: *Uncle Tom's Cabin* (1852)	75
4. IGNAZIO SILONE: *Fontamara* (1933)	114
5. ALEXANDER SOLZHENITSYN: *One Day in the Life of Ivan Denisovich* (1962)	146
6. SALMAN RUSHDIE: *The Satanic Verses* (1988)	189
BIBLIOGRAPHY	242

ACKNOWLEDGMENTS

▼ ▼ ▼

This book has taken many years to research and to write — in fact my daughter, Polly, who is twenty-one, claims she can't remember a time when I wasn't working on it! While this may be an exaggeration, it is certainly true that, over the years, a great number of friends and colleagues in different parts of the world have read or heard parts of it, and have offered insights and suggested improvements deriving from their own specialisms and experience for which I am deeply grateful.

In the United States, I thank especially: Ed Ahearn, Tony Oldcorn, Olga Ragusa, Frank Rosengarten, Eduardo Saccone, and Alberto Traldi. In Britain, I have received valuable assistance from Mike Caesar, Judy Rawson, and Adalgisa Giorgio. In Italy, Silvia Albertazzi, Giovanna Capone, Elvio Guagnini, and Geno Pampaloni have been most generous with their time and expertise. In Australia, John Gatt-Rutter, Alastair Davidson, and colleagues in the English department of La Trobe University have helped with detailed comments on early versions of my text. In New Zealand: David Bevan (now moved to Canada), Ian Carter, Jonathan Lamb, Nick Perry, Malcolm Read, Jane Schaverien, Laurence Simmons, and Terry Sturm have all contributed in crucial ways to the many stages through which this project has passed.

It is another sort of debt that I owe to the students on whom I have tried out ideas for this book over the years and whose responses and comments have helped to shape it. I am especially pleased to express my admiration and thanks to three graduate students with whom I have worked in recent years and from I have learned so much: Paula Green, Susan Jacobs, and Charlotte Wrightson.

There is another group of people again whose assistance I warmly acknowledge: the patient and skilled librarians of the many libraries around the world in which I have undertaken the research for this book. Most particularly I express my deep gratitude and appreciation to the

Acknowledgments

dedicated staff of the Information Services department, directed by Cathie Hutchinson, of the library at my own institution, the University of Auckland, New Zealand, who have solved knotty bibliographical problems for me on a daily basis over a very long period.

I wish also to thank the University of Auckland for several research grants and periods of study leave which have greatly facilitated the writing of this book.

I am most grateful to Marion Berghahn for the care and professionalism with which she has handled each stage of publication. Brian Johnson has been a splendid copy editor, in particular untangling some awkward sentences with an almost infallible sense of what I *really* wanted to say.

Finally I offer my love and my thanks to Marija Radić, whose confidence in this project has sustained me and whose critical acumen, as she has read drafts of each chapter, has helped me to avoid so many pitfalls.

1. NARRATIVE AND POWER

▼ ▼ ▼

The political "impact" of fiction

Can a novel start a war, free serfs, break up marriages, drive readers to suicide, close factories, bring about a law change, swing an election, or serve as a weapon in a national or international struggle? These are some of the large-scale, direct, social and political effects which have been ascribed to certain exceptional novels and other works of narrative fiction over the last two hundred years or so.[1] How seriously should we take such claims?

In their crudest form, assertions of this kind are obviously naive, oversimplifying the complex ways in which literary texts can be said to "work in the world" and oversimplifying, too, the causal processes required to account for a major social or political change. But is it possible to modify or refine such claims in the light of contemporary theory and historical research so that the mechanisms by which each text has engaged with the political forces of the time are adequately described? This book explores that general question through the close examination of five works, from several different countries and periods, for which remarkable direct political effects of one kind or another have been claimed. It is an inquiry both at the level of theory (in what sense, and by what mechanisms, might literary works conceivably be said to start wars, swing national opinion, and so on?) and at the level of history (what evidence can be gathered on the influence which a particular fictional narrative has had in a given place and at a given time?).

The first two works studied, Ivan Turgenev's *A Sportsman's Notebook* and Harriet Beecher Stowe's *Uncle Tom's Cabin* (both published in volume form in 1852), are probably the pieces of narrative fiction for which the most spectacular claims have been made. It was Turgenev's boast, echoed later by many historians and literary critics, that his *A Sportsman's Notebook*, a collection of short stories or sketches rather than a novel, was directly responsible for convincing Tsar Alexander II to abolish serfdom in Russia. And it was Abraham Lincoln, no less, who addressed Harriet Beecher Stowe, when they met in late 1862, with the words: "So this is the little lady who made this great war" (the American Civil War). Although Lincoln probably did not mean his words to be taken at face value, many politicians and historians in the years that followed independently attributed to *Uncle Tom's Cabin* a major role in bringing about the war and thereby hastening the abolition of slavery.

Ignazio Silone's novel *Fontamara* (1933), the third work studied, is remarkable not only for the fact that it is claimed to have played a significant role in turning around the broadly favorable opinion of Mussolini's Fascism still held by large numbers of political commentators in the United States and Europe in the early 1930s, but for having achieved several more, distinct, politically significant receptions since its first publication, including in Italy during the Second World War and in Third World countries in the postwar period.

In the case of Alexander Solzhenitsyn's *One Day in the Life of Ivan Denisovich* (1962), whose publication Khrushchev personally authorized to further his discrediting of Stalin, it is not a question of the novel's having achieved a specific reform (as Solzhenitsyn complained, the labor camps continued to operate fairly much unchanged) but of its having engaged in an extraordinarily dramatic way with the mechanisms of power of a relatively closed political system.

I doubt that the publication of any previous work of narrative fiction has engendered quite such immediate and dramatic reverberations on the level of international relations as the fifth work I examine, Salman Rushdie's *The Satanic Verses* (1988). Readers of this book will know of: the street protests, resulting in deaths, in several cities in Muslim countries; the demonstrations by members of the Muslim immigrant communities in Britain, Canada, and other western countries at which copies of the book were burned; the repeated calls made to devout Muslims by the Ayatollah Khomeini and, since his death, other Islamic religious leaders to "execute" Rushdie for blasphemy; which were followed, in turn, by counter-protests from western countries including the temporary withdrawal from Teheran of the heads of diplomatic missions of all the European Community countries; the killing of several individuals associated with translating, publishing, or defending the book, and so on. (The story took further twists in 1993 with the bombing of a hotel in Turkey where a publisher intending to bring out a Turkish translation of the novel was staying and the wounding of the novel's Norwegian translator.)

Of course, the mere fact that these events have followed the publication of *The Satanic Verses* does not necessarily mean that they should be thought of as causally connected consequences or effects of its publication. Indeed, the issue of the extent to which Rushdie can be held responsible for those events is, itself, a hotly debated topic. Unique though the case of *The Satanic Verses* might seem, it actually exemplifies a broad problem about causality which is common to all the works I shall be examining. When we talk loosely of the political *impact* of a novel, that metaphor implies that effects have followed from its publication by the simplest causal connection, like ripples moving outwards when a pebble is tossed into a still pool. It must be immediately obvious not only that Rushdie's novel possesses a quite un-pebble-like complexity as a cultural object but that the political pool into which it was tossed was already extremely turbulent. Much the same point would have to be made about each of the other works I shall be examining and the historical moments at which they first appeared. *One Day in the Life of Ivan Denisovich*, for instance, appeared in the Soviet Union at precisely the time of the Cuban missile crisis. This leads many commentators to a contrary oversimplification, according to which the literary work is treated as having no causal value, being no more than a symptom of an historical change already under way.

"A good book ... is a force a tool *a weapon* to make the dreams of today become the reality of tomorrow," wrote Roger Garaudy.[2] In several of the cases I shall be examining, the image of the fictional narrative as a weapon in a continuing struggle, a weapon for hitting at some institution or for striking a blow in favor of an oppressed group, will be seen to have considerable validity — *Uncle Tom's Cabin* as a weapon against slavery, *Fontamara* as a weapon against fascism, for instance. In his review of *One Day in the Life of Ivan Denisovich*, Cyril Connolly declared that "it is a blow struck for human freedom all over the world."[3] The particular aptness of the metaphor lies, however, in the fact that fictional texts, like other sorts of weapons, may be seized and used to serve the causes of different parties in a conflict and even, as we shall see, in several different conflicts.

The issue of *The Satanic Verses* as a weapon (and, at least as important, whose weapon and in which conflict!) is as contentious as every other issue surrounding this remarkable novel. While there can be little doubt that Salman Rushdie did intend certain episodes in the novel as satirical attacks on religious and political bigotry in general and the Ayatollah Khomeini in particular (*and* Margaret Thatcher, the racism of the British police force, and numerous other targets) he nevertheless strenuously and, to me, convincingly denies that he intended it to be an attack on Islam itself. (Making a somewhat similar distinction, Harriet Beecher Stowe insisted that her novel attacked slavery but not Southerners. Most Southerners, however, were not convinced.) At a certain point, however, authors' political intentions — which, like authorial intentions in general, are in any case ultimately unknowable — in a sense become irrelevant, as groups of readers wittingly or unwittingly appropriate the text for their own purposes. Writers have no means of limiting, let alone absolutely determining, the readings to which their works will be subjected. (I shall be examining in some detail the surprising discrepancy between Turgenev's apparently dilettantist intentions in writing *A Sportsman's Notebook* and the political seriousness with which it was subsequently interpreted.)

The openness of many fictional texts to quite widely divergent readings by distinct groups of readers, especially groups which differ in nationality, religion, gender or class, will be a recurrent theme of this book. And, as much contemporary literary theory makes clear, there is no reason to think of any of those readings as necessarily mistaken. *The Satanic Verses* has of course been read quite differently by Muslim and non-Muslim readers (as well as by different Muslim groups — though this point is usually ignored). The existence of several different constituencies of readers for some fictional works is an issue which is rarely examined. When I come to discuss Silone's *Fontamara*, for instance, I shall detail the significant political differences between the readings of it by American, Italian, and Third World readers. Many of those who have protested against *The Satanic Verses* (some of whom have died during demonstrations against it) have, it is well known, not read the novel — indeed refuse to read it on conscientious grounds — and base their protest on hearsay. Even in this respect, Rushdie's novel is not unique: southern anger against *Uncle Tom's Cabin* was probably fiercest amongst those Southerners who refused to read it. It will be one of the odder features of my book that, in at least these two cases, it will be necessary to study the impact of a fictional text on the political attitudes of *nonreaders* of the work!

In the eyes of many Westerners, *The Satanic Verses* only became a weapon of any seriousness when certain Islamic fundamentalist leaders made it into one. They, it is suggested, appropriated the novel and turned it into an instrument of terrorism against the tolerant, rational pluralism of the West. The deficiency in this argument is that it takes no account of the historical relationship between the West and the Muslim nations of the Middle East, which is characterized by gross inequalities of power and, on the side of the West, by an almost uniform ignorance, indifference and/or fear towards Islam. So, whatever Rushdie's intentions, it has been convincingly argued by, among others, Edward Said, that his novel offered to the West an opportunity for the further denigration of a religion and culture already at a disadvantage. More generally, it is true that any serious assessment of the political "impact" of any work must focus on the effects it has had on an already existing power relation.

The extent to which works of narrative fiction may be thus largely appropriated by a dominant political discourse is remarkable. George Orwell made clear that he intended in *1984* to denounce, from the perspective of a democratic socialist, the totalitarian features of both Soviet communism and western capitalism. Nevertheless, his novel was exploited, during the 1950s at least, almost exclusively as a source of propaganda material against any form of socialism, supplying terms like "Newspeak," "Thought Police," and so on for use in antisocialist newspaper articles and speeches. As Isaac Deutscher wrote: "A book like *1984* may be used without much regard for the author's intention. Some of its features may be torn out of their context, while others which do not suit the political purpose which the book is made to serve, are ignored or virtually suppressed."[4]

None of this means, of course, that *The Satanic Verses* has not also been appropriated as a weapon in several struggles by those fundamentalist Shi'ite leaders who have called for Rushdie's execution. Such attempts at antagonistic appropriation and exploitation of a narrative work are not so rare as might be supposed. As I shall be showing in a later chapter, proslavery Southerners sought to use *Uncle Tom's Cabin* as a rallying point for southern feeling against the North almost as much as abolitionists used it as a propaganda weapon against slavery. Harriet Beecher Stowe's novel, like Rushdie's, became, one might say, a piece of ambiguously located cultural territory over which conflicting parties claimed authority, a borderland, vulnerable, as such territory always is, to skirmishes, provocations and downright violent conflict.

Nevertheless, just as an author's intention may, on occasions, seriously misfire, so, too, may the attempts of those who consciously try to seize control of a literary text for their own political purpose. Since the instrumental political use of a work of literary fiction usually involves a narrow, even closed, reading of the text, it sometimes happens that the text opens out in ways which do not suit the interests of those who were seeking to appropriate its meaning to their sole use. As Nikita Khrushchev found, when he approved publication of *One Day in the Life of Ivan Denisovich* for the purpose of discrediting his Stalinist opponents in the Presidium, narrative fiction sometimes resists such opportunistic rough handling and blows up in the face of those who attempt it. Those who seek to appropriate the meaning of a literary work cannot necessarily impose that exclusive reading on other readers any more than the author can impose his or her intended meaning.

It should by now be clear that the title of this book, *The Power of the Story*, is deliberately provocative. Certainly, on one level, it is a study of the kinds of power which a number of exceptional works of narrative fiction are claimed to have exerted at moments of major political change. Nevertheless, it attempts to reframe those claims in terms of statements about the nature of the engagement each work achieved in an historical situation where certain patterns of distribution of political power already existed. Eventually it asks whether publication of that work facilitated, was a catalyst in, any shifts in the distribution of power.

My attitudes to many questions will doubtless emerge in the course of this book, but I feel I should make clear here my commitment on two issues, which I see as having considerable intellectual, educational and political implications. First, I aim in this book to demonstrate, in my own way of working, the necessity of integrating literary theory with critical practice, of constantly applying and testing theory on concrete historical instances, if theory is not to remain remote and hermetically self-contained, and if criticism is not to be theoretically unsound. Precisely because the particular pieces of narrative fiction examined here are, in one way or another, extreme cases, they severely test, and demonstrate the limitations of, the various theoretical approaches applied to them. Secondly, I am committed to writing in a nonelitist way about a subject that I believe to be intellectually demanding and politically significant. So, while I hope that I shall satisfy academic readers that I have developed convincing and — in some ways, quite new — arguments, that I have reflected the latest scholarship in a number of academic fields, that I have documented my sources of evidence carefully, I am also determined that this book should be accessible to a wider audience. By avoiding obscurantism and mystification, I hope that this book will serve to *empower* general readers, with no great previous knowledge of literary theory, in their thinking about just how, in some extraordinary instances, works of literary fiction have had a measurable effect in shaping political attitudes and events.

Narrative as a "primary cognitive instrument"

One way of defining the subject of this book is to say that it poses questions about how fiction relates to history, and specifically about the problem of locating certain kinds of fiction *in* history. It asks how social and political history can be written which takes due account of the role played by some exceptional works of narrative fiction in shaping particular political outcomes. It therefore begins with the simple reminder that novels and historical writing are both forms of narrative, both instances, among many other possible instances, of the universal human practice of storytelling. Whether in the form of dreams, myths of origin, memoirs, reports of scientific experiments, evidence given in court, tribal genealogies, novels, histories, printed or electronic news, economic predictions, biographies, folktales, soap operas, annual reports of corporations, feature films, diaries, erotic fantasies, medical case histories, or strip cartoons, there is no getting away from storytelling.

A number of thinkers have seized on this point over the last twenty years, among them Roland Barthes, who stated that "the narratives of the world are numberless ... narrative is present in every age, in every place, in every society; it begins with the very history of mankind [*sic*] and there nowhere is nor has been a people without narrative ... narrative is international, transhistorical, transcultural: it is simply there like life itself."[5] Even so, most commentators do not hold on to this recognition for very long, hurrying on to examine in isolation just one of the traditionally acknowledged narrative forms. Only occasionally do students of literary narrative pause for a moment to peer over the fence they have built around their chosen field. So Jonathan Culler ends a closely argued article on the analysis of literary narrative with the comment that "we still do not appreciate as fully as we ought the importance of narrative schemes and models in all aspects of our lives."[6] And Thomas M. Leitch ends his recent book, *What Stories Are: Narrative Theory and Interpretation*, with the suggestion that the great neglected question about narrative is "what stories do."[7] I aim to respond here to the challenges implied by both statements in that I examine the question of what certain fictional stories may be said to have "done" in terms of "narrative schemes and models" which cut across the traditional boundaries between the many forms of storytelling in which we are constantly entwined. I shall attempt to define just how each may be said to have "worked in the world" — using the term "worked" in all its possible senses: labored, succeeded, functioned, produced, fermented, and so on.

Storytelling, it must be recognized from the start, is always associated with the exercise, in one sense or another, of power, of control. This is true of even the commonest and apparently most innocent form of storytelling in which we engage: that almost continuous internal narrative monologue which everyone maintains, sliding from memory, to imaginative reworking of past events, to fantasizing about the future, to daydreaming.

Such internal storytelling is the radar-like mechanism we use to constantly scan the world around us, by which we give order to, and claim to find order in, the data of experience. If we cannot narrate the world in this everyday manner, we are unable to exercise even the slightest degree of control, or power, in relation to the world. It is our internal narrative faculty that makes it possible for each of us perpetually to construct and reconstruct our sense of ourselves as individuals, located socially and in time and space. Just occasionally, that narrative faculty fails for a moment — the traveler wakes in a hotel room in a foreign city and for a brief time is unable to construct any recollection of the immediate past, and so has no idea where he or she is, nor any anticipation of the day to come. Few moments are quite so bewildering.

One of the essential functions which such everyday telling of stories to oneself performs is that it enables us to discard massive quantities of material which we deem to be unimportant. In allowing us to *exclude* so much of our experience, it permits us to retain just a few items which we regard as significant, which have "point" for us. As Jean-François Lyotard paradoxically asserts, narrative is, in some respects, a mechanism for consuming the past, for forgetting.[8] In this sense, too, it involves an exercise by the narrator of a form of power, a sorting and reckoning-up of experience. Such storytelling, it should be emphasized, relates just as much to the future — to hopes, fears, plans, and alternative scenarios — as it does to the past.

It has been suggested by a number of recent thinkers that narration may, indeed, be the most fundamental of all human psychological operations. Fredric Jameson, for example, describes it as "the all-informing process ... the central function or *instance* of the human mind"[9] and

Hayden White observes that the word "narrate" derives from the same Sanskrit root *gna* as the Latin and Greek words for "know."[10] The implication would seem to be that there is, perhaps, no "knowing" which does not involve "narrating." And to assert that one "knows" something is to assert a kind of power over it. Louis O. Mink, a philosopher of history, develops this point, by arguing that "narrative is a primary cognitive instrument — an instrument rivalled only by theory and by metaphor as irreducible ways of making the flux of experience comprehensible."[11] And, while most modern scientists assert that they have left behind the fanciful storytelling of their predecessors in favour of rigorous "scientific method," some philosophers of science, P. B. Medawar for instance, insist that there is no such thing as scientific method and that a scientist is, above all, a person who "tells stories."[12]

Our psychological dependence on storytelling is perhaps best illustrated by the fact that most mental disorders, from amnesia to phobias, and from obsessional compulsions to schizophrenia, can be interpreted as breakdowns in the individual's capacity to construct and appropriately weave together the whole repertoire of internal narratives. It is widely recognized, for example, that criminals who are repeatedly caught and convicted for similar offences characteristically lack the general capacity to foretell accurately the consequences of their (and probably other people's) actions. They are poor at telling stories about the future. James Hillman, the psychotherapist, says more generally, "those who have a connection with story are in better shape and have a better prognosis than those to whom story must be introduced … to have 'story-awareness' is *per se* psychologically therapeutic."[13]

Storytelling is, of course, more commonly thought of as a communication between (at least) two people, narrator and narratee. In fact the simple definition of story offered by the literary theorist, Barbara Herrnstein Smith, is "someone telling someone else something that happened."[14] It involves, then, an interactional process, an assertion of power not only over the matter shaped into narrative but over the audience for the story. As Ross Chambers expresses it, "to tell a story is an act, an event, one that has the power to produce change, and first and foremost to change the relationship between narrator and narratee."[15]

Storytelling, indeed, is probably the prime mechanism by which we negotiate our way through the more demanding moments of our daily lives. We use stories to explain, to persuade, to justify, to propose, to accuse, to deny guilt, and so on. And, inevitably, such interaction by storytelling operates within already established contexts of power. Chambers, again, declares, "narrative mediates human relationships and derives its 'meaning' from them ... consequently, it depends on social agreements, implicit pacts or contracts, in order to produce exchanges that themselves are a function of desires, purposes and constraints."[16]

The metaphor used fruitfully by Chambers to describe the process by which a story exercises power over the narratee is "seduction."[17] The significance of the seductive nature of narrative is that the point of a story is established, indeed imposed on the narratee, in terms of the story's whole narrative form and development. So, for instance, it is much harder to counter a racist story (whether it purports to be a factual record of personal experience or a simple joke) than it is to demonstrate the nastiness and inaccuracy of more direct forms of racist statement. Narrators of racist stories will often simply deny that their story has racist implications, or insist that "it's just a story," or respond with "but I'm only telling you what happened." It is usually impossible to invalidate such a story by pointing out logical faults or statistical errors as one can with more abstract observations about, for example, the unwillingness of a particular racial group to do hard work. To counter the racist point of a story, it is necessary to combat the story in its totality. In fact listeners are often caught up in a story before it becomes entirely obvious that its point is racist or sexist. Chambers argues that a story typically has "the power to control its own impact through situational self-definition."[18] In other words, storytellers are seldom required to make explicit the presuppositions on which their story is based — and the story's "point" may also remain implicit.

Storytelling and social change

Much recent discussion of narrative has brought together evidence and argument to suggest that storytelling serves in general to reinforce an existing social order, existing power structures. Robert Scholes, a literary theorist, explores the notion that "traditional narrative structures are ... part of a system of psychosocial dependencies that inhibit human growth and significant social change."[19] Robert Anchor, a theorist of history, argues that all storytelling contributes to the reproduction of dominant ideology: "historical narratives, no less than fictional narratives, always serve in one way or another, to legitimize an actual or ideal social reality."[20] Louis O. Mink observes that narrative is central to the social transmission of culture, "storytelling is the most ubiquitous of human activities, and in any culture it is the form of complex discourse that is earliest accessible to children and by which they are largely acculturated."[21]

Evidence for such an argument is available in every field of storytelling. The part played by folktales, with their active young male heroes, passively beautiful maidens waiting for their prince to come, and wicked older women (stepmothers and witches), in acculturating young people to stereotypical gender roles has been very well documented.[22] The process by which news stories in the media purport to *inform* mass audiences, but function at least as much to *form* them in attitudes which *conform* to orthodox and politically conservative social conditions, has also been fully examined.[23] It is, likewise, not difficult to show that the annual reports of corporations are usually framed to tell the story of the previous year in a way which suggests that the corporation's health is entirely (and appropriately) defined by the interests of shareholders and management rather than those of the labor force, or that tribal genealogies perform the function of legitimating the dominant position of certain individuals or castes within the tribal organization.

Most work on this issue has been done in the historical field, where many (though by no means all) thinkers would agree with Nancy Whittier Heer's broad claim that "historiography functions in any political system to socialize the coming generation, to legitimate political institutions, to perpetuate established mores and mythology, and to rationalize official policies."[24] Hayden White has argued that historians construct the stories they tell around a moralizing "point," yet propagate, and often actually subscribe to, the illusion that they have merely uncovered stories which were somehow objectively there.[25] Feminists and activists from working-class and oppressed racial groups have demonstrated that history, as traditionally conceived, has excluded from its narration elements which would have given that narration a very different point — or, indeed, it has suppressed entire stories ("herstory", for instance) which might have been told. Historical writing by and large privileges the experience of the dominant class, race, and gender by failing to record the experience or perspective of subordinate groups.

The processes by which storytelling performs such a conservative, legitimating function are readily defined. Storytelling, it is argued, is a fundamentally *reductive* (as well as *seductive*!) process. It mystifies our understanding by giving a false sense of coherence and comprehensiveness to a selection of scattered events. Moreover every story necessarily operates in terms of one or another set of pre-existing (social) conventions — whether those of the folktale, or the television news report, or academic historical writing, and so on. Linguists Edward Sapir and B. L. Whorf have argued that all human utterances are constrained by the inherited language available to the person uttering them.[26] Not only is it impossible to express any concept that one's language is not structured to express, but the language of each society or social group even places limits on what members can perceive and think. This leads Sapir and Whorf to the aphorism that people do not speak languages, rather languages speak people. Similarly it may be argued that every piece of storytelling (even including stories one tells to oneself) is constrained by the storytelling codes or conventions available to the teller — conventions which are rooted in a particular historical situation and operate in relation to a particular social formation. So a further aphorism can be proposed: people do not tell stories, rather stories tell people.

A number of theorists, among them the philosopher Jean-François Lyotard, have, moreover, recently coined the useful term "metanarratives" (or "grand narratives") to denote certain overarching sets of religious, historical, and political assumptions structured in narrative terms: the belief in, for instance, decline after a golden age, or the expectation of a last judgement, or of reincarnation, the vision of history as progress or emancipation, and so on, the entire range of narratives which have functioned at certain times as legitimating frameworks shared by whole societies. They are controlling narratives of which the individuals and groups who live within them are not even perhaps consciously aware, though every lesser narrative bears the imprint of the metanarrative. Metanarratives can, in general, only be fully identified after they have ceased to be fully effective.[27]

Evidence for the argument that stories typically perform acculturating, mystifying or legitimating roles is, of course, massive and readily visible in every social arena: the schoolroom, the bar, the mass media, the hospital, the commercial world, the justice system, and so on. But are these really the *only* roles stories can perform? Both common sense and recent experience suggest many ways in which storytelling may also be disruptive, progressive, liberating.

To tell a previously "untold story" is an act which can be extraordinarily disruptive to the existing social order. This is perhaps most vividly illustrated by the work done by journalists in telling of events which governments or other kinds of authority want to keep hidden, such as the Watergate affair or the Iran-Contra scandal. Equally important, and disruptive of an existing power relation, are the actions of those women in western societies who have, in recent years, felt able for the first time to recount stories of the incest and other sexual abuses to which they have been subjected.[28] The psychological discomfort of feeling prohibited from retelling to others a story one regularly tells to oneself is well recognized. To tell such a story, especially, in the first instance to other women who have undergone the same experience, allows abused women to attribute blame appropriately (especially to stop blaming themselves), to raise their collective consciousness of gender issues, and eventually to convince a wider public of the existence of this large-scale, long-term social problem. Most importantly, once (potential) abusers realize that such stories are now "tellable," some, at least, are discouraged from continuing to abuse because of the criminal and other sanctions to which telling makes them subject. Telling untold stories may, in certain circumstances, positively empower oppressed people and diminish the offensive power of their oppressors. (Strictly speaking, as Hayden White has shown, there is no such thing as an untold story, since a story does not exist until it has been told.[29] So-called "untold stories" are stories whose elements are being shaped into narrative form for the first time, or stories which have previously only been told internally by people to themselves, or told in private, or, as frequently occurs, told but subsequently suppressed.)

There are many recent examples of historians who have contributed to a radical transformation of dominant ideology by writing history which includes factual material or perspectives previously excluded. The history of the United States has been rewritten by Mary Frances Berry and others in a black, rather than a white, key.[30] The story of the Industrial Revolution in Britain has been told by E. P. Thompson from the perspective of agricultural and industrial workers, rather than that of the bourgeoisie.[31] The history of western literature is being rewritten by Ellen Moers, Dale Spender and many other feminist critics in a woman-centered, rather than man-centered, form.[32] Feminists have also demonstrated the empowering effects of exposing young children to folktales and other stories with characters who offer a wider variety of role-models for boys and girls than were previously available.[33]

Study of previously untold stories leads to the recognition that storytelling is a fundamentally competitive activity. Whereas most stories are covertly competitive, in the sense that, as we have seen, their telling suppresses alternative or contrary emplotments of the same events, there are many social situations in which we expect to witness overtly competitive storytelling. Probably the most vivid example of overt competition in storytelling in a formally sanctioned setting is provided by the criminal courtroom, where, in the Anglo American adversarial system at least, prosecution and defense tell alternative stories of the same series of events. The summing-up and judgement with which the trial ends not only indicate which parts of each story the judge found well-formed and convincing but tell a third story which purports to narrate "the truth" of the matter and, because it is backed by the institutional power of the judicial system, entails serious practical consequences (a conviction or not, punishment or not). There are many other situations in public life where overtly competitive narratives are displayed in a framework which is supposed to facilitate decision-making. So, for example, city planners will offer a set of competing scenarios for the introduction of a rapid transport system, so that city councillors — and, hopefully, the public — may choose between them. By and large it seems true that the very act of making overt the competitive nature of the narration is progressive.

The claims which have been made for the political effectiveness of all of the first four works I examine here include assertions that they have told for the first time a story which had previously been suppressed: *A Sportsman's Notebook* is supposed to have told previously untold stories about serfdom, *Uncle Tom's Cabin* about slavery, *Fontamara* about Italian Fascism, *One Day in the Life of Ivan Denisovich* about the labor camps. The case of *The Satanic Verses* is much more complicated.

There are a number of other ways, in addition to the telling of untold stories, by which narrative can act in a productively disruptive way. Ross Chambers argues that the seductive character of narrative makes it, by its very nature, noncoercive and, indeed, a tool for use against coercion: "Such seduction, producing authority where there is no power, is a means of converting (historical) weakness into (discursive) strength. As such, it appears as a major weapon against alienation, an instrument of self-assertion, and an 'oppositional practice' of considerable significance."[34] The question then remains as to whether oppositional practices of this kind are merely *tactical*, in the sense that they achieve a temporary advantage without disturbing the underlying power relation, or whether they are *strategic* acts which really upset the existing structure of power.[35] (Incidentally, I believe Chambers overstates his case in suggesting that the seductive character of narrative means that it tends generally to be a tool against coercion. I shall argue that while the seductive force of storytelling may on occasions be used for oppositional purposes, it has much more often been used, like seduction in its literal sense, to reinforce a relationship of dominance. There are, sadly, many more misogynist than feminist anecdotes and many more racist than anti-racist jokes in circulation.)

Frequently in societies I am familiar with (and my guess is that this is a very nearly universal social practice), the telling of one story will trigger the telling of other stories by other members of a group, which illustrate the same theme or respond to the same question. Such sequential storytelling usually has a competitive element to it, involving "capping" a story that someone else has just told with another: my story is claimed to be more dramatic, or more extraordinary, or funnier than yours. The sociolinguist, William Labov, has done some remarkable work in collecting strings of stories told by members of clearly identifiable communities in, for instance, Harlem, to whom he has posed questions such as: "Were you ever in a situation where you thought you were in serious danger of getting killed?"[36] (Many fictional literary works — Boccaccio's *Decameron* is a wonderful example — imitate this naturally occurring pattern whereby stories develop in strings. The ten stories of each day of the *Decameron*, after the first, illustrate a new theme, defined at the start of the day. So all the stories of Day Four, for example, relate to "loves which ended disastrously.") The broad social function of such story strings may be seen as generally conservative, communicating traditional wisdom or widely held concerns or beliefs (life is perilous, love often does end disastrously, and so on). But it is clear that, in certain circumstances, the telling of a different kind of story (often a previously untold story) will trigger the telling of other stories of the same kind and a new, highly charged consciousness and solidarity will be created on the basis of the aggregation of similar stories, which results in a degree of empowerment of people who previously saw themselves as isolated and powerless. This typically occurs in therapeutic, consciousness-raising groups.

Several of the novels studied here are said to have triggered important episodes of linked storytelling among their readers. In the case of *Uncle Tom's Cabin*, this included not only the circulation among white Northerners of a vast number of additional stories, oral and written, factual and fictional, about the horrors of slavery, but the writing and publication in the South of many anti-Uncle-Tom novels, depicting slavery in a rosy light. *One Day in the Life of Ivan Denisovich* opened a previously closed door, prompting other former camp inmates to tell friends and a wider public for the first time of their experiences. In both cases, it is in this capacity to trigger related stories among a vast readership that the political force of the work has been located. The notion that certain fictional narratives serve to promote a kind of group (even mass) therapy among their readers is one that will recur in this book. *The Satanic Verses* is, however, a special case which, it will be argued, has, for the moment at least, provoked mass responses (and not only amongst Muslims) which are almost wholly nontherapeutic and dysfunctional.

A number of theorists, as has already been mentioned, see the reductive character of narrative as always and necessarily tending to inhibit human growth and social change. Some psychologists, on the other hand, make the very simple point that human beings *require* the reductive force of narrative if they are to make any sense of the world on an everyday basis. As Richard Bandler and John Grinder say (and their observation applies equally to individuals and to social groups) "when human beings create their linguistic models of the world, they necessarily select and represent certain portions of the world and fail to select and represent others."[37] Some narrative reductions, they point out, may lead to creative action, while others limit or immobilize those who subscribe to them. The main processes by which people create defective models, they suggest, are inappropriate generalization, deletion and distortion. So, for instance, an individual may generalize from an unhappy experience in the past to construct a narrative model of the future which shows that experience being infinitely repeated.

Bandler and Grinder's main interests are in the behavior of individuals and small groups, but their ideas have great relevance, also, to the narratives by which larger groups, and even whole societies, live. Their account of the role of the psychotherapist, for instance, which is to "challenge and expand the impoverished portions" of their clients' defective narrative,[38] has a good deal in common with the definition many political activists might give of their role in society at large. Once it is seen that narratives are functional only in relation to particular moments (whether personal or historical) and that they are (or should be) in a constant state of renewal, their reductive quality need no longer be feared.

Psychotherapists of different persuasions not only start from radically different primary narratives (in terms of which they account for functional and dysfunctional psychological development) but adopt quite different narrative strategies in their face-to-face therapeutic encounters. At one extreme, Freudian analysis involves a long series of consultations in which the patient is prompted to recount memories, dreams, and fantasies, which the analyst retells as he/she interprets them. In Roy Schafer's words: "The analyst establishes new, though often contested or resisted, questions that amount to regulated narrative possibilities. The end product of this interweaving of texts is a radically new, jointly authored work or way of working."[39] At the other extreme, the brief therapy interventions of, for instance, Milton Erickson, require only quite limited narrative probing into the conscious or unconscious world of the patients (who are typically interviewed as a couple or a family). The interactional therapist of the Ericksonian type comes quickly to the formulation of a "metanarrative" which captures the circular, self-sustaining, yet destructive nature of the patients' current behavior patterns.[40] (This use of the word "metanarrative" runs precisely counter to Lyotard's use of the same term, in that it refers to a conscious attempt to escape the limitations of a confining narrative.) Nevertheless, change is not attempted by acquainting clients with this metanarrative (since the self-sustaining nature of the doublebind they are in would cause them to resist the insight it would offer) nor is any major alteration of behavior recommended. The therapist's intervention involves, instead, the insertion of some new, often quite small, provocative, even paradoxical, element into the narrative presented by the clients. Clients who attempt to follow this prescription frequently discover, not only that they cannot sustain such an absurd charade, but that their old, dysfunctional pattern of behavior has been permanently disrupted.[41]

The process underlying such a maneuver, that is, the formulation of a metanarrative which escapes the limitations of existing narratives and yet makes possible a small intervention in those narratives to disrupt them in some crucial way, is readily identifiable also in certain kinds of political activism. The use of passive resistance or civil disobedience in the service of a wider political philosophy parallels the paradoxical nature of the intervention described above particularly closely. Partisan struggle against occupying forces and guerrilla activity against colonizers have likewise often achieved massive change with the judicious use of very limited resources. Even jokes about authority figures, and political cartoons, satire and other forms of story against oppressive regimes, have, in certain circumstances, and despite their clandestine nature, undermined the credibility of their targets to a quite devastating degree.[42]

I shall be suggesting in the case studies which follow that, whilst some of the works I deal with may be said to have had an effect on political behavior patterns by means akin to the prolonged, wide-ranging and gradual processes of the Freudian analyst, others have exercised extraordinary leverage in a particular historical situation, through an intervention which appears on the surface, like Erickson's, almost irrelevant to it.

In order to approach more directly the question of just how fictional texts may be said to contribute to political change, I need now to focus my attention more narrowly on the theoretical problems which arise when the terms "literature" and "power" are brought together. Nevertheless, it will be noticeable that a number of the issues which have come up in this brief discussion of storytelling in its broad sense will recur in a different guise in what follows.

The great writer as alternative government?

It is a curious thing that, in liberal democracies, the word "power" is used more frequently than any other by publishers and reviewers to indicate, and invite, approval of a work of narrative fiction. Glancing at the covers of paperback novels on just a single shelf in my local bookshop (novels written by authors whose names begin with the letter R), I found the following phrases, all of which were either quoted from newspaper or magazine reviews or written by the publishers themselves: "stinging authenticity and power," "powerfully claustrophobic," "powerful and tender first novel," "powerful writing which evokes the rancid and decayed inner-city setting so strongly you can almost smell it," "a superbly written first book ... few contemporary writers can have evoked so powerfully the temper and texture of the ocean."

This flooding of popular critical discourse with the term "power" does not, of course, indicate a widespread belief in the capacity of narrative fiction to "change the world." The use of "power" in these examples indicates little more than approval of the novel's capacity to involve and move the individual reader emotionally. Indeed the term is so devalued as to imply a denial that narrative fiction can exercise power in a wider social and political sense. Received opinion in most liberal democracies has long been that fictional writing involves an unproblematic personal communication from author to reader. To the extent that the major writer exercises "power" over the reader, this is seen as a legitimate, educative influence, with the writer conveying generalized human truths and the reader becoming, by reading, a better human being. As Toril Moi says, "the role of the reader or critic is to listen respectfully to the voice of the author as it is expressed in the text."[43] The notion of the writer's "power" is a curious blend of the medieval concept of the authority of the classical writer with the respect for inspired genius that derives from romanticism. On to this conception of the writer's power has been grafted, however, a notion of authority which derives from theories of liberal constitutional government. Just as it is assumed that the individual citizen concedes power to the government in some kind of social contract, so it is assumed that the reader submits willingly to the authority of the writer, thereby authorizing the writer's power over him or her. Power, as is usual in a liberal democracy, is treated as individual and unproblematic, rather than collective, structural, and problematic.

Two important corollaries follow from this: a) there is no public acknowledgement that literature plays a role in the maintenance of existing power structures and b) literature is seen as incapable of playing a seriously disruptive role within such a society. Fictional works may be deemed "offensive" or "indecent", but in that case they are not "literature." If, in a liberal democracy, a piece of imaginative writing seeks or achieves social or political influence that goes beyond such a limited conception of its proper power, it must either be nonliterature masquerading as literature or a literary work being manipulated and misused for nonliterary, propagandist purposes. This assumption, that serious social or political influence is not to be expected, or even desired, of a literary text, is nicely illustrated by the phrasing of the article on Harriet Beecher Stowe in the *Literary History of the United States* edited by Robert E. Spiller and others. Its author, George Whicher, does not deny that *Uncle Tom's Cabin* evoked a tremendous response in the United States, "the words set down by her hand appeared to convulse a mighty nation," but he quickly undercuts this statement by adding the general disclaimer that "in spite of the enormous vogue of Mrs Stowe's novel, it is doubtful if a book ever had much power to change the course of events."[44] These comments trap Harriet Beecher Stowe from two opposite sides: either her work did not change the course of events (because literature by definition can't) or it did, in which case it isn't literature!

In overtly authoritarian states whose form of government does not rely on liberal bourgeois conceptions of constitutionality, such as Russia under the Tsars or the Soviet Union under Stalin, these assumptions are entirely reversed. Literature is *required*, by a combination of censorship and patronage, to contribute to the maintenance of power as constituted at the time. The government's insistence on retaining tight control over what is written and published reflects the belief, which is most often shared by the regime's opponents, that fictional writing possesses an extreme potential for disruption. So the critic, Vissarion Belinsky, writing in the 1840s of the situation of poets and novelists in Tsarist Russia, declared that "the public is right, for it looks upon Russian writers as its only leaders, defenders and saviours against Russian autocracy, orthodoxy and nationality."[45] One hundred and thirty years later, Solzhenitsyn echoed Belinsky's optimism about the oppositional effectiveness of the writer of literary fiction when he had a character in his novel, *The First Circle*, state (and one can be sure that this reflected Solzhenitsyn's personal opinion), "for a country to have a great writer … is like having another government."[46] In his Nobel Speech of 1970, which makes extraordinarily grand claims for the political influence of literary fiction, Solzhenitsyn adds the assertion that "literature … nurses and preserves [a] nation's lost history, in a form which is not susceptible to distortion and slander."[47]

There is, of course, a considerable naivety about Solzhenitsyn's position. While fiction can tell stories untold by history (the story *Uncle Tom's Cabin* told about slavery, for instance) such fictional stories are just as subject to "distortion and slander" as history itself. Literature, I shall be seeking to demonstrate throughout this book, is always embedded in structures or networks of power. Consequently it is never *either* as impotently marginal as Whicher asserts, *or* as independently powerful and incorruptible as Solzhenitsyn suggests. What is true is that the widespread expectation in a society that literary works either can, or cannot, play a significant political role is largely self-fulfilling. Whereas in some countries, readers weigh every word in a literary work for its possible political implications, in other countries, readers remain insensitive to political allusions which are very thinly veiled. (A rejection note for *Animal Farm* sent to George Orwell by one American publisher simply stated that there was currently no market for animal stories!)

The question which will be posed in several of the cases I shall be examining is whether a fictional work can be said to have exercised significant *disruptive* power against a large scale *oppressive* form of power (serfdom, slavery, fascism, Stalinist terror). This question requires that I now address directly the issue of what is meant by "power."

Concepts of power

Debates about the nature of power have, of course, raged for centuries among philosophers, who have been joined in the last hundred years or so by thinkers from the newer disciplines of political science and sociology. I take an unashamedly eclectic approach to theory in this field, as also in the area of literary theory, being unconvinced that any of the theorists whose work I have met has developed a framework which makes other theories superfluous, and believing that most theoretical perspectives offer valuable insights for the purposes of my present enterprise.

It is widely agreed that slavery, fascism, patriarchy, and many other forms of oppressive power relations can usefully be grouped together as "asymmetric" relations.[48] All imply inequality, control, dependence, and actual or potential conflict. The power relation involved is typified by the notion that one group has *power over* another. As Max Weber wrote, power, in this sense, may be defined as "the probability that one actor within a social relationship will be in a position to carry out his [*sic*] own will despite resistance."[49] Nevertheless, such power can rarely be described in simple individual terms and recognition of the structural nature of power becomes essential. Frank Parkin, for instance, writes of power as "a concept or metaphor which is used to depict the flow of resources which constitute the system."[50] Political philosophers have argued vigorously in recent years about whether it makes better sense to view human beings as mere bearers of structural power (Nicos Poulantzas) or as having a degree of independence as agents within power systems (C. Wright Mills and Ralph Miliband).[51] Such concepts are relevant to the present study, firstly because it asks what roles certain works of narrative fiction have played in relation to pre-existing structures or systems of power, secondly because it examines the extent to which it is appropriate to talk of writers *and readers* as exercising power independent of the social, institutional and discursive systems within which they operate.

Several recent theorists have proposed modifications to traditional thinking about power as an asymmetric relation. Perhaps it is a mistake, for instance, to think of power as a single system. In his later writings, Roland Barthes developed a concept of power as multiple, all-pervading, and infinitely resistant to attack: "And yet, what if power were plural, like demons? 'My name is Legion,' it could say; everywhere, on all sides, leaders, massive or minute organizations, pressure groups, or oppression groups, everywhere 'authorized' voices which authorize themselves to utter the discourse of all power: the discourse of arrogance .... Exhausted, defeated here, it reappears there; it never disappears. Make a revolution to destroy it, power will immediately revive and flourish again in the new state of affairs."[52]

This view appears to admit of no possibility either that nonoppressive forms of power could exist or that oppressive power might in any way be undermined or reduced. Michel Foucault in one sense develops and in another sense counters these arguments by declaring that power can only be analyzed as something which circulates or functions in the form of a chain: "It is never localized here or there, never in anybody's hands, never appropriated as a commodity or piece of wealth. Power is employed and exercised through a net-like organization. And not only do individuals circulate between its threads; they are always in the position of simultaneously undergoing and exercising this power."[53]

This is a very subtle and, in certain respects, fruitful account. For instance, it illuminates the situation of a man who is in a subordinate position in class terms but who exercises brutally oppressive power over his wife. Nevertheless it should not be allowed to obscure the commonsense observation that power is overwhelmingly concentrated at certain points of the network, rather than others.

An important feature of most descriptions of power as structure or network is the notion of "ideology" as developed by thinkers within the Marxist tradition (especially Gramsci and Althusser), and as elaborated and transformed by other thinkers including, notably, recent feminist theorists. "Ideology" in this usage denotes the way in which the dominance of a given social group is maintained not only by coercion, but by the manner in which its interests are built into all social institutions and into the very discourse (the ways of talking, writing, even thinking) of the whole society, including the oppressed groups.[54] As Marx and Engels wrote, the ruling ideas of an epoch "are nothing more than the ideal expression of the dominant material relationships grasped as ideas."[55] So, the law, religion, the education system, the mass media, and so on, whilst they give the appearance of being independent bodies of ideas and social practice, are all, in fact, "ideological forms" which essentially reflect and contribute to sustaining the fundamental economic, race and gender relations. Working-class people, women and colonized or enslaved racial and national groups unwittingly learn patterns of thought — stereotypes about their own group — which serve to intensify their own (and each other's) subordination by making it seem natural.

Much recent thought, on a mainly empirical level in English-speaking countries and on the level of theory in France, has identified the central mechanism of ideological control as language. Dale Spender, for instance, declares in connection with gender oppression that: "The

English language has been literally man made and ... it is still primarily under male control ... This monopoly over language is one of the means by which males have ensured their own primacy, and consequently have ensured the invisibility or 'other' nature of females, and this primacy is perpetuated while women continue to use, unchanged, the language which we have inherited."[56] (Her point is well illustrated by the number of times in this book that I have, in passages quoted from academic writers, inserted "sic" to draw attention to the use of exclusively masculine pronouns and possessive adjectives in contexts where women as writers, as readers, or even as human beings were thereby made invisible.) Roland Barthes, in a lecture shortly before he died, went so far as to declare in the most general terms that "language — the performance of a language system — is neither reactionary nor progressive: it is quite simply fascist."[57]

These, then, are some of the threads spun by thinkers concerned with describing power as an asymmetric relation. Many theorists and activists, however, have felt the need to identify and develop concepts of power which are distinct from the oppressive concepts of power which predominate in colonial, postcolonial, class, and patriarchal relations. Socialists envisage a radical political and economic transformation which will construct a society founded on collective or communal power. Anticolonialists struggle towards self-determination for their people. Modern conceptions of power as nonoppressive derive from a long and wide-ranging tradition of political philosophy going back to Plato which sees power as implying, not control and competition, but communal achievement. Within this tradition, power is a "collective capacity,"[58] or, as Hannah Arendt has expressed it, "the human ability to ... act in concert."[59] There is a good deal of disagreement within and between activist groups about whether power as "collective capacity" is merely a goal to be aspired to, with the path to that goal frequently necessitating the use of power as "asymmetric relation" — the position taken by many socialists and anticolonial fighters — or whether it is essential for the means employed to be always informed only with power as "collective capacity," never oppressive power — the position taken by Gandhian pacifists and many anarchists and feminists.

Indeed, it is feminists who have, in recent years, probably articulated most clearly their rejection of the prevailing concept of power as an exclusively "asymmetric relation." As Toril Moi expresses it, "feminism is not simply about rejecting power, but about transforming the existing power structures and, in the process, transforming the very concept of power itself."[60] Hélène Cixous develops this argument by distinguishing what she calls "masculine" and "feminine" forms of power (making clear, however, that she does not mean that men always operate in terms of masculine power or women always in terms of feminine power.) Masculine power, she says, is: "always and only a power over others. It is something that relates back to government, control, and beyond that, to despotism. Whereas if I say 'women's powers', first it isn't one power any longer, it is multiplied, there is more than one … and it is a question of power over oneself, in other words of a relation not based on mastery but on availability."[61]

Cixous's positive notion of multiple power, it should be noticed, runs directly counter to Barthes' notion of the multiplicity of *oppressive* power. Similarly, Julia Kristeva counters Barthes' notion of language as "fascist" by arguing that it is better understood as an arena of conflict. While, in many societies, everyone uses the same language, different groups within the society have different interests which intersect in language. While it is in the interests of the dominant power group to ensure that language operates only "univocally", that is, conveys single, fixed meanings, which allow no space for dissenting thought (let alone action), subordinate groups will always manage to introduce a "polysemic" (multiple) quality into the construction of meaning. Language is therefore, according to Kristeva, not merely a reflection of existing social relations, but a productive area of struggle.[62]

Theories about literature and power

Theorists have taken up a great variety of positions on the question of the relations between literature and power, literature and ideology. It was, not surprisingly, in the works of Marx and Engels that the earliest, major theoretical challenge was offered to the liberal model of the interaction of author and reader as a personal communication, unproblematic in terms of power. In the first place, they demonstrated that, whereas bourgeois ideology would have it that literary works are conceived in isolation by inspired individuals and offered directly to the waiting world, in fact literary works are products of a labor which is constrained by essentially the same set of power relations, economic and otherwise, as other forms of labor. As such, literary works are produced, marketed, distributed, sold, exported and imported, kept and discarded, within the context of national and international economic (and political) systems. Fictional writing is processed, at different stages, by the mass media (in both advertising and criticism), the law (in censorship), and the education and library systems. (This means that it is necessary for me, in the present book, to examine the power relations implicit in every aspect of the production, rhetorical structure, distribution, and consumption of each of the works I am studying.)

A second relevant observation of Engels is that a text's political meaning is not determined by its author's conscious political stance or intentions for the work. So, he argued, a great novelist like Balzac, writing in a period in France at which economic and political power was shifting rapidly from the aristocracy to the bourgeoisie, could not but reflect in his novels the inevitability of that shift, even though, in conscious political terms, he opposed it.[63] The capacity to represent the underlying social forces of the historical moment is therefore, for Marx and Engels, the great "power" of literature. Engels developed this point by arguing that any attempt by a fictional writer, such as Zola in the 1880s, to hasten or lead the coming to power of the emerging class (in Zola's case, the proletariat) is "tendentious writing" and doomed to failure.[64] Lucien Goldmann, a Marxist writing in the 1960s, followed a parallel track in arguing that the validity of a work of art may be judged by the degree to which its structure embodies the world vision of the social class or group to which the writer belongs — with Goldmann, too, the criterion is the extent to which the work demonstrates "the way things really are."[65] While there are major theoretical difficulties about any argument which depicts art as, in any simple sense, "reflecting" life, it remains the case, as psychotherapists well know, that "if people define situations as real they are real in their consequences."[66] It will become clear in the case studies that follow that the impact of several of the works I study resulted from the fact that readers in large numbers *read* them as conveying vital new information about social and political conditions, even if subsequent readings make clear that they mirrored reality in a distorted or incomplete manner.

A number of theorists, both inside and outside the Marxist tradition, explore the notion that literature may perform a positively empowering or liberating role. For Bertolt Brecht, theater and literature were capable of exercising a strongly subversive function. While he avoided simplistic conceptions of art as reflection, insisting that "if art reflects life it does so with special mirrors,"[67] he nevertheless saw the empowering possibilities of literature as lying in its capacity to reveal hidden realities to the oppressed class (in other words, to tell untold stories), by: "laying bare society's causal network / showing up the dominant viewpoint as the viewpoint of the dominators / writing from the standpoint of the class which has prepared the broadest solutions for the most pressing problems afflicting human society / emphasizing the dynamics of development ... "[68]

To achieve this, Brecht employed what he called "alienation effects" which, rather than inviting the audience to become absorbed in his plays as illusions, would regularly break the continuity of the action, insisting that the audience reflect actively on what was happening and being said.

The problem of literature and power is illuminated by a further theoretical development within the Marxist tradition. Pierre Macherey argues that, far from constituting rounded, coherent unities, literary texts are essentially fragmentary, self-contradictory, distinctive for what they omit as much as for what they include, and are therefore capable of working on our ideological experience, distancing us from its illusory qualities. Whilst literature cannot operate outside ideology, it can demonstrate the limits of ideology by offering scattered, diverse, and conflicting meanings.[69] Literature can thus be seen as yet another arena for struggle.

Macherey, along with other literary theorists, Marxist and non-Marxist, has moved away from assumptions about the unity and stability of the meaning of a literary text and the centrality of the *writing* process towards an assertion of the instability of literary meaning and the importance of the *reading* process. Interestingly, these theorists are actually developing the cultural implications of Marx's statement that "a product becomes a real product only by being consumed. For example a garment becomes a real garment only in the act of being worn; a house where no-one lives is in fact not a real house; thus the product, unlike a mere natural object, proves itself to be, becomes, a product only through consumption. Only by decomposing the product does consumption give the product the finishing touch."[70]

It is the "consumption" of the fictional text, the reading process, which German and American reception theorists have focused their attention on and while the reception theorists have been criticized by Marxists, and others, for failing to confront the problem of power and the fictional text, in my view they have, often unwittingly, illuminated the problem in some very important ways and I make considerable use of their insights in the studies that follow. Wolfgang Iser, for instance, argues that the fictional text "should be understood as a combination of forms and signs designed to guide the imagination of the reader" and that the interaction of text and reader involves "the prestructuring of the potential meaning by the text, and the reader's actualization of this potential through the reading process."[71] Iser's choice of the word "guide" for the action of the text on the reader's imagination makes the relationship seem unproblematic in terms of power (indeed, in this sense, Iser takes a very traditional, liberal position), but it requires only a moment's thought to see that it disguises a very strong interaction. Another writer has described the act of reading in these terms: "Here I am thinking a thought which manifestly belongs to another mental world, which is being thought in me just as though I did not exist."[72] The formulation proposed by an American reception theorist, Lowry Nelson, illustrates this point more fully. He suggests that the fictional text is most usefully regarded as being like a musical score, or the text of a play, which must be "performed" if the work is to be realized. He elaborates the notion of "a reader's role written in the text as part of the fiction, to which the existential (real-life) reader, in order to become an adequate or 'optimum' reader, must conform, thus playing a role, becoming a collaborator, an accomplice."[73]

The relevance to the discussion of politically loaded texts, such as those under consideration here, of the terms "perform," "collaborator," and "accomplice" will be obvious. The text *requires* a form of participation from the reader (as Chambers' term "seduction" suggests) and, as is well known in the fields of education and psychotherapy, active role-playing can be enormously influential on the person doing it. Reading, it may be argued, is capable of promoting the same kind of more or less permanent change in readers which psychotherapists tells us therapeutic role-playing sometimes produces in their clients: the radical reframing of a familiar situation. (This accounts for the familiar remark: "After that I could never see it in quite the same way again.") This sense of the term "reframing" is defined by Paul Watzlawick and his associates as follows: "To reframe ... means to change the conceptual and/or emotional setting or viewpoint in relation to which a situation is experienced and to place it in another frame which fits the 'facts' of the same concrete situation equally well or even better, and thereby changes its entire meaning."[74] (This notion of reframing can be seen, in turn, as having a good deal in common with Thomas Kuhn's account of how radical breaks in scientific thinking occur, with the substitution of one explanatory paradigm with another.)[75] It is noteworthy that one of the claims that have been made for the political effect of *Uncle Tom's Cabin* is that it brought about a complete "reframing," or reconceptualization, of slavery in the minds of a large proportion of the northern white population of the United States. Similar claims are made for some of the other fictional works studied.

Inviting the participation of the reader as an accomplice is (like "seduction") an act which has very different connotations in terms of power, according to the location within existing power structures of the person doing the inviting and the person who is invited, as well as the form in which the invitation is made. (The case of the, at least nominally, all-powerful Tsar "performing" *A Sportsman's Notebook* as "collaborator" or "accomplice" illustrates this point particularly vividly.) It is, of course, possible to refuse an invitation to perform a literary work, by refusing to read any further. Another reception theorist, Susan Suleiman, has posed the very interesting question as to whether it is possible for a reader to continue reading and yet avoid a full collaboration with the value system implicit in a work of fiction. She argues that a kind of reading is possible which involves the reader in a full performance of the text, yet with an "ideological dissent," a recognition of "certain formal devices as masks for the novelist in his [*sic*] role as a manipulator of values."[76] The seducer is thereby unmasked.

This argument has been further developed, and given great importance, in the work of feminist literary critics who describe themselves as "reading against the grain" of texts, usually by men, which they find offensive to women. Kate Millett, for instance, picked up the novels of male writers, D. H. Lawrence, Henry Miller, Norman Mailer, and others and then, rather than collaborating with their particular forms of male erotic fantasy, demonstrated their profoundly misogynist character.[77] This notion of the assertive, disobedient reader who refuses to acknowledge the authority of the author and *his* text is seen as a crucial weapon against patriarchy, but is of course transferable to opposition against other forms of oppressive power. Such critics are insisting on the subversive power of the reader of (or against) distinctly nonsubversive texts, turning the text into a weapon to be used against the interests of the oppressive group it would otherwise serve (in somewhat the way that teachers of martial arts instruct their students to turn around the force of an attacker). This formulation attributes an independent power to the reader (feminist critics use the term "the resisting reader") which has great significance in the present study. Resisting reading may well involve disobeying not only signs within the text, but disobeying signs erected around the text by publishers, reviewers, educators, and so on. Some intriguing cases will be documented of "reading against the grain" by Southerners who came across *Uncle Tom's Cabin* in the 1850s, and by former camp guards who wrote to tell Solzhenitsyn about their interpretations of *One Day in the Life of Ivan Denisovich*. The case of *The Satanic Verses* will once again prove to be the most problematic: have Muslims claiming to be offended by Rushdie's novel misunderstood it (as the author and many of his defenders argue) or willfully read against its profoundly anti-Islamic grain (as they, themselves, argue)?

The literary text as "theatre of a production"

Nevertheless there are many kinds of literary theory which deny that fictional works have a (single) "grain" which the reader is invited to follow. Theorists of various schools emphasize what they variously call the "multivalence" or "polyvalence" (reception theorists),[78] or "openness" (Umberto Eco),[79] or "polysemousness" (Barthes and Kristeva)[80] of fictional texts. In Barthes's words, the text is no longer to be considered as: "the product of a labour ... but the very theatre of a production where the producer and the reader of the text meet: the text 'works,' at each moment and from whatever side one takes it. Even when written (fixed), it does not stop working, maintaining a process of production."[81]

For some theorists, "openness" is one of the distinguishing characteristics of literary texts. The reception theorists, for example, assert that it is in the very nature of fictional texts that they offer "a multiplicity of varying, contrasting and, to a certain degree, mutually exclusive strands of meaning ... which stand on an equal footing as far as their validity is concerned."[82] Other theorists, Eco for instance, emphasize the difference between texts which are relatively "open" to multiple interpretation and those which are relatively "closed." And it has become a commonplace of discussion amongst politically engaged novelists and critics over the last thirty years or more that, to be politically progressive, to contribute towards upsetting the monolithic certainties of an oppressive political system, a literary work must be formally complex, even ambiguous.

The ramifications of the argument about the "openness" of literary texts run in a number of different, in some cases quite contrary, directions, all of which have some importance for the kinds of study undertaken in this book.

The reception theorists, on the whole, depict the reader as possessing relative autonomy to select amongst the "mutually exclusive strands of meaning in the text." Meaning is, one might say, "negotiated" between text and reader. Some reception theorists, however, emphasize that each reader's capacity to generate meanings from a text is constrained, not only by the nature of the text itself, but the "syndrome of expectations" the reader brings to the text. That syndrome of expectations is, in turn, determined by the reader's particular linguistic experience, experience in dealing with texts, and individual emotional, social, and cultural experience.[83] Most reception theorists are unwilling to acknowledge how closely their concept of a "syndrome of expectations" parallels the Marxist and feminist concepts of "ideology" and so miss its relevance to the discussion of literature and power.

On the other hand, a line of argument about the relative openness of fictional texts developed by some reception theorists has great usefulness in the examination of how a particular fictional text has "worked in the world." Interesting studies have been undertaken, especially by Manfred Durzak, of the broad shifts in interpretation which occur when a fictional work is read in another country than the one in which, and for which, it was written. Durzak has shown, for instance, that while West German critics of Günter Grass's story, *Ballad of a Badgerdog*, viewed it (rather unfavorably) as a literal depiction of political events in their own country, "American critics interpret the story right from the beginning in a nonliteral way: for them it is a veiled portrayal in parable form of domestic political events of a specifically American kind."[84] I shall be showing, in a later chapter, how Ignazio Silone's *Fontamara*, conversely, achieved remarkable political influence in the United States in the mid-1930s because its American readers interpreted it as being a very literal, concrete rendering of life under Mussolini's fascism, whereas readers closer to Italy read it much more metaphorically. And, as we have already seen, differences of interpretation between cultural and religious groups have played a major part in the disputes over *The Satanic Verses*. In fact, the political importance of shifts in interpretation of a fictional work as it crosses national, cultural, and religious frontiers will be a recurrent theme of this book.

Then there is the issue of shifts in the reception of the fictional work over time. It is Hans Robert Jauss who has explored this question most fully. He argues that what occurs is an ongoing "dialogue" between a work and successive groups of readers, in which the work provides new "answers" to new generations of readers, because they, with their different syndromes of expectations, read it with different "questions" in mind.[85] Where the "power" lies in this formulation (and what kind of power it might be) is not easy to decide. It is almost as if the reception theorists regard the text as a multipurpose resource (a kind of versatile power-tool!) which later readers may use in ways they choose on the many situations in which they find themselves. Some illumination of this issue on the empirical level will occur when I examine the complex histories of the reception by different social groups, in different countries, and at different historical moments of, in particular, *Uncle Tom's Cabin* and *Fontamara*. What one can be sure of is that the wonderfully grand and simple image of how literary works supposedly convey their message across time and national boundaries, which Solzhenitsyn expressed in his Nobel Speech, does not accurately reflect the complex processes involved. Solzhenitsyn declares that literature has a miraculous facility: "that of overcoming differences of language, custom and social system, and conveying life experience from one whole nation to another. And this national experience, painfully built up over many decades by one nation, when conveyed to a second nation which has never had it, can perhaps save it from taking an unnecessary, mistaken or even ruinous path ... There is another immensely valuable channel along which literature conveys human experience, in condensed and authoritative form: from one generation to another."[86]

Solzhenitsyn's position contrasts strongly with that taken by a large number of politically active writers and critics over many decades who have identified the political force of fictional texts as lying precisely in their ambiguity and openness, which, they say, tends to disturb the certainties of totalitarian political systems. The productive energy of the text is associated with a concept of power as collective, multiple, and subversive of oppressive forms of power. Elio Vittorini, Italian author of the richly ambiguous anti-Fascist novel *Conversation in Sicily*, developed a particularly attractive formulation of this argument. He accounted for his complex and elusive style, not only by referring to the need to fool the Fascist censors, but by insisting on his desire to reject as authoritarian any writing "in which the truth is administered to the reader from on high, under the *technical fiction* that the writer is demiurgic, the center of the the world, the spirit, God" in favour of writing which is "democratic, dialectical, conjectural."[87] In a totalitarian regime, to use words in a way which allows for a variety of conflicting interpretations and responses is to cast serious doubt on the regime's own handling of language. (This line of argument ties in interestingly with the proposal of the Russian theorist Mikhail Bakhtin that the novel is, because of the very mixed character of the language it uses, by nature a "dialogic" literary form.)[88] Some feminists have developed this argument in important ways. Hélène Cixous grafts ideas about the text as open and productive onto her own account of masculine and feminine power to develop the notion of "feminine writing." Feminine texts are those which "split open the closure of the binary opposition and revel in the pleasures of open-ended textuality."[89]

This argument, that "openness" in fictional texts (and for that matter "openness" in reading strategy) necessarily tends to foster power as "collective capacity" and undermine power as "asymmetric relation," is a very attractive one. But when tested in the case studies which follow, it will be found to need considerable qualification. Without anticipating the detail of my findings, I can say here that, in examining the apparently progressive political impact of a number of fictional works, I am struck by the fact that, on some occasions, it is a relatively *closed* reading that has given the work its political sharpness, its subversive quality. (As the interactional psychotherapists and guerilla fighters know well, an apparently *reductive* intervention may be most effective at inducing change.) More generally, it needs to be said that any discussion of how specific literary texts might have contributed to social and political change has to take account of the context in which the work was received and of the way in which it actually meshed with the current situation and preoccupations of its readers.

It is in the work of Roland Barthes and the poststructuralists that the issue of the productive openness of literary texts is taken to its furthest extreme. Barthes, we have seen, usefully describes the literary work as "productive" of meanings; it might be expected that he would have extremely relevant things to say about how the energy of literary texts converts into political power. In my view, however, his arguments on this topic lead down what is nearly a blind alley. His oracular statements are expressed in such absolute terms that they sometimes obscure as many important issues as they reveal.

In his seminal essay "Theory of the Text," Barthes defines the productive working of texts as a kind of infinite, erotic, combinative, self-referential play of meaning, and he concludes: "the signifier belongs to everybody; it is the text which, in fact works tirelessly, not the artist or the consumer."[90] Vaguely democratic though that sounds, Barthes avoids locating the work done by texts in an historical context and so avoids relating his theory of textuality to issues of power. Indeed, having, as I said earlier, developed a concept of power as all-pervading, multiple and uniformly oppressive, and a concept of language as fascist, Barthes, in a characteristic intellectual back-somersault, argued, in the same lecture, that literature, because it is capable of employing language in infinitely playful and self-reflexive ways, is a "permanent revolution of language" which somehow evades power. He calls literature "this salutary trickery, this evasion, this grand imposture which allows us to understand speech *outside the bounds of power*" (my italics).[91] This not only goes against the broad argument I have advanced so far about the intimate relationship which will always exist between narrative (including literary narrative) and various forms of power, but surely contradicts Barthes's own conception of power as totalitarian and ubiquitous. There is another level on which Barthes and practitioners of deconstruction are frequently — and to my mind rightly — criticized, but which I can refer to here only in passing. The kind of brilliantly rich and playful reading which Barthes proposed is profoundly elitist, because it is only available to readers with not only his richness of intellect, but also his economic and educational privilege and leisure. At the same time, it can be said that it actually diffuses any political energy the text may be capable of by splitting it — just as the force of a big river is diminished if it divides into a hundred streams. My interest is in seeing what sorts of meaning large numbers of people of quite varied educational and economic background have found in certain fictional texts at moments of acute historical — and sometimes personal — stress. I could not disagree more with the novelist and critic Luce d'Eramo, who declared that "the critic's job is to penetrate a book, forgetting everything else, otherwise one's judgement of a book would change if one read it in prison or on holiday."[92] The role which a work of fiction may play in the complex mechanisms of social and political power is eventually determined precisely by the circumstances in which it is read, and often — to come back to Barthes — by the constraints on playful reading which they impose.

The notion developed by some American feminist theorists that certain literary texts are not infinitely productive of meaning, but productive of politically significant *double-meaning* has great relevance to the present study. Sandra Gilbert and Susan Gubar, in their book, *The Madwoman in the Attic*, look at the problem of women writers who appear to conform in large part to patriarchal ideology, but have written "literary works that are in some sense palimpsestic, works whose surface designs conceal or obscure deeper, less accessible (and less socially acceptable) levels of meaning. Thus these authors managed the difficult task of achieving true female literary authority by simultaneously conforming to and subverting patriarchal literary standards."[93]

This line of argument brings together Macherey's notion of gaps in, and fragmentariness of, the text with the reception theorists' conception of the text as containing mutually exclusive strands of meaning. The idea that an author may, by transmitting a double message, establish a kind of conspiratorial, subversive relationship with the activist section of his or her readership, while satisfying the rest of the readership (including censors, reactionary publishers, and reviewers) that the work conforms to the demands of the dominant ideology, is, of course, not only relevant to works by women, as will become clear in the studies that follow. A variation on this argument, which I develop particularly in relation to *A Sportsman's Notebook*, suggests that a text capable of being read in somewhat divergent ways may actually contribute to uniting, for political action, groups who have previously thought of themselves as distinct and even opposed, because they see it as constituting common ground between them.

Fiction and history

It will be very evident that I have, until this point, avoided reiterating the traditional distinction between supposedly factual storytelling (history, journalism, biography, the writing of a diary, medical case-histories, and so on) and supposedly fictional storytelling (folktales, feature films, jokes, novels ...). This has of course been deliberate and some of the reasons for it will already be obvious. It has been the argument of much of the historical theory I have been referring to that all historical writing is in large part fictional, not only in that historians sometimes get their facts wrong, but also because the facts they "get right" are only given shape and meaning in the telling. At the same time, what we call narrative fiction is, in large part, factual, not only in that much of its content refers accurately and recognizably to real places, times, objects, events, but also because much of the interest of fictional stories derives from the fact that readers perceive them to be accurate representations of real human and social processes. Louis O. Mink expresses it very simply, "histories are full of things that are not so, just as fiction is full of things that are so."[94]

This, naturally, does not mean that no distinctions can be made between history and narrative fiction. History and overtly fictional narratives make different claims on, and contracts with, the reader. A history is required not to include material that the historian knows to be untrue. There is no such obligation on the writer of fictional narrative.

Historians must provide, or be able to provide, evidence for the accuracy of their stories. Fictional writers do not. It is assumed that a historical narrative should be compatible with, and complement, existing historical narratives on the same topic — otherwise one or other must be invalid. We make no such assumption about the compatibility and complementarity of, for instance, novels. Most importantly, while many elements in a fictional narrative will be factual, it is also the case that, as Louis O. Mink again states, "for fiction, there is no claim to be a true representation *in any particular respect*" (my italics).[95] I shall suggest that it is just this slipperiness of narrative fiction, the uncertainty of the claims that any work of fiction makes on its readers, that provides a key to understanding the social and political influence of which it is capable.

The argument about the closeness of history and narrative fiction is by no means just a theoretical nicety. It is also a practical question of how people actually use historical and fictional narratives. Most people (and not just naive or poorly educated people) derive more of their sense of the history of other countries over the last two hundred years from reading novels (and watching films) than they do from reading the works of historians. It would be absurd to deny that large numbers of educated people have obtained most of their knowledge of French society in the 1830s from Balzac, their sense of Russia in the 1840s from Gogol and Turgenev and of Victorian England from Dickens and George Eliot, their understanding of the United States in the 1920s and 1930s from Dos Passos and Steinbeck, their grasp of the Soviet Union under Stalin from Solzhenitsyn, and so on. We derive general impressions of living conditions of different classes, forms of social interaction, political processes, all of which we take to be typical of the period and place, from the fictional narratives we read, despite our awareness that most of the characters and events included in the story did not exist outside it. Moreover, we check the reliability of these impressions against our reading of historical narratives — normally (but not always) giving precedence to the histories where there is conflict, but otherwise treating the fictional narrative as a complementary source of historical information.

This book is concerned with a still stronger kind of interaction between narrative fiction and history. It looks at the extent to which fictional narratives have (through their publication, distribution, and consumption) served as significant agents in social and political history. And it asserts that there is a need to write history in a way which acknowledges the role of particular fictional texts in causing social and political change (in addition to the more diffuse structural role of literature as an institution).

Collective human action is, in very large part, shaped by the interaction of, even slippage between, such diverse narrative forms as religious and national metanarratives, written history, collective memory, shared fantasies about the future, and so on, all of which have fictional elements in them. Conscious decision-making about the future is inevitably done in relation not just to anticipatory narratives about what is necessary, desirable, or possible for the future, but to the many forms of retrospective story which serve to tell us where we have come from and who we are. To the extent that literary fiction contributes to social and political change, it does so primarily in terms of its interaction with other significant forms of human narrative. It works by complementing and aggregating with the narratives of other kinds (particularly history and imaginative anticipation) from which political and social action primarily derives, or in competition with them by a process of capping or reframing or disruption. In some striking instances, narrative fiction may insert a new provocative element into one or more of the controlling metanarratives of a particular society and so contribute to radical change by a process which might be termed mass psychotherapy.

I made clear, early in this chapter, that I would be eclectic in my use of critical methods deriving from a wide variety of theoretical schools. It will be evident by now that, in the studies that follow, I shall, likewise, be taking a thoroughly relativist position in treating the question of literature and power (to the disappointment of some readers and the satisfaction of others). In examining the circumstances of the publication and reception of each of the narrative works that I study, I try to identify some of the many, complex large- and small-scale forms of power in operation at the time. I suggest, in each case, the extent to which the narrative text should be seen as a mere channel through which major structural forces have worked and the extent to which independent power can be attributed, at different points and in different ways, to the author, to the text and to groups of readers, as well as to the many agents who mediate between texts and readers. I aim to show that the political productivity of relatively open and relatively closed *texts* (as of relatively open and relatively closed *reading*) is much more dependent on historical circumstances than is generally supposed. And I am particularly interested in tracing both continuity in, and shifts of, political effects from the same work over a period of time.

To anyone who is skeptical about the assertion that narrative fiction, in certain circumstances, plays a central role in the lives and political thinking of ordinary people, I recommend the earthy reminder provided

Narrative and Power
▼▼▼

in a letter to Solzhenitsyn by a reader of *One Day in the Life of Ivan Denisovich* living in the Ukraine, who wrote to the author: "In Kharkov I have seen all kinds of queues — for the film *Tarzan*, butter, women's drawers, chicken giblets and horse-meat sausage. But I cannot remember a queue as long as the one for your book in the libraries."[96]

NOTES TO CHAPTER 1

1. One of the earliest, and best known, examples of a novel which is claimed to have exercised a massive, direct, social influence is Goethe's story of hopeless love, *The Sorrows of Young Werther* (1774), which is said to have so stirred the feelings of a whole generation of young readers all over Western Europe that a number were recorded as committing suicide in imitation of its lovesick hero. Of a very different kind is the impact claimed for the novels of Dickens and Charles Kingsley, which have been credited with contributing, through the exposure of some of the social evils of mid-nineteenth century Britain, to the most important pieces of reform legislation enacted in the later part of the century. Perhaps the most specific (and best-documented) claim for a novel's leading to significant legislative change relates to the publication in 1906 of Upton Sinclair's *The Jungle*, which, through its depiction of the lives of workers in the Chicago meat-packing industry, is reliably said to have been instrumental in ensuring the passage of the Pure Food and Drug Act in the U.S. Congress a few months later. (See Ronald Gottesman, "Introduction" to Upton Sinclair, *The Jungle* [New York: Viking Penguin, 1985]: 24. A curious knock-on effect of the widespread anxiety about the health risks associated with canned foods provoked by *The Jungle* was the immediate collapse of whole communities based on canning quite remote from Chicago — including those in my country, New Zealand. See Dick Scott, *Seven Lives on Salt River* [Auckland: Hodder and Stoughton, 1987].) The equally specific impact claimed for the French edition of Arthur Koestler's *Darkness at Noon* in early 1946 is that, through its representation of the supposedly corrupt essential logic of communism, it directly contributed to the defeat of the French Communist Party in a crucial referendum later that year (see Goronwy Rees, "*Darkness at Noon* and the 'Grammatical Fiction'" in *Astride the Two Cultures: Arthur Koestler at 70*, ed. Harold Harris [London: Hutchinson, 1975]: 118). While Koestler gloried in his novel's apparent political influence, George Orwell, had he lived to see it, would almost certainly have been much less pleased at the way in which his *1984* served the United States and its allies, in the first decade after its publication, as a propaganda weapon against all forms of socialism. In the area of gender politics, Fay Weldon has described Marilyn French's novel, *The Women's Room* (1977) as "the kind of book that changes lives" (cover of Sphere paperback edition, 1978) referring not just, in a general sense, to the way in which it introduced feminist ideas and arguments to a wider readership of English-speaking women than was reached by more theoretical feminist works, but to the plentiful anecdotal evidence that reading *The Women's Room* gave some women the courage they needed to leave unsatisfactory marriages.

– 37 –

2. Quoted in David Caute, *The Illusion: an Essay on Politics, Theater and the Novel* (London: Andre Deutsch, 1971): 72-73.

3. Cyril Connolly, cover of Penguin edition.

4. Isaac Deutscher, "*1984* — The Mysticism of Cruelty," in his *Heretics and Renegades* (London: Hamish Hamilton, 1956): 35.

5. Roland Barthes, "Introduction to the Structural Analysis of Narratives," in his *Image — Music — Text*, trans. Stephen Heath (Glasgow: Fontana/Collins, 1977): 79.

6. Jonathan Culler, "Story and Discourse in the Analysis of Narrative" in his *The Pursuit of Signs: Semiotics, Literature, Deconstruction* (Ithaca: Cornell University Press, 1981): 186.

7. Thomas M. Leitch, *What Stories Are: Narrative Theory and Interpretation* (University Park and London: Pennsylvania State University, 1986): 198-201.

8. Jean-François Lyotard, *The Postmodern Condition*, trans. G. Bennington and B. Massumi (Minneapolis: University of Minnesota Press, 1984): xii.

9. Fredric Jameson, *The Political Unconscious: Narrative as a Socially Symbolic Act* (Ithaca: Cornell University Press, 1981): 13.

10. Hayden White, *The Content of the Form: Narrative Discourse and Historical Representation* (Baltimore and London: Johns Hopkins University Press, 1987): 215.

11. Louis O. Mink, "Narrative Form as a Cognitive Instrument," in *The Writing of History: Literary Form and Historical Understanding*, ed. Robert H. Canary and Henry Kozicki (Madison: University of Wisconsin Press, 1978): 131. See also his "History and Fiction as Modes of Comprehension," *New Literary History* 1 (1969-70): 541-558.

12. P. B. Medawar, *The Art of the Soluble*, 6th ed. (London: Methuen, 1967): 116.

13. James Hillman, "A Note on Story," in his *Loose Ends: Primary Papers in Archetypal Psychology* (Dallas: Spring Publications, 1975): 1.

14. Barbara Herrnstein Smith, "Narrative Versions, Narrative Theories," in *Critical Inquiry* 7 no. 1 (Fall 1980): 232.

15. Ross Chambers, *Story and Situation: Narrative Seduction and the Power of Fiction* (Minneapolis: Manchester and Minneapolis University Presses, 1984): 74.

16. Chambers, *Story and Situation*: 4.

17. Chambers, *Story and Situation*: 218.

18. Chambers, *Story and Situation*: 211.

19. Robert Scholes, "Language, Narrative, and Anti-Narrative," *Critical Inquiry* 7, no. 1 (Fall 1980): 212.

20. Robert Anchor, "Narrativity and the Transformation of Historical Consciousness," *Clio* 16, no. 2 (1987): 133-134.

21. Mink, "Narrative Form as a Cognitive Instrument": 133.

22. See, for instance, Marcia Liebermann, "Some Day My Prince Will Come: Female Acculturation through the Fairy Tale," *College English* 34 (December 1972): 383-395.

23. See, for instance, *The Manufacture of News*, ed. S. Cohen and J. Young (London: Constable, 1973) and *People, Society and Mass Communications*, ed. L. A. Dexter and D. M. White (Glencoe, Illinois: Free Press of Glencoe, 1964).

24. Nancy Whittier Heer, *Politics and History in the Soviet Union* (Cambridge, Massachusetts and London: M.I.T. Press, 1971): vii.

25. Hayden White, *The Content of the Form*: 23-24.
26. For a good account and assessment of the work of Sapir and Whorf in this field, see George Steiner, *After Babel: Aspects of Language and Translation* (London: Oxford University Press, 1975): 87-94.
27. See, especially, Lyotard, *The Postmodern Condition*.
28. See, for instance, *I Never Told Anyone: Writings by Women Survivors of Child Sexual Abuse*, ed. Ellen Bass and Louise Thornton (New York: Harper and Row, 1983); Oralee Wachter, *No More Secrets for Me* (Ringwood, Australia: Penguin, 1986).
29. Hayden White, "The Value of Narrativity in the Representation of Reality," *Critical Inquiry* 7, no. 1 (Fall 1980): 5-27.
30. Mary Frances Berry, *Long Memory: The Black Experience in America* (New York: Oxford University Press, 1982).
31. E. P. Thompson, *The Making of the English Working Class* (London: Gollancz, 1963).
32. Ellen Moers, *Literary Women* (Garden City, New York: Anchor Press/Doubleday, 1977); Dale Spender, *Women of Ideas and What Men Have Done to Them: From Aphra Behn to Adrienne Rich* (London and Boston: Routledge and Kegan Paul: 1982); Elaine Showalter, *A Literature of Their Own: British Women Novelists from Brontë to Lessing*, revised edition (London: Virago, 1984), and many others.
33. See, for instance, Kay F. Stone, "The Misuses of Enchantment: Controversies on the Significance of Fairy Tales," in *Women's Folklore, Women's Culture*, ed. R. Jordan and S. Kalcik (Philadelphia, University of Pennsylvania Press, 1985): 125-145.
34. Chambers, *Story and Situation*: 212.
35. For discussion of this broad question, see Michel De Certeau, "On the Oppositional Practices of Everyday Life," *Social Text* 3 (Fall 1980): 3-43.
36. William Labov and Joshua Waletzky, "Narrative Analysis: Oral Versions of Personal Experience," in *Essays on the Verbal and Visual Arts: Proceedings of the 1966 Annual Spring Meeting of the American Ethnological Society*, ed. June Helm (Seattle and London: University of Washington Press, 1967): 12-44.
37. Richard Bandler and John Grinder, *The Structure of Magic I: A Book about Language and Therapy* (Palo Alto: Science and Behavior Books, 1975): 49.
38. Bandler and Grinder, *The Structure of Magic I*: 156.
39. Roy Schafer, "Narration in the Psychoanalytic Dialogue," *Critical Inquiry* 7, no. 1 (Fall 1980): 35-36.
40. Milton H. Erickson, *The Nature of Hypnosis and Suggestion* (New York: Irvington Publishers, 1980).
41. See, for instance, Stephen R. Lankton, *Enchantment and Intervention in Family Therapy: Training in Ericksonian Approaches* (New York: Brunner/Mazel, 1986).
42. See, for instance, Luisa Passerini's discussion of jokes and satirical comments which circulated in Mussolini's Italy, "Oral Memory of Fascism" in *Rethinking Italian Fascism: Capitalism, Populism and Culture*, ed. David Forgacs (London: Lawrence and Wishart, 1986): 185-196.
43. Toril Moi, *Sexual/Textual Politics: Feminist Literary Theory* (London: Methuen, 1986): 78.

44. George F. Whicher, "Literature and Conflict," in *Literary History of the United States*, ed. Robert E. Spiller, Willard Thorp, Thomas H. Johnson, Henry Seidel Canby, Richard M. Ludwig, 3rd. (New York: Macmillan, 1963): 563.

45. Vissarion G. Belinsky, *Selected Philosophical Works* (Moscow: Foreign Languages Publishing House, 1956): 543.

46. Alexander Solzhenitsyn, *The First Circle*, trans. Michael Guybon (London: Collins and Harvill, 1968): 361.

47. Alexander Solzhenitsyn, *One Word of Truth: The Nobel Speech on Literature 1970* (London: Bodley Head, 1972): 15.

48. For an excellent survey of theories of power and an introduction to the related terminology see Stephen Lukes, "Power and Authority," in ed. T. Bottomore and R. Nisbet, *A History of Sociological Analysis* (New York: Basic Books, 1978): 633-676.

49. Max Weber, *Economy and Society*, ed. G. Roth and C. Wittich (New York: Bedminster, 1968), vol. 2: 927.

50. Frank Parkin, *Class, Inequality and Political Order* (London: MacGibbon Kee, 1971): 46.

51. Nicos Poulantzas, *Political Power and Social Classes*, trans. T. O'Hagan (London: New Left Books and Sheed and Ward, 1973; C. Wright Mills, "The Structure of Power in American Society" in *Power, Politics and People: The Collected Essays of C. Wright Mills*, ed. I. L. Horowitz (New York and London: Oxford University Press, 1963; Ralph Miliband, *Marxism and Politics* (Oxford: Oxford University Press, 1977).

52. Roland Barthes, "Lecture in Inauguration of the Chair of Literary Semiology, Collège de France, January 7, 1977," trans. R. Howard, *October* 8 (Spring 1977): 4.

53. Michel Foucault, *Power/Knowledge: Selected Interviews and Other Writings 1972-1977*, ed. Colin Gordon (Brighton: Harvester Press, 1980): 98.

54. For a discussion of the concept of ideology which is both acute and readable, see Janet Wolff, *The Social Production of Art* (London and Basingstoke, 1981): 49-70.

55. Karl Marx and Friedrich Engels, *The German Ideology*, (London: Lawrence and Wishart, 1963): 39.

56. Dale Spender, *Man Made Language*, second edition (London, Boston, Melbourne and Henley: Routledge, 1985): 12.

57. Barthes, "Lecture": 5.

58. See Stephen Lukes, "Power and Authority": 639.

59. Hannah Arendt, *On Violence* (London: The Penguin Press, 1970): 44.

60. Toril Moi, *Sexual/Textual Politics*: 148.

61. Hélène Cixous, "Entretien avec Françoise van Rossum-Guyon." *Revue des Sciences Humaines* 168 (1977), 483-4, quoted in Toril Moi, *Sexual/Textual Politics*: 124-5.

62. Julia Kristeva, *Desire in Language: A Semiotic Approach to Literature and Art*, trans. Alice Jardine, Thomas Gora, Léon Roudiez (Oxford: Blackwell, 1980): 23 ff.

63. Friedrich Engels, "Letter to Margaret Harkness (April 1888)," in *Marx and Engels on Literature and Art*, ed. Lee Baxandall and Stefan Morawski (New York: International General, 1974): 115-17.

64. Engels, "Letter to Minna Kautsky," in Baxandall and Morawski, eds., *Marx and Engels on Literature and Art*: 113-14.

65. Lucien Goldmann, *Towards a Sociology of the Novel*, trans. Alan Sheridan (London: Tavistock Publications, 1975) and his earlier *The Hidden God: a Study of Tragic Vision in the 'Pensées' of Pascal and the Tragedies of Racine*, trans. P. Thody (London: Routledge and Kegan Paul, 1964).
66. Paul Watzlawick, John H. Weakland, Richard Fisch, *Change: Principles of Problem Formation and Problem Resolution* (New York: W.W. Norton, 1974): 56.
67. Bertolt Brecht, "A Short Organum for the Theater," in *Brecht on Theater: The Development of an Aesthetic*, ed. J. Willett (New York: Hill and Wang, 1964): 204.
68. Brecht, "The Popular and the Realistic", in *Brecht on Theater*. 109.
69. Pierre Macherey, *A Theory of Literary Production*, trans. G. Wall (London and Boston: Routledge and Kegan Paul, 1978).
70. Karl Marx, *Grundrisse* (Harmondsworth: Penguin, 1973): 91.
71. Wolfgang Iser, *The Implied Reader: Patterns of Communication in Prose Fiction from Bunyan to Beckett* (Baltimore and London: Johns Hopkins University Press, 1974): 58.
72. Georges Poulet, "Phenomenology of Reading," *New Literary History* 1 (1969): 56.
73. Lowry Nelson, "The Fictive Reader: Aesthetic and Social Aspects of Literary Performance," *Comparative Literature Studies* 15, no. 2 (1978): 206.
74. Watzlawick et al., *Change*. 95.
75. Thomas S. Kuhn, *The Structure of Scientific Revolutions* (London: University of Chicago Press, 1962).
76. Susan Suleiman, "Ideological Dissent from Works of Fiction: Toward a Rhetoric of the Roman a Thèse," *Neophilologus* 60 (April 1976): 173.
77. Kate Millett, *Sexual Politics* (Garden City, New York: Doubleday, 1970).
78. For a thorough study of the German theorists, see Robert C. Holub, *Reception Theory* (New York and London: Methuen), 1984.
79. Umberto Eco, *The Role of the Reader: Explorations in the Semiotics of Texts* (London: Hutchinson, 1981).
80. See Roland Barthes's work from *S/Z* (New York: Hill and Wang, 1970).
81. Roland Barthes, "Theory of the Text," trans. Ian McLeod, in *Untying the Text: A Post-Structuralist Reader*, ed. Robert Young (Boston, London and Henley: Routledge and Kegan Paul, 1981): 36.
82. Werner Bauer et al., *Text und Rezeption: Wirkungsanalyse Zeitgenössischer Lyrik am Beispiel des Gedichtes "Fadensonnen" von Paul Celan* (Frankfurt: Athenäum, 1972): 12, quoted in D. W. Fokkema and Elrud Kunne-Ibsch, *Theories of Literature in the Twentieth Century: Structuralism, Marxism, Aesthetics of Reception, Semiotics* (London: C. Hurst and Co, 1977): 157-160.
83. Bauer, *Text und Rezeption*: 9.
84. Manfred Durzak, "Plädoyer für eine Rezeptionsästhetik: Anmerkungen zur Deutschen und Amerikanischen Literarturkritik am Beispiel von Günter Grass *Örtlich Betaübt*," *Akzente* 6 (1959): 487-504. For a more recent example of such a study, by a sociologist, see Wendy Griswold, "The Fabrication of Meaning: Literary Interpretation in the United States, Great Britain, and the West Indies," *American Journal of Sociology* 92, no. 5 (March 1987): 1077-1117, which examines the varying reception in each country of the novels of the Barbadian novelist George Lamming.

85. See especially his "Literary History as a Challenge to Literary Theory" in *New Directions in Literary History*, ed. Ralph Cohen (London: Routledge and Kegan Paul, 1974): 11-41.

86. Solzhenitsyn, *One Word of Truth*: 15.

87. Elio Vittorini, *Le due tensioni: appunti per una ideologia della letteratura*, ed. Dante Isella (Milan: Il Saggiatore, 1967): 27.

88. Mikhail Bakhtin, "Discourse in the Novel," in *The Dialogic Imagination: Four Essays by M. M. Bakhtin*, ed. Michael Holquist, trans. Caryl Emerson and Michael Holmquist (Austin, Texas: University of Texas Press: 1981).

89. Moi, *Sexual/Textual Politics*: 108.

90. Barthes, "Theory of the Text": 37.

91. Barthes, "Lecture": 6.

92. Luce d'Eramo, *L'opera di Ignazio Silone: saggio critico e guida bibliografica* (Milan: Mondadori, 1971): 242.

93. Sandra M. Gilbert and Susan Gubar, *The Madwoman in the Attic: The Woman Writer and the Nineteenth-Century Literary Imagination* (New Haven: Yale University Press, 1979): 73.

94. Mink, "Narrative Form as a Cognitive Instrument": 130.

95. Mink, "Narrative Form as a Cognitive Instrument": 130.

96. See Chapter 5.

2. IVAN TURGENEV:
A Sportsman's Notebook (1852)

▼ ▼ ▼

The nature of the claim

The spectacular claim made for Turgenev's collection of stories, *A Sportsman's Notebook*, is that Tsar Alexander II's reading of that work was instrumental in his decision to abolish serfdom in Russia. It is the apparent simplicity of this claim — that a work of narrative fiction helped to inspire an autocrat to exercise his unlimited powers in the liberation of 50 million people — which makes it an ideal subject for the first of these case studies.

Turgenev's biographers are remarkably consistent in their references to the part played by *A Sportsman's Notebook* in bringing about the abolition of serfdom. The individual stories which came to make up *A Sportsman's Notebook* were published one-by-one in a literary periodical between 1847 and 1851, and the collection was first published in volume form in 1852, when Alexander's father, Nicholas I, was still Tsar. The usual assertion is that Alexander read them as they first appeared, was deeply moved by them, and, at least partly under their influence, resolved to abolish serfdom at the earliest opportunity. He succeeded to the throne in 1855 and almost immediately initiated moves to bring about emancipation, which finally came about in 1861. Leonard Schapiro, one of Turgenev's most serious biographers, is typical in stating: "It is ... quite certain that the future Emperor Alexander II was influenced by *A Sportsman's Notebook* in his final decision to put through the emancipation of the serfs."[1]

Almost identical assertions are found in the studies of Turgenev by Avrahm Yarmolinsky and Henri Granjard.[2] Turgenev himself expressed pride in later years at the effect his book had had on Alexander, claiming that the Tsar personally ensured that his gratitude was conveyed to him.[3]

Significantly, and perhaps surprisingly, Tsar Alexander's biographers also vouch for the truth of these claims.[4]

It should be immediately obvious that these assertions, as they stand, are founded on the highly debatable assumption that emancipation came about primarily as a consequence of Alexander's personal decision, rather than through the agency of wider social and political forces. Yet that issue is the subject of major disagreement amongst historians. As Terence Emmons has said, the emancipation of the serfs poses in an extraordinarily vivid way the difficult and persistent general problem for historians of "establishing causal relationships between broad socioeconomic developments and specific historical events (such as revolutions) or deliberate human actions (such as reforms)."[5] So this study of *A Sportsman's Notebook* will, from the beginning, treat the issue of causality in the process of emancipation as complex and problematic rather than simple. More particularly, it will be concerned not only with Alexander's personal response to *A Sportsman's Notebook*, but with the way in which the work seems to have insinuated itself in a remarkable way into the consciousness of a great number of the landowners and bureaucrats who participated, pursuing what they perceived to be their own various interests, in the long and complex process of the movement toward emancipation. There are, it is interesting to discover, several accounts of Turgenev as an old man being accosted by strangers, and introduced to large gatherings, as the author of *A Sportsman's Notebook* (even though he had by then published a number of novels, including *Fathers and Sons* and *A Nest of the Landed Gentry*, which were very widely read) and of his still being applauded for the part played by that early work in bringing about emancipation. During a visit he made to Moscow University in 1879, for instance, the students even applauded Turgenev on the improbable grounds that he had foreshadowed in *A Sportsman's Notebook* their demands for a Russian constitution.[6] The tradition that the work had a direct influence on events, not only through its particular impact on Alexander but through its wider effect on public opinion, was evidently well established in Turgenev's own time.

The problem of Turgenev's intentions

While there is no necessary connection between the political intentions of a writer and the political outcomes which may follow a work's publication, the question of Turgenev's intentions in writing *A Sportsman's*

Notebook is still a useful starting point. Although Turgenev declared himself, as he got older, very proud of the contribution his book was supposed to have made to the coming of emancipation, he nevertheless recounted, on different occasions, two almost contrary (certainly competing) stories about how and why he had written it. On the one hand, he went so far as to claim that he had written *A Sportsman's Notebook* as a political manifesto, and even on one occasion in 1868 that his departure from Russia for several years in 1847 had been with the specific intention of fighting serfdom by writing the stories.[7] On the other hand, he frequently asserted his complete detachment from social and political concerns, except in that, as a writer, he could not avoid them. For instance, in a letter to Countess Yelizaveta Lambert, he declared: "I'm not a political person ... I have never been and never will be involved in politics: that business is alien to me and uninteresting, and I pay attention to it only as much as is necessary for a writer called upon to paint pictures of contemporary life."[8]

Moreover he was always dismissive towards what he regarded as tendentious literary works, such as D.V. Grigorovich's novel, *Anton the Hapless* (1847), whose main theme was criticism of serfdom.[9] He disapproved of *Uncle Tom's Cabin*, which he read within months of its first publication, for the same reason. And in a letter to a friend, Pavel Vasilyevich Annenkov, in 1853, he wrote of his concern that a character in one of his longer stories, "The Inn" (of the same period as *A Sportsman's Notebook* but not included in the collection), was "of the same calibre" as Uncle Tom, that both were "polemics" and he "promised never to write like that again." (It is an indication of how great a potential for political influence was attributed to narrative fiction in Russia during this period, even in translation, that *Uncle Tom's Cabin* was banned till 1855. By a curious coincidence, *Uncle Tom's Cabin* was first published in volume form in precisely the same year as *A Sportsman's Notebook*, and the abolition of slavery in the United States occurred just one year after the emancipation of the serfs in Russia. The coincidence is all the stranger because the differences, in every other respect, between the two books and between the two societies within which they had their respective impacts were so stark.)[10]

In any case, it emerges that in the 1840s Turgenev's attitudes to serfdom itself were far from being as clearcut as he sometimes later suggested. He was of an aristocratic, landowning and serfholding family, and he inherited vast estates, with their two thousand serfs, on his mother's death in 1850. He had loathed her brutal and capricious treatment of the serfs and had often come into conflict with her on this issue. But an essay he wrote in 1842, entitled "Some Remarks on the Russian Economy and the Russian Peasant," recommended only modest reforms of serfdom, including controls on arbitrary serfholders, rather than its abolition.[11] And, whereas he later claimed that he had always had a deep hatred for the whole institution of serfdom and always longed above all else to see emancipation brought about, a friend from his years at Berlin University (1839-1840) remembered his stance at that time rather differently: "In all our conversations he never departed from the purely historical soil, and I never heard him express ardent hopes or wishes on the subject of the abolition of serfdom, as many now assert."[12] (I shall several times in this book be noting a tendency for writers, in recalling their early years, to suggest that they developed their current views at an earlier date than was actually the case. Whether writers of narrative fiction are any more prone than other people to this retrospective smoothing of their life story into a unified, homogeneous narration, I am not sure.)

It seems evident, too, that Turgenev had no commitment at that time (if ever) to the absolute desirability of human liberty. As he commented after the events of 1848 in France: "If it comes to that, who said that man is intended to be free? History proves the opposite."[13] While it seems likely that by 1845 he had become convinced that abolition, rather than the reform of serfdom, was required, it also appears that he had no expectation that it would happen in his lifetime. Moreover, his commitment to the freedom of his own serfs, when he inherited them in 1850, only extended to freeing the relatively small number of household serfs, who then stayed on as servants. He did not free the field serfs, though he permitted them to switch from the more onerous obligation to work in his fields (*barshchina*) to the less onerous system (which was less profitable to him) whereby they made him an annual payment (*obrok*). He also allowed them to buy their freedom if they could afford it.[14] The limits to Turgenev's sense of responsibility towards his serfs are also indicated by his sexual exploitation of serf women, by whom he had one, and possibly two, children. (He did acknowledge responsibility for his daughter by one of these women and arranged her education and upbringing in France.)[15]

As for his management of his estates and serfs (and, after Emancipation in 1861, free peasants), he was, by the standards of the time, a humanitarian and relatively generous landowner who did not, however, take the trouble to equip himself with the skills to undertake the agricultural modernization and efficient administration that he knew were required, and who lived abroad as much as he could, delegating his authority to a series of inefficient managers. It is true that, with a number of like-minded intellectuals, he put money and energy into a large-scale proposal for spreading literacy and primary education amongst peasants, but nothing came of it.[16] (And, later still, he founded a peasant school on his own estate.)

So, while there is no doubt at all of Turgenev's enthusiasm for emancipation as, after 1850, it came to seem more and more likely, any assertion that, in the late 1840s, he was a radical who worked for the abolition of serfdom through his writing is, on several grounds, unconvincing. The view taken by most Soviet critics that Turgenev was a liberal who, throughout his life, supported proposals concerning the peasantry which would ultimately bring economic advantage to his own, landowning, class has a good deal of justification.[17] Certainly his income during the twenty-two years of his life after emancipation, which he spent mostly outside Russia, continued to derive primarily from the labor of his former serfs. And a letter he wrote to Annenkov in 1853 (still some years before emancipation came about) illustrates the strict limits, even at that crucial time, of his interest in serfs as literary subjects: "the peasants have absolutely overpowered us in literature ... It's time to send the peasants into retirement."[18] This comment seems, in turn, to confirm the assertion of Eva Kagan-Kans that "the significance of serfdom for Turgenev in *A Sportsman's Notebook* was purely structural,"[19] a device for developing a rural version of the existing "physiological sketches" of typical characters to be found in the city, rather than the subject of any burning political commitment.

The nature of the sketches

The discovery that Turgenev may not have written *A Sportsman's Notebook* as a manifesto against serfdom does not in itself invalidate claims for its actual influence in that direction. So what kind of works are these stories and how, precisely, has it been suggested that they achieved such a remarkable impact? *A Sportsman's Notebook* as we now read it consists of twenty-four stories (and a brief concluding landscape description, entitled "Forest and Steppe") of which three were inserted for the first time only in the edition of 1874 and so do not concern us here. The twenty-one original stories are linked, as their eventual collective title suggests, by purporting to recount experiences from the life of a hunting enthusiast. The narrator, who is never named, is a landowner and so, no doubt, a serfholder. In each story he describes a particular character or group of characters encountered, almost always, in the course of a hunting expedition, usually on foot, in different parts of rural Orel province, two hundred miles south of Moscow. He sometimes has a hunting dog with him and, in four of the stories, he is accompanied by Ermolai, a serf belonging to one of his neighbors, who is enormously knowledgeable about the countryside and the game to be found in it.

Though there is great variety amongst the stories, most of them belong to one or other of two main types. There are eight or nine stories which depict encounters with people of more or less the same class as the narrator, mostly gentry landowners, but including a doctor ("The Country Doctor"), an elderly woman ("Tatyana Borisovna and her Nephew"), and a prince buying horses at a fair ("Lebedyan"). These are essentially character sketches which evoke figures in their social context with extraordinary vividness. The landowners are mostly impoverished, having, we are told, lost their money by extravagance or bad management (in, for instance, "Pyotr Petrovich Karataev" and "Chertopkhanov and Neopyuskin"). The very few prosperous landowners tend to be either supercilious or brutal (or both) in their treatment of their serfs. The narrator never comments directly on such behavior, but conveys a subtle distaste for this kind of landowner. So, for instance, having described the young Arkady Pavlich Penochkin (in "The Bailiff") in apparently flattering detail ("he gives excellent dinners ... he is a judicious steady fellow ... to use his own words, is strict but just, has the good of his serfs at heart, and punishes them — for their good"), he adds that "a strange uneasiness takes hold of you in his house" linking this to the cowed attitude of the man's house serfs (*Sportsman's Notebook*: 120).[20] Nevertheless, in the three or four stories of this type where relations between landowners and their serfs are directly depicted, it is in the context of a closely observed psychological portrait of the landowner, rather than as the central subject of the story.

In the second, and more famous, type of story from *A Sportsman's Notebook*, the narrator relates his encounters with individual serfs, or groups of serfs, from whom he usually seeks some kind of assistance as he walks or rides across the landscape in search of wildfowl. He needs shelter from the sun (in "Raspberry Water") or the rain (for instance, in "The Bear", "The Estate Office"), or help with a broken axle on his carriage ("Kasyan from Fair Springs"), or assistance to get out on a lake to shoot duck ("Lgov"), or somewhere to sleep ("Ermolai and the Miller's

Wife" and "Bezhin"). He usually comes across the serfs without even meeting their owners but learns a good deal from them about their relationship with their owners.

Some of the more obviously barbaric features of serfdom are referred to in the course of these stories: serfs who have been flogged or sent off to the army for displeasing their master, serfs who have been prohibited from marrying, serfs who are sent to work in a factory and whose wages are paid to their owner. In "Ermolai and the Miller's Wife," a young maidservant is prohibited by her master and mistress from marrying the footman she loves and, when she falls pregnant by him, is sold off to be the wife of an old rich miller. In "The Bailiff," a landowner allows his bailiff to beat and cheat the serfs. As one serf explains: "'He's sent two of my sons out of their turn to join the army, and now he's taking the third one away too. Yesterday, sir, he took my last cow out of my yard and he beat my old woman'" (*Sportsman's Notebook*: 149).

One or two stories show serfs quite degraded by the capricious treatment they have received from their masters or mistresses. In the story "Lgov," for instance, an old serf tells of having been owned by five different landowners, prohibited from marrying, renamed and required to learn (successively) the skills of page, postillion, gardener, whipper-in, cobbler, cook, coffee-server, actor, coachman and fisherman in a pond which has no fish. He is paid no wages but is entirely accepting of this state of affairs: "'Wages? Certainly not, sir ... they give me food — and I am quite content, thank God. May God give the mistress long life!'" (*Sportsman's Notebook*: 89). In several stories we see serfs behaving brutally to each other in protection of their masters' interests (for instance, "The Bear"), but often serf overseers are intent on gain for themselves too (for instance, in "The Estate Office"). However, all such features of serfdom are referred to incidentally and without any great emphasis or overt moral comment.

There are, by contrast, a number of stories in which peasants, while nominally remaining serfs, have established themselves in a profitable farmlet, such as Khor from "Khor and Kalinich," or a small business, for instance the innkeeper who presides over the singing contest in "The Singers." While the owner of the busy little tavern, indeed of the whole village and its inhabitants, remains anonymous, being referred to only as "some German or other from Petersburg," the serf innkeeper emerges as a fully developed character with his own name and sphere of influence: "Nikolai Ivanich ... forced a well-known horse-thief to return a horse stolen from someone of his acquaintance; he made the peasants of a neighboring village listen to reason when they had refused to accept a new factor, and so on. Incidentally, it mustn't be supposed that he did this from love of fair play, from any zeal for his neighbor's interests; no, he is simply at pains to avert anything that might in any way disturb his own peace" (*Sportsman's Notebook*: 231-232).

A number of others, while not prosperous, have a striking independence of character and a wisdom that is impressive (the gentle Kasyan in the story "Kasyan from Fair Springs" is well known as a healer, reproaches the narrator firmly for killing for sport, and appears to be able to warn the birds to keep away from him).

The narrator's interactions with the serfs are minimal. The demands he makes on them are modest — shelter from a storm, directions, a little black bread. Typically circumstances allow him to observe interactions between serfs who are largely unaffected by his presence. In several stories ("Ermolai and the Miller's Wife," "Bezhin Meadow," "The Estate Office," "The Rendezvous") the serfs believe he is asleep and he overhears their conversation. In "The Estate Office," he is caught in the rain in a remote place, takes shelter in a room attached to the estate office, and overhears the conversations of those who work there. They reveal corruption and extortion against other serfs by the serf clerks who run the office. In "Bezhin Meadow," he has lost his way and, having to sleep outside, lies under a bush as five young serfs sit around a fire, cooking potatoes and keeping an eye on some grazing horses. They tell tales, which make them increasingly frightened, of water-fairies, of goblins, of snakes and wolves, and the ghost of a drowned man which has taken possession of a lamb. This story, like many others, is suffused with an almost idyllic appreciation of the beauty of the landscape that is far from polemical. Here is the narrator's description of the view from beside the fire: "From the lighted circle it was difficult to make out what was happening in the shadows, and therefore everything close at hand seemed hidden by a blackish curtain; but farther off, towards the horizon, long shapes could be discerned dimly as hills and woods. The clear, dark sky stood, solemn and immeasurably high above us, in all its mysterious magnificence. It caught one deliciously at the heart to breathe that unmistakable, languorous, cool breath — the breath of a summer night in Russia" (*Sportsman's Notebook*: 99).

It is not, in general, suggested that the main impact of *A Sportsman's Notebook* on its first readers, whether the Tsar or others, was in terms of the stories' conveying new information about the awful conditions under which serfdom, and individual serfholders in particular, required peasants to exist. There was no shortage of such information, whether in the countless official reports which had been compiled over the previous thirty years, or in the polemical fiction of Grigorovich and others. It is in a different sense that *A Sportsman's Notebook* may be said to have recounted "untold stories." The feature of the work which seems to have so radically shifted the attitudes to serfdom of many of his readers (and these stories made Turgenev in his lifetime "the best known, most widely read and most controversial writer in Russia")[21] is simply the degree of attention which it accords to the serfs and the closeness and detail with which the serfs are observed. This went not only against Russian *literary* convention, in which serfs were traditionally treated as mere background figures, or stock comic characters, but, more importantly, against every *social* convention. It was a matter of foregrounding characters traditionally thought of as literary and social background. Whatever their legal and economic status, the serfs are shown as having a lively rounded humanity. As Victor Ripp writes, in his excellent book, *Turgenev's Russia*, Turgenev had the "ability to impart a particularity to each of his characters, even those one expects to have been crushed to insipid flatness."[22] Leonard Schapiro's observation is that "Turgenev had, for the first time probably, shown members of his own social standing that peasants were individual human beings, with intellectual and spiritual potentialities — a fact which very few landowners were accustomed to recognize."[23] So, for instance, whereas to the neighboring landowner, Mr Polutykin (in the story "Khor and Kalinich"), Kalinich is just "a keen obliging fellow," indispensable on his hunting expeditions, the narrator invites the reader to see him through his more perceptive eyes: "Kalinich was a man of the gayest and gentlest character imaginable; he was constantly humming below his breath and throwing carefree glances in all directions; he spoke in a slightly nasal voice, smiling and screwing up his pale blue eyes and often passing his hand over his scanty wedge-shaped beard ... his attitude to his master was one of fatherly supervision" (*Sportsman's Notebook*: 7).

P. V. Annenkov, a famous literary critic as well as Turgenev's friend, stated that the stories of *A Sportsman's Notebook* contributed in no small measure to a general change of attitude towards the peasants and their mental processes, adding specifically that they put an end to the tendency, which had been widespread even among liberals desiring emancipation, to treat the peasant with a degree of derision and contempt.[24] The educated and largely landowning readership of *A Sportsman's Notebook* were familiar enough with "the serf problem" as an abstraction, but what Turgenev required of them in the course of reading these stories, was to perform the quite unfamiliar social role of studying serfs closely as individuals.

The context for publication

The years 1847 to 1851, in which Turgenev published the single sketches which make up *A Sportsman's Notebook*, were a period of widespread peasant unrest and growing clandestine activity by intellectuals (many from the landowning class) opposed to serfdom, and in some cases, to the autocracy. Tsar Nicholas I (Alexander's father), appalled at the prospect that the massive uprisings occurring throughout Western Europe around 1848 might be repeated in Russia, used military repression on the serfs and the weapons of "super-censorship" and exile on writers and intellectuals who showed liberal tendencies. (Dostoevsky was arrested in 1849 with other members of the Petrashesky circle and taken as far as the execution yard before being informed of his reprieve.)

In this period of extreme repression and censorship, there was a quite remarkable sensitivity to indirect political reference in certain cultural forms. It has been pointed out, for instance, that after 1842 economists were prohibited from writing about the possibilities for agricultural reform, but that literary writers could, if they were prudent, still do so.[25] Lectures on English parliamentarianism by the historian T. N. Granovsky were widely interpreted as an attack on Russian autocracy.[26] And it was at this time that Belinsky wrote his famous letter to Gogol declaring that the public looked on Russian writers as "its only leaders, defenders and saviours against Russian autocracy, orthodoxy and nationality."[27] This was the atmosphere of extreme sensitivity into which Turgenev drip-fed the stories which were to make up *A Sportsman's Notebook*. The fact that they appeared one-by-one over a period of several years meant, on the one hand, that they slipped past the censor's scrutiny more easily but, on the other, that they struck a certain note in their readers' minds *repeatedly and at intervals.*

Alexander's reading of the sketches

It is known that Alexander (Grand Duke until his father's death in 1855) read the sketches avidly as they first appeared in *The Contemporary* and discussed them enthusiastically with his wife. One of his biographers,

E. M. Almedingen, refers to his reading the first story, "Khor and Kalinich," to her in 1847 and notes that this "glimpse into the depths of peasant life" was "never forgotten by either of them."[28] Her unfamiliarity with serfdom (she was Marie of Hesse and did not come to Russia until her marriage to Alexander in 1841) must have given a particular flavor to their joint readings of the sketches, with Alexander having the difficult task of explaining this peculiarly Russian phenomenon to her. (A piece of fictional narrative shared in this way between readers often acts as a focus or catalyst for significant wider debate.) The French Turgenev scholar, Henri Granjard, insists that this reading of *A Sportsman's Notebook* was crucial because, he says, Alexander was hostile to "any plan for the reform of serfdom" until at least 1847, and his change of mind coincided precisely with the publication of the earliest sketches.[29] The reality was almost certainly more complicated.

The desirability *in principle* of the emancipation of the serfs was quite widely agreed on through much of the first half of the nineteenth century in Russia, agreed on even by Alexander's uncle, Alexander I (Tsar from 1801 to 1825) and by his father, Nicholas I (1825-1855). Alongside, and vitally linked to, moral distaste for serfdom was the growing realization that Russia needed to develop a more entrepreneurial form of agriculture and manufacturing which, in turn, required a more mobile and more productive labor force. So what stopped these autocrats from abolishing serfdom? As Lionel Kochan and Richard Abraham express it: "Nicholas himself was quite clear about the desirability of its abolition. However, he was inhibited by the complementary fears that emancipation on terms favorable to the serfs would secure his assassination, while emancipation on terms unfavorable to them might provoke a peasant war."[30] This is an indication of the real constraints on even the autocrat's supposedly absolute power. Nicholas himself, as late as 1846, stated to a plenary sitting of the State Council that serfdom was an evil, "yet to interfere with it in any way would result in a worse evil. At the moment any thought of emancipation would be a criminal attempt against the tranquillity and wellbeing of the State ..."[31] One of his specific concerns was that the serfs would, if emancipated, rapidly be transformed into the kind of dangerous proletariat he saw in the industrialized nations of Western Europe.[32]

As for Alexander's own position, his tutor as he grew up had been the poet, Vassily Zhukovsky, who, though not rich, had chosen to free all his serfs, and there is no doubt that in the case of serfdom, as in many other fields, Zhukovsky had a great influence on Alexander. In 1837, when

Alexander was only 19, Zhukovsky was instructed by Nicholas I to take him on a seven-month tour of the Empire, during which, against Nicholas's wishes, Alexander insisted on stopping frequently to enter peasant huts and talk to the serfs. One biographer, E. M. Almedingen, refers to his having displayed "obvious anguish" as he discovered the conditions of existence of many of the serfs.[33] Another, Schumacher, notes that during that tour "the people's sorrow became Alexander's sorrow."[34] So, ten years before he read the first stories of Turgenev's *A Sportsman's Notebook*, Alexander had had a series of direct encounters of his own with serfs and been deeply moved by the desperate conditions in which he saw many of them living.

In 1842, Nicholas appointed Alexander to chair a committee on serfdom, in the course of which Alexander read a large number of documents, some dating back to the turn of the century, which stated that serfdom was the greatest evil in the Empire. At this time, Zhukovsky wrote several letters reminding him that: "Slavery is abhorrent in God's eyes and runs counter to his truth ... Don't forget that supreme power rests upon an acknowledgement of that truth ... It alone is the law ... To break with [that truth] would be the suicide of autocracy ... It may take ten, twenty, twenty-five years, but come it must — just as it must come in the United States."[35]

At the same time, of course, Alexander received memoranda from a large number of landowners, both within and outside the State bureaucracy, insisting on the practical impossibility of abolishing serfdom, and from Philaret the Orthodox Metropolitan of Moscow and many archbishops and bishops insisting that serfdom was entirely compatible with God's will.[36] Alexander is reported to have taken all the submissions, on both sides of the question, seriously. His committee made some minor recommendations for the reform of serfdom, but it seems clear that Alexander, himself, would, on economic, political, and moral grounds, have gone much further even at that stage, if Nicholas had allowed it.[37] In the long term, it can be said that chairing the commission made him more acutely aware of all the arguments for emancipation, but equally brought the obstacles to emancipation very fully to his attention.

At most, therefore, *A Sportsman's Notebook* was only one element, though perhaps an important one, in Alexander's long consideration of the problem of serfdom in preparation for his succeeding to the throne in 1855. The question as to how (or why) the stories might have moved Alexander's mind (and the minds of liberal intellectuals in the late 1840s and early 1850s) further along the path towards the emancipation of the serfs has traditionally been answered by saying that, for the first time, they showed the serfs to be, in Leonard Schapiro's words, "individual human beings, with intellectual and spiritual potentialities." This line of argument can certainly be developed further than it has been. The "normal" relationship between landowner and serfs (especially house serfs) was for the serf to observe and attend to the landowner and his or her wishes and demands. As far as possible, the serf aimed to avoid attracting the attention of the landowner. (Peter Kropotkin cites the example of a landowner who, when another landowner drew to his notice the fact that his peasants were reproducing rather slowly, called for a list of five young female and five young male peasants and, arbitrarily pairing the names off, ordered them to marry ten days later.)[38] What Turgenev did so remarkably was to reverse the normal direction of observation and attention within Russian rural society. The landowning narrator observed individual serfs closely, and so directed the attention of the (mostly) landowning readers to do the same. The argument therefore appears to be that the stories made it extraordinarily difficult for such readers to achieve any kind of congruence between what they knew perfectly well to be the legal and social status of serfs, and the lively, rounded humanity of the serf characters they saw through the eyes of Turgenev's narrator. Moreover, it seems highly likely that, for Alexander himself, these stories of encounters with serfs in their own environment recalled the moving encounters *he* had had with serfs during his tour of the empire ten years before and which his status (and his father) had not allowed him to repeat. This would have been particularly significant, since the 1842 committee on serfdom, which he had chaired, neither invited nor received any submissions from serfs. Alexander may well have felt that, through *A Sportsman's Notebook*, the voices of the serfs were again brought directly to his ears as they could have been by no other means.

Absences and ambiguities in the depiction of rural society

While this account of the impact of *A Sportsman's Notebook* in terms of its inclusion and foregrounding of a social group previously excluded or treated as background has considerable validity, it is hardly sufficient, on its own, to account for the influence which has been claimed for the book. The foregrounding of the serf characters needs to be related to a number of features in this work which have not yet been mentioned. The key to understanding more fully the nature and mechanisms of the influence achieved by *A Sportsman's Notebook* is to be found in a number of important absences and ambiguities in Turgenev's depiction of rural society and serfdom.

Commentators have always noted with some bemusement that *A Sportsman's Notebook* was greeted warmly by readers with very different views, by Westernizers and Slavophiles, radicals and moderates, with only "right-wing critics with close links to officialdom" actively disliking it.[39] It will be my argument that the absences referred to above came to be filled, and the ambiguities resolved, in significantly different ways by different groups of readers — in other words, that it was precisely the relative openness of the text which made it "seductive" to such a wide readership. This also explains its initial acceptability to the censors. (I shall also be speculating that Alexander developed a particular reading of his own that derived from his unique position, but for the moment I am leaving aside the question of Alexander's individual response to the work.) Once it had been accepted, internalized, by such diverse groups, it came to work on them over the years leading up to emancipation in ways they could not have anticipated. (The image of the work of fiction as a kind of Trojan horse, whose subversive force only bursts out once the work has gained initial admission to its readers' mental world, is one which will recur in connection with other works to be studied here.)

In the first place, *A Sportsman's Notebook* omits from its depiction of serfdom the two major groups of Russian serfs of the period — peasant or field serfs in private hands attached to their master's estate, and peasant serfs settled on state lands — in favour of the depiction of types of serfs who constituted a small minority and were marginal to the actual institution of serfdom. So Turgenev's serf characters include many house serfs (Mitrofan in "Raspberry Water," Suchok in "Lgov," Viktor in "The Rendezvous," the cowed servants in "The Bailiff" etc); some peasants who have, quite exceptionally, established themselves in a successful business (such as Nikolai Ivanich, the tapster, in "The Singers") or become overseers or bailiffs (such as Sofron in "The Bailiff" and several characters in "The Estate Office"); and a number of idiosyncratic, often almost derelict, serfs existing on the edges of estate life (Styopushka in "Raspberry Water," the woodsman in "The Bear," Kasyan in "Kasyan from Fair Springs" and so on). Historically all the groups from which Turgenev took his examples constituted only a very small fraction (at the most two million) of the fifty million serfs alive in Russia in the late

1840s, the vast mass of whom were peasant or field serfs, who are almost entirely unrepresented in *A Sportsman's Notebook*.

More generally, it is true that serfdom is not represented *as a system* in *A Sportsman's Notebook*. So, for instance, the few peasant serfs the narrator does come across and describe are *never* seen at work in the fields and, if the narrator visits their house, it is always situated on the edge of, or remote from, a village. As Eva Kagan-Kans comments: "The ordinary Russian village with its physical appearance and its external way of life did not draw his attention. The descriptions of the village, when they are given, are sketched rapidly and impressionistically, mainly emphasizing the squalid and gloomy character."[40] In "The Knocking," for instance: "The village in which we found ourselves was solitary and out of the way; all its inhabitants seemed to be desperately poor; with difficulty we had found a single cabin that had no chimney, certainly, but was quite roomy" (*Sportsman's Notebook*: 376). And in "Kasyan from Fair Spring": "The hamlet of Yudiny consisted of six little low cabins, which had already managed to take a list to one side, although they had probably not been standing long; some of the backyards were not even fenced-in. As we drove into the hamlet, we met not a single living soul" (*Sportsman's Notebook*: 119). Consequently the reader is never reminded of the communal dimension of serf existence, whereby the village *mir* (or communal council), in many areas, took official responsibility for, amongst other things, allocating agricultural plots and collecting taxes.

There are few references to the intricacies of the laws relating to serfdom — even though Turgenev had considerable expertise in such matters and discussed them in some detail in his letters. Similarly, the vast, corrupt bureaucracy, which was almost as directly responsible for the sufferings of the peasants as the landowners, does not figure in *A Sportsman's Notebook*. (A practical reason for this omission is that an unflattering depiction of the bureaucracy would have been interpreted as criticism of the Tsar and have attracted the wrath of the censors.) Nor is there any allusion to the violence of serfs against landowners which occurred regularly in the 1840s. While a number of serfs express anguish or despair at the particular treatment they have received from their masters, none appears even to think of the possibility of individual or collective revolt against them. Even the serfs who have been treated least well tend to conclude their stories with a comment such as "'May God give the mistress a long life!'" (Again there is no question of Turgenev's being ignorant of the many peasant revolts that occurred in the late

1840s, one of which touched him directly: his friend's father, and a close neighbor of the family, was hanged by his own serfs.)

Significantly, too, the reader of *A Sportsman's Notebook* is never confronted with the vital issue of the economics of serfdom as a system. We often meet or are told of landowners who manage their estates poorly, but their bad management is always depicted as deriving from their personal idiosyncrasy or extravagance, rather than from the widely acknowledged economic inefficiency of serfdom itself. A typical portrait is that of Count Pyotr Ilyich, in the story "Raspberry Water," "a rich magnate of the old days who was famous for his hospitality ... For long years the Count continued to give banquets and to walk about with a welcoming smile among the throng of obsequious guests. But, alas, his fortune was not enough to outlast his lifetime. Ruined beyond repair, he went place-hunting in St Petersburg and died in an hotel bedroom before he knew the result of his quest" (*Sportsman's Notebook*: 35). Victor Ripp contrasts Turgenev in this respect with Dickens: "Dickens' novels ... are crowded with the paraphernalia of the legitimized political structure. The actions of judges, policemen, lawyers, and businessmen of the City drive his plots along, and it is often a will, neat symbol of established law, that serves as the instrument of his narrative climaxes."[41]

Turgenev's stories (and novels) conspicuously lack equivalent Russian features. And, because *A Sportsman's Notebook* avoided detailed depiction of serfdom as a system, it offered no overt comment on what measures might be required for reform. At most, Victor Ripp argues, it can be said that it offered insights into three aspects of the psychological mechanism sustaining serfdom: that it appeared reasonable, even to those it most oppressed; that it was all-encompassing; and that it did not oppress all peasants equally.[42]

While Turgenev can be rightly credited with telling "untold stories" in this work, it is also true that he consistently *suppressed* some very important stories that he might have told about serfdom.

Different groups of readers, then, will have brought their own experience, interests, and attitudes to bear to fill these gaps. At one end of the continuum along which readers who found the stories acceptable might be arranged were those who believed only in the desirability of some reform of the detail of laws relating to serfdom. From their point of view, Turgenev's concentration on serfs who were, in one sense or another, peripheral to serfdom as a system reflected their belief that the "problem of serfdom" (and almost everyone agreed that there was a problem) lay more or less exclusively in that periphery, with those serfs who had in some way fallen outside the "protection" of good master-serf relations. It was, for instance, accepted by many landowners opposed to emancipation that there had to be a reform to improve the often slave-like existence of house serfs. So, partial though its representation of serfdom might be, *A Sportsman's Notebook* must have been seen, by such readers, as touching precisely its sorest areas. For those readers, field serfs could be omitted from *A Sportsman's Notebook*, in a sense, because *they* were not seen as constituting the problem. At the other end of the readership continuum, those who were already committed to the abolition of serfdom were able to read the stories as implying that the whole institution of serfdom, indeed the whole of Russian life, was infected with a disease whose symptoms were manifested most vividly in those marginal areas which are depicted. In other words, *A Sportsman's Notebook* suggests unequivocally only that serfdom was a problem, leaving open to quite diverse interpretations the precise nature of that problem.

Westernizers, Slavophiles, and Russian history

A different kind of gap in Turgenev's depiction of serfdom and rural life is the absence of a consistent historical perspective on serfdom and the consequent ambiguity not only about whether conditions for serfs are better or worse than they used to be, but also about whether there has been an improvement or a deterioration in rural life in general. The brief narratives of *A Sportsman's Notebook* almost never intersect with broader historical forms of narrative. A key story in this respect is "Ovsyanikov the Freeholder," whose central character, precisely because he is neither serf nor serfholder, is able to comment more freely on serfdom than any other character from the whole collection. On the one hand, he describes vividly the brutality and injustice of landowners in the old days; on the other, he shows he has no more admiration for the young landowners of the present: "'They treat the peasant like a doll: they turn him this way and that, they break him and throw him away'" (*Sportsman's Notebook*: 72). Nevertheless he strongly disapproves of his nephew's composing petitions on behalf of peasants who have been treated unjustly. When asked directly whether things were better in the old days, he answers contradictorily: "'Some things were certainly better, I should say ... We had a quieter life; things were easier, certainly ... but all the same, it is better now; and for your children it will be better still, please God'" (*Sportsman's Notebook*: 64). Elsewhere, he makes the curious comment: "'Must I really die without seeing the end of it? Must I really die without seeing any new system in action? ... It's a strange thing when the old order passes and there's no new one to take its place!'" (*Sportsman's Notebook*: 72). It is as if the stories, and the world they depict, are situated in a kind of hiatus between an ill-defined past and a quite unpredictable future.

The absence of an historical perspective is particularly significant for an understanding of just how *A Sportsman's Notebook* was read by different groups of readers in the 1850s because it was in their thinking about history — the historical metanarratives to which they subscribed — that the two major groups of Russian intellectuals of the period, the Westernizers and the Slavophiles, were most strongly divided. The debate between the two groups sprang from the polemically negative description of Russia in the first of the *Philosophical Letters* written by Peter Chaadaev in the 1830s, in which he declared the Empire to be intellectually and spiritually bankrupt. In a phrase which corresponds closely to the atmosphere that pervades *A Sportsman's Notebook*, he added: "We live in only the most narrow kind of present, without a past and without a future, in the midst of a shallow calm."[43] The parallel with the words of Ovsyanikov the freeholder is remarkable.

The Slavophiles, partly at least in reaction to Chaadaev's views, developed a kind of conservative romantic nationalism which idealized Russian Orthodoxy and the old institutions of Muscovite Russia, especially the assembly of the lands (*zemskii sobor*) and the peasant commune (*mir*). They rejected constitutional government as alien and divisive in favor of the absolute power of the Tsar while recommending that freedom to express opinion be guaranteed at all levels and that the *mir* decide all matters relating to peasant administration (an interesting coexistence, on different planes, of contrasting forms of power). In their view, Russian life had declined as a consequence of the reforms undertaken in the late seventeenth and early eighteenth centuries by Tsar Peter I, which they saw as having introduced false Western principles which had wrought spiritual damage on the Empire. As K. S. Aksakov wrote in a memorandum to Alexander in 1855: "For Russia to fulfill her destiny, she must follow her own ideas and requirements, and not theories which are alien to her."[44] There was no agreement amongst the Slavophiles, however, on whether serfdom (which had only existed formally for two centuries) should continue to exist, or be abolished, in their vision of a restored, old order.

The Russian historical narrative constructed by the Westernizers ran contrary to that of the Slavophiles. They repudiated Orthodoxy (most excluding a religious perspective altogether from their historical vision) and argued that Russia's current problems came from the fact that it had diverged from the paths of development established by Western Europe. The task for the future was therefore to ensure that Russia regained one or other of those paths. In fact, however, within the Westernizing camp, there were a number of views about which path was most appropriate, ranging from liberal constitutionalism to socialism, though almost all Westernizers were committed to the abolition of serfdom.

Turgenev generally associated himself with the Westernizers, yet, in the late 1840s and early 1850s particularly, he maintained much closer links with individual Slavophiles than did most Westernizers. While *A Sportsman's Notebook* makes history acutely problematic, it endorses neither the grand historical narrative of the Slavophiles nor that of the Westernizers, remaining oddly compatible with both. Far from contributing to change by acting as a divisive influence on traditionally opposed groups (as several of the novels to be examined later in this book did) *A Sportsman's Notebook* functioned, to an extraordinary degree, as a gentle, unifying influence, bringing together in the movement toward emancipation groups who, in all other respects, could be relied on to contradict each other.

The figure of the narrator

The other thoroughly ambiguous, even anomalous, feature of *A Sportsman's Notebook* is the peculiar figure of the landowning, serfholding narrator. The stories are all narrated by a gentry landowner, with serfs of his own, who, nevertheless, hunts on land owned by other members of the gentry and describes his encounters with other people's serfs. Though he evidently possesses his own estate, household, serfs, wealth, and resources, he is, in these stories, not only physically, but mentally, it seems, almost wholly detached from them. In his own environment, the unnamed narrator must have considerable personal power, yet, wandering over great distances and away from home for days at a time, he has, to a great extent, temporarily renounced that power, frequently placing himself in the hands of those he meets, without any apparent fear that they will take advantage of him. So, for instance, in "Bezhin Meadow," he misses his way and sleeps out in the open with a group of young serfs and in "The Bear," he takes shelter from a thunderstorm in the miserable cottage of a burly forester. This, in turn, makes it possible for him to gain a perspective on rural life which would not otherwise be available to him. Moreover, as he observes the serfs, the landowners, and the estates he comes across, it is never, as one might expect, to recall or make comparisons with his own situation, his own estate, his own serfs, his own ways of managing land and peasants. And, while judgements on what he sees are sometimes implied, they are never overtly stated. He is, himself, one might say, almost entirely a "reader" of the serfs' stories, rather than an agent in them. His failure to intervene in any of the episodes of injustice that he witnesses makes him an accomplice in that injustice to a far greater degree than we, as his readers, can ever be. (One of the minor exceptions to his habit of nonintervention occurs in "The Bear," when he persuades the poor forester to release a hungry serf who has been cutting down one of his master's trees.) He leaves the serf characters and the situations in which he finds them almost entirely as he found them at the beginning of the encounter.

In contrast to the range of vivid characters he describes, whether serfs, landowners, or others, the sportsman/narrator, who is after all present in every story, hardly emerges as a character at all. He is perceptive, sympathetic, mildly humanitarian but otherwise almost transparent. The reader is given little sense of his life beyond hunting (whether he is married, has children, has a large or small estate, many or few serfs, etc.) And while the serfs are strongly located in, and knowledgeable about, the particular landscape in which he meets them, he is no more than an appreciative observer of it and them; he is literally *displaced*, neither owner of, nor in any other way at home in, the land in which he finds himself. The near-transparency of the figure of the narrator is both a formal device which makes it possible for the lives of the serfs to be discovered and represented with the appearance of almost anthropological objectivity and a comment on the problematic situation of landowners at the time. A passage from the very first of the stories, "Khor and Kalinich," illustrates this latter point well. Khor, a serf who, with his family has worked hard to develop a successful smallholding, asks the narrator:

"'Have you got an estate of your own?'
'Yes.'
'Far from here?'
'A hundred versts.'
'And do you live there, sir?'
'I do.'

'But I expect you spend most of the time shooting?'
'I suppose I do.'
'And quite right, too, sir; shoot blackcock to your heart's content, and change your agent every so often.'" (*Sportsman's Notebook*: 16).

Irrelevant to the day-to-day workings of his own estate, this kind of landowner is one example of the so-called "superfluous man" who figured in so much of the literature of the 1840s in Russia.[45]

Irrelevance to, and frequent absence from, his own estate is therefore presented as the only alternative for a landowner to, on the one hand, the cold brutality and, on the other hand, the bumbling ineffectiveness of the landowners who actively run their estates in *A Sportsman's Notebook*. Turgenev's stories, it has often been said, highlighted the profoundly problematic social role of the Russian landowner of his period. But did they suggest to the readers of the time any processes by which that role might be made less problematic? Victor Ripp says not: "The constraints on the Russian political imagination is the unstated theme of Turgenev's [*A Sportsman's Notebook*] ... in the end the work is an illustration of how political positions in Russia were rendered incoherent and ineffectual."[46] Certainly the stories offer no simple recipe for transforming the role of the landowner. But, in contrast to Ripp, I would suggest that, once again, the very incompleteness of Turgenev's stories as a picture of rural life made it possible for contemporary readers to reconcile them with their several different, even mutually exclusive, visions of the future. So, it accommodated equally well, at one end of the readership continuum, those conservative groups who believed in the desirability of reestablishing, as they saw it, the landowners' proper power in the countryside, with stronger legal requirements for its reasonable exercise, and in the possibility of restoring health and centrality to the landowner-peasant relationship in Russian life, and, at the other, the radicals who envisaged a sharp reduction in, or even the eradication of, the landowners' power. The importance of literary works which make themselves acceptable (as successful political parties so often do) to groups which hold strongly divergent political views should not be underestimated.

A Sportsman's Notebook and emancipation

A Sportsman's Notebook, I have conceded, could have been only one element in Alexander's thinking about serfdom in the period leading up to his succession to the throne in 1855. The point has also been made that the two preceding Tsars had already both accepted that emancipation would have to come eventually. What distinguished Alexander II was, of course, that *he* was the one to carry out the reform, early in his reign, which all three of them believed, in principle, to be desirable. The question to ask here is: what influence, if any, did *A Sportsman's Notebook* have on the actual decision to attempt full emancipation and on the long process by which the legal form of emancipation was determined? Just as the process of working towards emancipation was long, and had different phases to it, so, too, did the process of publication and reception of *A Sportsman's Notebook*. It will be my argument here that the political influence of the work can be best understood in terms of the interweaving of these two processes over a considerable period of time.

The second phase in the history of *A Sportsman's Notebook* was the collection of the stories and their publication in volume form in 1852. This form of publication not only made the stories available to a much larger (but still predominantly landowning) audience than before, but also meant that they achieved a greater concentration of effect than when published singly. This was particularly the case because of the extreme delicacy of the political situation in that year (just before the outbreak of the Crimean War) and the increased censorship and repression ordered by Nicholas. As Henri Granjard has written, stories which appeared innocuous separately, were incendiary when published together.[47]

In fact Turgenev was arrested and confined to the central St. Petersburg police offices for a month, then exiled and confined to his estate at Spasskoe for a further eighteen months. He wrote, years later, that his arrest and exile were a consequence of the publication of *A Sportsman's Notebook* in volume form, but the precise chronology of events makes clear this was not the case. Turgenev was arrested in April 1852 for publishing an obituary for Gogol (whose death the authorities wanted to pass unmarked) in a Moscow magazine the previous month, even though he had received the Moscow censor's permission to publish it![48] (Nevertheless it is probably true that the government's anger at the public response to the earlier publication of Turgenev's individual stories relating to serfdom lay behind its excessive reaction to the obituary.) Meanwhile arrangements were under way for the publication of *A Sportsman's Notebook* in volume form and it came out in August when Turgenev was already in exile. This, in turn, provoked a further hostile reaction from the regime, and in 1853 *A Sportsman's Notebook* was banned, but not before the whole edition had sold out. It, too, had in fact been passed for publication by one of the Moscow censors, Prince

V. V. Lvov, but when the Minister of Education saw it, he disapproved and ordered an investigation. The official in the ministry who conducted the investigation reported that the book would be read by literate peasants and, since it idealized the peasants, showing them to be oppressed, and represented landowners as "vulgar savages and half-wits" who behaved in an arbitrary and illegal manner, it would do a great deal of harm.[49] (The claim that it would stir serf readers to revolt paralleled, and was just as implausible as, the claim made at just the same time by slaveholders in America that *Uncle Tom's Cabin* was dangerous because it would be read by slaves. Whatever claims can be made for political impact in either case, there is *no* question of these books having directly reached the enslaved group in any large numbers.)

The Minister passed these comments to Tsar Nicholas I, adding that "a great part of the stories in the book is a direct incitement to the destruction of the Russian landowner"[50] and the Tsar personally ordered the dismissal of the censor, Prince Lvov, with loss of pension. (Turgenev, in his characteristically kindly manner, gave some financial assistance to the elderly prince until his death.) This personal intervention by Nicholas gives a good indication of the seriousness with which the volume was regarded. But *A Sportsman's Notebook* had by this time been widely read, discussed and applauded. All this would have brought it to Grand Duke Alexander's attention again, and it is suggested that the removal of the exile order on Turgenev in November 1853 was probably a result of Alexander's direct intercession on his behalf with the Tsar.[51]

The outbreak of the Crimean War in 1853 and the failure of the Russian military forces by 1855 naturally altered the whole political climate. Nicholas died in 1855 and Alexander came to the throne, widely welcomed as a new force by all classes. He extricated Russia from the war as quickly, and with as little additional pain, as possible. Within a year he announced his intention to abolish serfdom. But it wasn't until 1861, five years later, that he was able to carry out that intention.

In theory, of course, the Tsar was an absolute monarch, an autocrat, with total, unquestionable power in relation to his vast empire and his seventy-four million subjects. There were no constitutional controls on his power, no parliamentary or representative mechanisms by which even the one hundred thousand "noble" or "gentry" landowners might participate in the exercise of power at the national level. In reality, the Tsar's freedom of action was ultimately restricted by the fear of assassination by the landowners on the one side, and peasant revolution on the other. Nevertheless, apart from this ultimate power, the influence of the landowners, as a class, on national politics was very slight. (This fact is one of the sources for the creation of the literary figure of the "superfluous man".) On the other hand, as some stories from *A Sportsman's Notebook* illustrate (especially "Ermolai and the Miller's Wife", "Ovsyanikov the Freeholder", "Lgov" and "The Bailiff") the landowners themselves had autocratic, very nearly absolute, powers over the lives of the twenty-two million serfs whom they directly controlled. (Turgenev's mother had her own police force for the control of her two thousand serfs and, like the Tsar, used exile as a punishment for any of her "subjects" who displeased her.) This represented a significant interruption of, or constraint on, the Tsar's personal power over his subjects, as, in a different sense, did the fact that landowners did not have to pay taxes or undertake military service as the serfs did. The larger estates may, in fact, be thought of as having been little autocratic regimes within the greater autocracy of the Russian Empire. (Nevertheless, the imperial family did have direct control of two million serfs of their own and another twenty million serfs lived on lands administered by the State.)

The main limitation on the personal autocratic power of the new Tsar, and the other major factor which must be taken into account in considering just how the emancipation of the serfs came about, is the existence of the massive State bureaucracy. The bureaucracy's nominal function was to execute the wishes of the autocrat in every corner of his empire, but in reality the bureaucrats were very much more than neutral bearers of the Tsar's personal power. Some historians go so far as to reverse the nominal position and refer to the Tsar's power as "a mere sector of the bureaucratic regime" and the Tsar himself as "a kind of supreme functionary."[52]

The bureaucracy has been described by recent scholars as being composed of two major groupings with competing objectives. On one side there was a relatively dynamic, liberal group of professional bureaucrats, well-educated, deriving mostly from the families of minor landowners, advocating emancipation of the serfs. On the other side were the high-ranking dignitaries of State and Court, with links to the provincial governors, most of whom strongly resisted any further reform of serfdom. Both groups, it should be noted, saw their position as reinforcing the autocracy itself.

On one level, then, the story of the abolition of serfdom can be narrated as a victory of the "liberal" grouping (and the broad economic and social forces they represented) over the "conservative" grouping (and the forces they stood for). The liberals represented those forces which undoubtedly contributed to emancipation: an increasingly entrepreneurial form of agriculture and manufacturing; the associated demand for a freer supply of labor and the expectation that unforced labor would be more productive and cheaper; the need for the development of a proletariat capable of consuming, as well as producing, the new manufactured products; the pressure of spontaneous peasant uprisings; discontent among the intellectuals; and so on.

To the extent that emancipation may be read as an outcome of economic and social forces at work in the 1850s, for which the liberal bureaucrats were agents, the great popularity of *A Sportsman's Notebook* amongst that group after 1852 is a further indication of the book's political influence.

Alexander's "unshakeable firmness"

All the evidence nevertheless makes clear that Alexander's personal role in bringing about emancipation was, in fact, crucial. It was in a speech to the Moscow gentry in Spring 1856, within a year of coming to the throne, that he first declared his definite intention to bring it about: "You yourselves are certainly aware that the existing order of serfdom cannot remain unchanged. It is better to abolish serfdom from above than to wait for the time when it will begin to abolish itself from below."[53] A great deal of his energy over the next five years (and that of his brother Constantine) was devoted to removing the many obstacles which were put in the way of reform. Alfred J. Rieber has written of Alexander: "His firm resolution during the period preceding the reform amazed his contemporaries even as they puzzled over its source and inspiration. D. A. Miliutin recalled vividly that 'the Tsar showed at this time such unshakeable firmness in the great state undertaking which he had personally conceived, that he could ignore the murmurings and grumblings of the clear opponents of innovation. In this sense, the soft and humanitarian Emperor Alexander II displayed greater decisiveness and a truer idea of his own power than his father who was noted for his iron will.'"[54]

What were the sources of that "unshakeable firmness" and did they include his reading of *A Sportsman's Notebook*?

Consideration of all the social and economic factors already mentioned undoubtedly entered Alexander's thoughts on emancipation. A new element, however, was the poor performance of the Russian armed forces in the Crimean War: the great Russian Empire had been humiliated. And serfdom was seen as one of the reasons for that humiliation. The system whereby serfs were signed up for military service for twenty-five years resulted in the existence of a large, ageing, underskilled, expensive standing army which did not have the flexibility of the armies it fought against. Moreover, supplies and munitions, manufactured mainly by serf labor, were of poor quality and slow in arriving. The absence of good roads and of a proper railway system for shifting troops and equipment was seen as a further disadvantage of the traditional serf economy. One of Alexander's first preoccupations, when he came to power, was the rebuilding of Russia's military strength and international prestige. The abolition of serfdom must have seemed to him an indispensable factor in that rebuilding. (It was, for instance, difficult to conceive of a major reform of the organization of the army without the abolition of serfdom, since that would have involved returning large numbers of serfs, with training in the use of arms, to villages where there was already considerable unrest — a recipe for peasant revolution.) So, it can be said, moral considerations, broad social and economic issues, and the specific practical demands of the post-Crimean historical moment would all have meshed together in Alexander's mind.

One thing that is quite certain is that Alexander saw his plans for reform as strengthening, rather than weakening, the autocratic regime. He utterly rejected any suggestion that the abolition of serfdom be linked to the development of a constitutional, representative, or parliamentary system of government. For instance, immediately after emancipation was proclaimed, a group of landowners in the province of Tver wrote a letter to Alexander arguing that the moral basis of the reform required further significant measures: "The only way to have it all settled peaceably and permanently is to call together an assembly of deputies to be elected without any regard to birth or civil status. That would seem the only means to answer problems raised but not resolved by the Manifesto.... Nobility and gentry are now exempt from many taxes ... Sir, we consider it a mortal sin to enjoy such benefits at the expense of others. It is indeed an unjust order of things where a poor man has to pay a rouble and a wealthy man does not pay a copper ..."[55]

Such arguments went far beyond Alexander's conception of emancipation, and the signatories were arrested, taken to St. Petersburg, and kept at the Fortress for five months. Alexander did not in the least see emancipation as being designed to assist the development of any mechanisms for the exertion of power upwards through the political system. It is significant that, among the thousands of documents recording consultations with groups of landowners, committees of bureaucrats, and the clergy in the period leading up to emancipation in 1861, there is not a single reference to the views of the serfs having been sought.

It seems likely that *A Sportsman's Notebook* functioned in a variety of ways to assist Alexander to come to a definite decision on emancipation by 1856, to maintain his (uncharacteristic) firmness of intention in the face of the stubborn resistance he encountered from many landowners and senior bureaucrats, and to influence the deliberations about the form that the emancipation document was to take in 1861. It is evident that *A Sportsman's Notebook*, especially after its publication in volume form in 1852, stood as a kind of enduring reference point for a whole generation of readers, including Alexander, a memory which could be re-created afresh, but with modifications, every time the reader picked it up. (I shall be arguing throughout this book that certain fictional narratives have a potential for durability in the individual and collective consciousness, for acting as a kind of touchstone to which readers can constantly return, which far exceeds that of the history or the documentary report as a force for change.) I suggest that the richness of the text brought Alexander back to it constantly over the dramatic years 1852 to 1861 with a sense both of returning to something familiar and of exploring its further possibilities.

A Sportsman's Notebook posed the problem of serfdom without, apparently, insisting on any particular solution to that problem. Instead, it insisted on the humanity of the serfs, and doubtless reminded Alexander of his own earlier encounters with them. Most importantly, Turgenev's stories permitted Alexander the sense of a direct and tranquil contemplation of the serfs he was trying to free which must have helped recharge his determination. The very absence of references in *A Sportsman's Notebook* to those areas which made the consultations over emancipation (and eventually its actual consequences) so problematic would have increased its effectiveness in this respect. There is no peasant unrest; the landowners are far too disorganized to pose any threat to autocracy; there is no discussion of the economics of serfdom or its alternatives, as well as very little reference to the problems associated with the bureaucracy, the state administration, or the judicial system. *A Sportsman's Notebook* must have served to keep the moral pressure on Alexander without addressing the practical, economic, and administrative measures which were so difficult for him to deal with. It is clear, incidentally, that when, in 1856, he first declared his intention to bring about emancipation, he had no definite plan about how it was to be done and what form it was to take. So, for instance, he only decided on the necessity for emancipation to include a grant of land in 1857. It was, then, precisely the openness, in all these respects, of *A Sportsman's Notebook* which allowed it to engage so productively with Alexander's own uncertainties at this time. Any attempt to lead an autocrat more firmly (even an autocrat whose freedom of action was in reality quite circumscribed) would have been doomed to failure.

There is, moreover, one further, very important feature of *A Sportsman's Notebook* which meshed vitally with Alexander's concerns. The Tsar, through the eyes of the narrator, would have found himself in direct contact with, or able to observe directly, that portion of his subjects, the privately owned serfs, who were to a considerable degree insulated by the institution of the private ownership of serfs from the autocrat's personal power. All the evidence suggests that Alexander's major objective for emancipation, alongside and inextricable from his belief in the moral and economic necessity of it, was to remove this interruption of his autocratic power over a group of his subjects, by removing the landowners as intermediaries between himself and the privately controlled serfs. Paradoxically as it must seem now, he sought in the abolition of serfdom to unify, make more nearly absolute, his personal exercise of power. It has been widely recorded that large numbers of privately owned serfs were under the misapprehension that emancipation meant the transfer of their ownership from the local landowner to the Tsar. The marshal of the aristocracy in the province of Podolsk reported, in August 1861:

> The peasants expect everything to come direct from the Tsar, to whom they give the character of a natural force, blind and implacable. They have completely given up believing in the simplest rules of respect for the property of others and for the general economic rules which are laid down in the manifesto of 19th February ... According to them, because for once fate has turned the natural force of supreme power to their advantage, they now have the right to expect from it every kind of benefit and generosity.[56]

In an odd sense, then, Alexander's attitude to emancipation involved a very similar delusion, a mystical belief in the infinite moral value of autocracy, that can be traced back to his former tutor's words (and beyond): "Slavery is abhorrent in God's eyes and runs counter to his truth ... Don't forget that supreme power rests upon an acknowledgement of that truth ... It alone is the law."

So it seems probable that *A Sportsman's Notebook* presented to Alexander, over the years leading up to emancipation, a constantly available symbolic image of a possible future relationship between himself, as all-observing, all-attentive, God-like autocrat and the whole body of his subjects. Indeed, this image may have contributed greatly to the firmness with which he maintained his intention to bring about emancipation. *A Sportsman's Notebook* fed into the grandiose delusion of a Tsar who said, in his speech to the State Council presenting the final draft of the emancipation document in January 1861, that on the liberation of the serfs would depend "the growth of [Russia's] forces and power."[57]

The consequences of emancipation

A month later the emancipation resolutions were read out from the pulpits of Russia's churches. The realities of emancipation failed to live up to the anticipations of almost everyone from the serfs themselves to the Tsar. While the serfs' legal status was immediately transformed — they could no longer be bought and sold, they were free to own property and trade in their own name and to marry — they remained heavily dependent on the landowners economically. Not only did they have to buy from the landowner the allotment of land granted to them, but most ended up with considerably *less* land for their own use than they had previously held. There were hundreds of cases of peasant rioting and a widespread expectation among the peasants that "true" emancipation was still to come. The landowners, for their part, were alarmed by the disruption to rural life and dissatisfied with the financial settlements they received. (Many had already mortgaged all their serfs to the banks, and a large proportion of the redemption payments they received went to pay off their debts.) Their decline as a class was now irreversible. What is more, in the short term, revenue to the State was dramatically reduced. Alexander, it is true, undertook other reforms, in the fields of local government, education, and the judicial system, but these, too, satisfied very few of the many interested parties. The reforms opened up new political and social spaces which were occupied by new forces. The great paradox is that, far from strengthening autocracy and empire, as Alexander had hoped, his signing of the the final act of emancipation, actually "sealed the doom of the old order."[58] To the extent that *A Sportsman's Notebook* facilitated the move toward emancipation, it also contributed to the eventual destruction of autocracy. But that is the beginning of another story.

NOTES TO CHAPTER 2

1. Leonard Schapiro, *Turgenev: His Life and Times* (New York: Random House, 1978): 66.

2. Avrahm Yarmolinsky, *Turgenev: The Man — His Art — His Age* (London: Hodder and Stoughton, 1926) and Henri Granjard, *Ivan Tourguénev et les courants politiques et sociaux de son temps* (Paris: Institut d'études slaves, 1966), 2nd ed.: 199.

3. See, for instance, Charles A. Moser, *Ivan Turgenev* (New York and London: Columbia University Press, 1972): 9.

4. See, for instance, E. M. Almedingen, *The Emperor Alexander II* (London: Bodley Head, 1962): 68 and 144.

5. Terence Emmons, ed., *Emancipation of the Russian Serfs* (New York: Holt, Rinehart and Winston, 1970) : 4.

6. Schapiro, *Turgenev*: 274-75.

7. See, for instance, Frank Friedeberg Seeley, *Turgenev: a Reading of His Fiction* (Cambridge: Cambridge University Press, 1991): 102.

8. April 27 1863, in *Turgenev Letters*, ed. and trans. David Lowe, 2 vols. (Ann Arbor: Ardis, 1983) 2: 11.

9. Schapiro, *Turgenev*: 64.

10. Quoted by Schapiro, *Turgenev*: 90. The banning of *Uncle Tom's Cabin* is referred to in Granjard, *Ivan Tourguénev*: 154.

11. Schapiro, *Turgenev*: 32.

12. Schapiro, *Turgenev*: 34.

13. Schapiro, *Turgenev*: 64.

14. Schapiro, *Turgenev*: 94.

15. Schapiro, *Turgenev*: 99-101.

16. Schapiro, *Turgenev*: 181.

17. See Victor Ripp, *Turgenev's Russia: From "Notes of a Hunter" to "Fathers and Sons"* (Ithaca and London: Cornell University Press, 1980): 23.

18. Quoted in Eva Kagan-Kans, *Hamlet and Don Quixote: Turgenev's Ambivalent Vision* (The Hague and Paris: Mouton, 1975): 24.

19. Kagan-Kans, *Hamlet and Don Quixote*: 23.

20. I refer throughout to Turgenev, *A Sportsman's Notebook*, trans. Charles and Natasha Hepburn (New York: The Ecco Press, 1986, first published New York: Viking, 1950). Other translations have appeared over the years variously entitled *A Sportsman's Sketches, Annals of a Sportsman, Sketches from a Hunter's Album, Hunter's Sketches* etc.

21. Anthony V. Knowles, *Ivan Turgenev* (Boston: Twayne, 1988): 129.

22. Ripp, *Turgenev's Russia*: 45.

23. Schapiro, *Turgenev*: 66.

24. Schapiro, *Turgenev*: 66.

25. Granjard, *Ivan Tourguénev*: 156.

26: Kochan and Abraham, *The Making of Modern Russia*: 171.

27. Vissarion Belinsky: *Selected Philosophical Works* (Moscow: Foreign Languages Publishing House, 1956): 543.
28. Almedingen, *The Emperor Alexander II*: 68.
29. Granjard, *Ivan Tourguénev*: 199.
30. Kochan and Abraham, *The Making of Modern Russia*: 162
31. Almedingen, *The Emperor Alexander II*: 78.
32. See Almedingen, *The Emperor Alexander II*: 84; and M. V. Nechkina, "The Reform as a By-product of the Revolutionary Struggle," in Emmons, ed., *Emancipation of the Russian Serfs*: 66-71.
33. Almedingen, *The Emperor Alexander II*: 52-54.
34. Quoted in Almedingen, *The Emperor Alexander II*: 52.
35. Almedingen, *The Emperor Alexander II*: 76.
36. Almedingen, *The Emperor Alexander II*: 155-156.
37. Almedingen, *The Emperor Alexander II*: 75-76.
38. Quoted in W. E. Mosse, *Alexander II and the Modernization of Russia* (London: English Universities Press, 1958): 15-16.
39. Schapiro, *Turgenev*: 88.
40. Kagan-Kans, *Hamlet and Don Quixote*: 20.
41. Ripp, *Turgenev's Russia*: 84. Turgenev, incidentally, read Dickens from an early age, see Schapiro, *Turgenev*: 7.
42. Ripp, *Turgenev's Russia*: 62-64.
43. *The Major Works of Peter Chaadaev*, trans. Raymond T. McNally (Notre Dame and London: 1969): 30. For a full account of the debate which followed publication of this letter in 1836, see Andrzey Walicki, *The Slavophile Controversy*. (Oxford: Clarendon Press, 1975).
44. Konstantin S. Aksakov, "On the Internal State of Russia," in Marc Raeff, ed., *Russian Intellectual History: An Anthology* (New York, Chicago, San Francisco, Atlanta: Harcourt, Brace and World, 1966): 233.
45. Indeed it was a work of Turgenev, *The Diary of a Superfluous Man* (1849), which gave wide circulation to the term.
46. Ripp, *Turgenev's Russia*: 42.
47. Granjard, *Ivan Tourguénev*: 174. See also David Magarshack, *Turgenev: A Life* (London: Faber, 1954): 143.
48. Schapiro, *Turgenev*: 87-88.
49. Schapiro, *Turgenev*: 87.
50. Quoted in Magarshack, *Turgenev*: 143.
51. Schapiro, *Turgenev*: 103.
52. The words are those of Boris Nolde, quoted by Alfred A. Skerpan, "The Russian National Economy and Emancipation" in Alan D. Ferguson and Alfred Levin, eds., *Essays in Russian History: A Collection Dedicated to George Vernadsky* (Hamden, Connecticut: Archon Books, 1964): 177.

53. Kochan and Abraham, *The Making of Modern Russia*: 182.

54. Alfred J. Rieber, "Raison d'état: Military," in Emmons, ed., *Emancipation of the Russian Serfs*: 75-76.

55. Almedingen, *The Emperor Alexander II*: 167; see also Terence Emmons, *The Russian Landed Gentry and the Peasant Emancipation of 1861* (Cambridge: Cambridge University Press, 1968): 321-349.

56. Quoted in Franco Venturi, *Roots of Revolution* (Chicago: University of Chicago Press, 1983): 212.

57. Quoted in Skerpan, "The Russian National Economy and Emancipation": 186.

58. Rieber, in Emmons, ed., *Emancipation of the Russian Serfs*: 72.

3. HARRIET BEECHER STOWE:
Uncle Tom's Cabin (1852)

▼ ▼ ▼

Harriet Beecher Stowe meets "Father Abraham"

When biographers and literary critics quote Abraham Lincoln's greeting to Harriet Beecher Stowe, "So this is the little lady who made this big war," they almost always interpret it as either a wholly serious or a wholly frivolous comment. In either case they miss the point that the greeting was a tactical shot fired by Lincoln in the context of an ongoing struggle between himself and the advocates of the immediate abolition of slavery.[1]

The meeting at which Lincoln is recorded as having spoken these, or similar, words to Stowe occurred in November 1862, just over eighteen months into the Civil War. It was the only occasion on which they ever met. Stowe had thought war unlikely even as late as 1860,[2] but when it did come she welcomed it as a holy crusade against the institution of slavery. In an article of April 1861 in *The Independent*, she wrote: "It is one part of the last struggle for liberty — the American share of the great overturning which shall precede the coming of Him whose right it is — who shall save the poor and needy, and precious shall their blood be in his sight."[3] Her explicitly religious, millenarian conception of American history was distinctly at odds with Lincoln's more secular, pragmatic sense of his historic mission. While he had, since the early 1850s, vigorously opposed the extension of slavery into states in which it was not already established, he had also written, as late as August 1862: "My paramount object in this struggle *is* to save the Union, and is *not* either to save or destroy slavery. If I could save the Union without freeing *any* slave, I would do it; and if I could save it by freeing *all* the slaves, I would do it; and if I could do it by freeing some and leaving others alone, I would also do that."[4] Nevertheless, only a month later, in September

1862, he had decided that, to relieve pressure from the abolitionists within his Republican Party (and to preempt foreign intervention in the war), it would be expedient to issue the Emancipation Proclamation.

In November 1862, Harriet Beecher Stowe, the most famous woman in America following the publication of *Uncle Tom's Cabin* in book form ten years before, was preparing an article on the war for a British women's magazine. She wanted to argue that the whole purpose of the war, as far as the North was concerned, was to free the slaves and that Britain should therefore, on moral grounds, support the Union. But it was still not clear how seriously the Proclamation was to be taken. So she went to Washington in November, "to satisfy myself that I may refer to the Emancipation Proclamation as a reality and a substance not to fizzle out at the little end of the horn as I should be sorry to call the attention of my sisters in Europe to any such impotent conclusion ... I mean to have a talk with 'Father Abraham' himself among others."[5] The President would have known very well that Harriet Beecher Stowe was going to press him on the seriousness of his intentions concerning emancipation, as every other abolitionist at that period did.

Lincoln's greeting to Stowe was not, then, an affirmation that abolitionism in general, let alone Harriet Beecher Stowe in particular, had been primarily responsible for bringing about the Civil War. It was a provocative quip, and by making it Lincoln acknowledged the extraordinary manner in which, over the preceding ten years, the question of the political and economic interests of the Union, with which Lincoln was preoccupied, had become intertwined with the moral and religious issues relating to slavery, which the abolitionists had been pressing for so long. It was a reluctant admission that the Union cause could not do without the abolitionists, yet, at the same time, a polite reminder that the abolitionists would never have brought the nation to the threshold of emancipation without the political, economic, and military pragmatism of the Republican Party. The meeting between Lincoln and Stowe epitomized the curious blend, not only of different human motives, but of contrasting emplotments of historical narrative embraced by the different parties in the North who were committed to the war.

The "power" of Uncle Tom's Cabin

If Lincoln's words to Stowe constituted only a limited and grudging acknowledgement of the role played by *Uncle Tom's Cabin* in preparing public opinion for a war between North and South, in part over slavery, much less ambiguous testimony to the novel's political importance came from many anti-slavery contemporaries of Stowe. Charles Sumner, the abolitionist Massachusetts senator, declared that, without *Uncle Tom's Cabin*, there would have been no Lincoln in the White House.[6] Another abolitionist commentator wrote in 1872 that the novel had been the chief force in developing support for the Republican Party in the 1850s.[7] Frederick Douglass, the black antislavery campaigner, stated after the Civil War that Stowe's novel had been "a flash to light a million camp fires in front of the embattled hosts of slavery" (though he also suggested that her role as an activist had been less significant than that of a dozen other women abolitionists).[8] A number of northern historians later in the century argued that the novel had been the most important source of opposition in the North to slavery. James Ford Rhodes was interestingly specific about the mechanisms by which it might have contributed to the building of support for the Republican Party:

> The great influence of Mrs Stowe's book was shown in bringing home to the hearts of the people the conviction that slavery is an injustice; and, indeed, the impression it made upon bearded men was not so powerful as its appeal to women and boys. The mother's opinion was a potent educator in politics between 1852 and 1860, and boys in their teens in the one year were voters in the other. It is often remarked that previous to the war the Republican Party attracted the great majority of the schoolboys, and that the first voters were an important factor in its final success.[9]

Of course all these commentators shared an interest in stressing, as Stowe herself did, the moral, crusading basis of the war. But Southerners, too, and that group of later historians from both North and South who have taken the view that the abolitionists whipped up public opinion in the North toward an unnecessary war, have credited Harriet Beecher Stowe with immense influence — but in order to blame her rather than to pay her tribute. Avery O. Craven, for instance, writing in the early 1940s, stated: "When argument and appeal to reason failed, the abolitionists tried entertainment and appeal to emotion. *Uncle Tom's Cabin* ... became a best seller in the most complete sense. Only the Bible exceeded it in numbers sold and in the thoroughness with which it was read in England and America."[10] (It is unanimously accepted that *Uncle Tom's Cabin* reached a massive white readership, in every social class, even including people who otherwise read very little, and that some of the most unlikely readers admitted to being moved by it. In ten months between 1852 and 1853, it sold an astonishing 300,000 copies in the United States alone, and, within a year, two-and-a-half million copies around the world. As Elizabeth Ammons has recently expressed it, "her novel riveted the nation ... kept the printing presses running night and day, making grown men weep and preachers rail."[11])

In this century, there has been a tendency to downplay, in one way or another, the causal link between *Uncle Tom's Cabin* and the war and emancipation. This has resulted partly from a sensible trend towards acknowledging the multiplicity of factors which contributed to the Civil War, with the issue of slavery being viewed as only one element in the clash between an agrarian culture in the South and a rapidly modernizing, industrial culture in the North, a conflict which as a consequence of institutional deficiencies and the personal failings of the political leaders of the time was not resolved before war became inevitable. But the belittling of the influence of *Uncle Tom's Cabin* also reflects ongoing struggles in the United States over race, gender, and the social function of literature.

Mainstream critics, mostly white, male, and formed in the tradition of the New Criticism, have generally written in a dismissively patronizing way of Stowe's work. This is partly due to their insistence on detaching literature from the hurly-burly of political life, raising it to a distinct, no doubt higher, realm of its own. An article in a major history of American literature is typical in asserting that "in spite of the enormous vogue of Mrs Stowe's novel, it is doubtful if a book ever had much power to change the course of events."[12] But it is also part of a very successful attempt, until quite recently, to marginalize and trivialize the whole tradition of sentimental novels by women to which *Uncle Tom's Cabin* belongs. The same article concludes with the astonishing comment that "obviously Harriet Beecher Stowe was neither a great personality nor a great artist."[13]

Recent criticism of *Uncle Tom's Cabin* by African-American and feminist commentators has not so much denied its contribution to the coming of war and emancipation as cut across that claim with other sorts of claims. African-American writers have emphasized the reactionary, racist features of the novel: the destructive, limiting stereotypes of black passivity (in the case of Uncle Tom) and foolish clowning (of Sam and Andy on the Shelby estate, Topsy in the St. Clare household, and other minor slave characters) which it has offered black and white readers in the century and more since the Civil War. As Richard Yarborough has expressed it, "although Stowe unquestionably sympathized with the slaves, her commitment to challenging the claim of black inferiority was frequently undermined by her own endorsement of racial stereotypes."[14] They have also lamented Stowe's enthusiastic reiteration of the colonizationist argument: that blacks, once freed, would prefer to leave the

United States, because they did not feel it was *their* country, for a nation of their own in Africa, especially Liberia: "Heavenly salvation might indeed be possible for blacks but a truly just interracial society was inconceivable."[15] James Baldwin's devastating attack on *Uncle Tom's Cabin*, in an essay entitled "Everybody's Protest Novel," implies that, even if it did contribute to emancipation, it would have been better, in the long term for blacks, if this "very bad novel" had never been written.[16] While there is very little doubt that, for almost a century *after* the Civil War, the existence of *Uncle Tom's Cabin* (and especially the numerous crudely reactionary stage adaptations of the novel) served almost entirely the forces obstructing black aspirations, this does not affect the seriousness of claims for its contribution to emancipation and the war.

Women and the abolitionist movement

It is modern feminist analysis which offers the most fruitful perspective for discussion of the "power" of *Uncle Tom's Cabin*. The wording of Lincoln's greeting (his patronizing reference to her as a "little lady") and of Stowe's account of seeking an audience with Lincoln (her reference to him as a patriarch and to herself as representing her "sisters in Europe") indicates the gender basis for the group of problems which I see *Uncle Tom's Cabin* as posing. Did a novel *by a woman* contribute to major change in activities (lawmaking and the declaration of war) which were supposed, at that time, to have have been exclusively the preserve of men? If so, how great a contribution did the novel make and how was it achieved? And was the kind of power exercised by Stowe through *Uncle Tom's Cabin* similar to, or essentially different from, the power exercised by her "sisters," those abolitionist women who worked toward emancipation by other means?

The abolitionist movement, it is well known, was the arena within which feminism came so spectacularly to self-conscious life in mid-nineteenth-century America. The involvement of educated white women in the struggle against slavery illuminated, for many of them, the parallel between the enslavement of blacks and their own lack of liberty. The meeting at Seneca Falls in 1848, which can now be seen as the founding convention of modern American feminism, grew out of the discontent felt by Elizabeth Cady Stanton and Lucretia Mott at being prohibited from taking their seats at an antislavery congress in London. But abolitionism posed for all women participating in it, whether they regarded themselves as feminists or not, a number of specific dilemmas about the kinds of action it was appropriate for women to undertake in furthering the cause of abolition. Should women speak in public against slavery, should they sit alongside men on the committees of abolitionist organizations, should they petition state and federal legislatures as men did?

The most radical feminist abolitionists, most notably Angelina and Sarah Grimké, who had, for some years, demanded full participation in American life for white women as well as the end of chattel slavery, affirmed that women should not only do all of the above, but even break state laws by emancipating their slaves, teaching them to read and write, and so on. Other women who opposed slavery, among whom Harriet's sister Catharine Beecher was one of the most articulate, insisted on a strict division of male and female roles: "A man may act on society by the collision of intellect, in public debate; he may urge his measures by a sense of shame, by fear and by personal interest; he may coerce by the combination of public sentiment; he may drive by physical force, and he does not outstep the boundaries of his sphere."[17] A woman, on the other hand, was limited in her activity on a matter such as slavery to the domestic circle, where it was her role, by kindly persuasion, to convince the men in her life of the unchristian nature of slavery, as well as mediating when conflicts arose in her household between opponents and advocates of slavery. Women were to exert not political *power*, which would have involved them in entering a properly male sphere, but their own "wise and appropriate influence ... which will most certainly tend to bring an end, not only of slavery, but unnumbered other evils and wrongs."[18] Discredited though this view now is, it has to be recognized as a feminist (that is, woman-centered) stance — it has been termed "domestic feminism" — and the grandeur of its claim concerning women's capacity to transform the world acknowledged.

The problem of Stowe's intentions

Part of Harriet Beecher Stowe's achievement in writing *Uncle Tom's Cabin* is that, as the quotation from James Ford Rhodes above about the novel's having made an impression mostly on women and boys suggests, she made it seem that she was working wholly within the domestic sphere prescribed for women, while, in reality, she was to a startling degree breaking out of that sphere. The vastness of her readership, the degree to which her book stimulated public debate, and the sheer fact of her requesting and obtaining an audience with Lincoln must be immediate evidence of that. But there will be more evidence to come.

Nevertheless, an immediate difficulty arises about the direction of the influence that *Uncle Tom's Cabin* exercised. There are numerous indications both from within the body of the novel and in letters to various correspondents that Harriet Beecher Stowe's intention in writing *Uncle Tom's Cabin* was to assist the cause of emancipation by means quite other than war. She emphasized her wish that her novel might serve to persuade Northerners to cease their direct or indirect involvement in slavery and Southerners to renounce slavery of their own accord. In a letter to Lord Shaftesbury in England, for instance, she wrote: "It was my hope that a book so kindly intended, so favorable in many respects, might be permitted free circulation among [the Southerners] ... and that the gentle voice of Eva and the manly generosity of St. Clare might be allowed to say those things of the system which would be invidious in any other form."[19]

There are many statements in the novel itself to the effect that it should not be read as an anti-Southern work. The first of these is in the Preface, where she wrote "the author can sincerely disclaim any invidious feelings towards those individuals who, often without any fault of their own, are involved in the trials and embarrassment of the legal relations of slavery" (*Uncle Tom's Cabin*: iv).[20] How are these words to be reconciled not only with the claim that *Uncle Tom's Cabin* contributed to the coming of the war, but with Stowe's enthusiasm, less than ten years later, for a military solution to the problem of slavery? More particularly, how is one to account for the discrepancy between her stated position in 1852 and these words on slavery written only four years later for the Preface to the British edition of her novel, *Dred: A Tale of the Great Dismal Swamp*:

> Meanwhile ... the great EVIL has marched on to its results with a terrible and undeviating tread. The foolish virgins, who all slumbered and slept, the respectable and tenderhearted, who, in ignorant sincerity, cried peace when there was no peace, have one by one been awakened in wild surprise; and the foolish have said unto the wise, Give us of your oil, for our lamps have gone out.
>
> The few who then fought the battle of liberty almost single-handed, those Cassandras who for many years saw the coming evil and prophesied to unheeding ears, now find themselves at the head of a mighty army, and in a crisis that must speedily determine what shall be the working out of this great evil, whether it shall issue peaceably or in blood.[21]

The Power of the Story
▼ ▼ ▼

A number of feminist critics, notably Jane P. Tompkins and Elizabeth Ammons, have examined the problem of the discrepancy between Stowe's statements of intention for *Uncle Tom's Cabin* and its supposed contribution to the coming of war. They accept those statements at face value and identify the central message of the novel as being essentially the "domestic feminism" of Catharine Beecher. Jane P. Tompkins argues that the idyllic scene in the Quaker settlement, in which Rachel Halliday radiates motherly love to resolve every potential conflict, is central to both the novel's structure and its political meaning. That scene (as well as the scene in which Mary Bird persuades her senator husband that their Christian belief requires them to break state law and give assistance to a fugitive slave), she suggests, offer a vision of a new matriarchy which would make the loving, peaceful Christian household, presided over by the mother, the model for wider American society. (This would be the Catharine Beecher model developed to its furthest extreme.) According to Tompkins, this "constitutes the most politically subversive dimension of Stowe's novel, more disruptive and far-reaching in its consequences than even the starting of a war or the freeing of slaves."[22] So she concludes that, while "*Uncle Tom's Cabin* ... induced a nation to go to war," it did so against its author's intentions and against the central message of the book, and that "in terms of it own conception of power, a conception it shares with other sentimental fiction, the novel was a political failure."[23]

While this focusing on the role of the female characters in the novel, and the model of "feminized Christianity" they propose, was long overdue, Tompkins' conclusion, that a novel whose central value is maternal love came to be appropriated for the patriarchal purpose of starting a war, must surely be flawed, since it takes no account of the discrepancy between Stowe's own declarations of 1852 and 1856. Did Harriet Beecher Stowe really take an entirely pacific, loving attitude to the practitioners of slavery in 1852 which she abandoned by 1856? If the central message of the novel was subverted by patriarchy in the years after its publication, so it seems, must Harriet Beecher Stowe's own stance have been!

Stowe's changing attitude to slavery

A rather more complex argument will be developed in this chapter. Examination of the evidence suggests that, at the time of writing *Uncle Tom's Cabin*, in 1851 and 1852, Harriet Beecher Stowe was at the midpoint of a long transition from actual disapproval of the abolitionist movement (in a letter of 1837, for instance, she had referred to "the excesses of the abolition party")[24] to passionate support (by 1861) for the Civil War as a crusade to abolish slavery. By 1851, when she started *Uncle Tom's Cabin*, she had reached the point of clearly supporting the demand for immediate emancipation, yet with much more uncertainty than her pacifist rhetoric at the time would suggest about the means by which emancipation was to be achieved. The novel contains a profound ambivalence about how slavery was to be defeated. Below the surface of the novel's almost consistently benevolent authorial comment are to be found the seeds of an antagonistic, even militaristic, stance on slavery. I shall argue that, over the years that followed its publication, these seeds rapidly grew, not only in the mind of its author, but also in the minds of the vast number of its white northern readers who kept it by them. In addition to drawing many Northerners into the debate over slavery for the first time by emotive means (as it is widely agreed it did), I shall suggest that *Uncle Tom's Cabin* in quite complex ways specifically fueled the antagonism between North and South in the mid-1850s.

Stowe's personal journey in regard to slavery and its abolition had many interesting features, some peculiar to herself, others common to the experience of large numbers of northern whites in the same period. That journey is worth tracing for a while. It is not that Stowe had ever approved of slavery itself, but that, like her father, the famous Presbyterian pastor, Lyman Beecher, she had taken the view, probably until 1850, that slavery should not be given any greater priority than other pressing moral and social problems, and that the most that could be hoped for was gradual emancipation with the consent of the slaveholders. Harriet Beecher Stowe came to abolitionism a good deal later than other prominent women abolitionists, many of whom had been carrying on the struggle, though gaining only limited support, since the mid-1830s. It seems very probable that Stowe was able to achieve the influence she did precisely because she was, in some important respects, less far ahead of those she led than the people who had worked for many years within the abolitionist organizations.

It was the passing of the Fugitive Slave Act by Congress in 1850 which nudged Harriet Beecher Stowe into giving priority to the issue of slavery. This act strengthened a law of 1793, requiring the return of fugitive slaves from all states, by denying jury trials to escaped slaves, barring their testimony, requiring federal officials to aid in their capture, and providing heavy fines for those who aided them in their escape. It not only confronted Northerners with the existence of slavery as a system, but enforced their collaboration in it. The act represented a concession by the North to the slave states, some of whose representatives in Congress were already talking of secession, and was strongly opposed by the abolitionists. There are numerous references to the Fugitive Slave Act and its practical implications in the novel.

The Fugitive Slave Act also moved vast numbers of other Northerners, far less advanced in their thinking about slavery than Harriet Beecher Stowe, some distance along the path toward an outright antislavery position. Abolitionism, it should be remembered, remained, until the early 1850s, a minority position to which most Northerners were antagonistic. The main issues which had arisen in the 1840s relating territory to slavery had been resolved, by 1850, in ways which gave some benefit to both southern and northern interests: Oregon, Iowa, and Wisconsin had been admitted as free states, while Texas and Florida had both been admitted as slave states. The so-called Compromise of 1850, which included the passing of the Fugitive Slave Act, was intended to reduce antagonism between North and South. In fact, the serial publication of *Uncle Tom's Cabin* in 1851 coincided with a presidential election campaign in which both major parties (the Democrats and the Whigs) expressed their support for the Compromise. Once elected, Franklin Pierce was able to say in his inaugural address: "I fervently hope that the question [of slavery] is at rest, and that no sectional or ambitious or fanatical excitement may again threaten the durability of our institutions or obscure the light of our prosperity."[25] This moment of illusory calm was, in fact, the turning point for northern white opinion on slavery. While its purpose was to give some assistance to slaveholders in the South, the Fugitive Slave Act "angered many Northerners who hitherto had been cool to abolitionism, and gave the abolitionists a real propaganda weapon."[26] It posed, in the starkest manner, moral dilemmas for white Northerners in relation to their own collaboration with slavery which most of them had previously been able to ignore. So when, in 1852 (the year of publication of *Uncle Tom's Cabin* in volume form), an escaped slave, Anthony Burns, was captured in Boston and marched to the train in irons, the streets were lined with silent white citizens, flags were flown at half-mast and church bells tolled.[27]

Another event occurred in 1850, personal to Harriet Beecher Stowe, which contributed to her adopting an outright abolitionist stance in *Uncle Tom's Cabin*. This was her moving, at the age of thirty-nine, with her children, from Cincinnati back to New England, where she was born and had lived until she was twenty-one. That relocation represented a move away from a city which was, for abolitionists, a frontline city in the struggle against slavery — its economy was closely tied in with the economies of the slave states through trade along the Ohio and Cincinnati rivers, and escaping slaves often passed through the city. Abolitionism was very much a minority stance in Cincinnati, most of the white population being hostile to the abolitionists, and Stowe had not joined the movement there. New England, on the other hand, was a stronghold of abolitionism.

The shift back to New England also represented a move out from under the direct domination of her father, Lyman Beecher. Harriet had accompanied him to Cincinnati eighteen years before, when he was appointed president of the Lane Theological Seminary. Her marriage to Calvin Stowe, one of the professors at his seminary, in 1836, did little to reduce her subordination to his influence. Specifically relevant in this case were the constraints of Beecher's disapproval of the abolitionists.

Beecher had crossed paths with both William Lloyd Garrison, the leading figure in the New England abolitionist movement, and Theodore Dwight Weld, leader of the other wing of the abolitionist movement which was active in Ohio, western New York State, and western Pennsylvania. Garrison had, as a young man, been a member of Beecher's congregation in Boston, but once Garrison developed his absolutist antislavery position, between 1828 and 1830, Beecher opposed him frequently in public, arguing that "you must take into account what is expedient as well as what is right."[28] Beecher took a similarly conservative, expedient line in 1834, when Theodore Dwight Weld, a student at the Lane Seminary, led an intense series of debates on slavery at the seminary, which were accompanied by educational and welfare work by the white students among the black population of Cincinnati. The trustees of the seminary banned these activities, Beecher put the ban into effect, and Weld led a walkout of a majority of students, who went to study at another college. Beecher argued the need "to make emancipation easy instead of difficult, to make use of the current of human fears and passions and interests when they may be made to set in our favour instead of attempting to row upstream against them."[29] Weld was to become the leader of one branch of the abolitionist movement and to marry Angelina Grimké.

Harriet Beecher Stowe's move back to New England made it possible for her to shed the conservative influence of Lyman Beecher on the issue of slavery in much the same way as Garrison and Weld had done. From that point on, she demonstrated a much stronger form of abolitionism than would have been possible in Cincinnati, so close to her father. (It may also be relevant that, during the first months of her return to New England, the other man to whose wishes she was subject, Calvin Stowe, had to stay back at the seminary in Cincinnati!) John R. Adams has linked Stowe's writing of the novel and her embracing of abolitionism to her experience of personal subjugation to the demands of her father, Lyman Beecher, and her husband, Calvin Stowe: "Her resentment toward the repressive influences in her own life, which she never dared admit to herself, attached itself to the symbol of the black race."[30] What she did admit vividly in letters was her frustration at the way in which domestic drudgery interfered with her writing, and her determination that her independent creative activity would not be stifled: "It is a dark, sloppy, rainy, muddy, disagreeable day, and I have been working hard (for me) all day in the kitchen, washing dishes, looking into closets, and seeing a great deal of that dark side of domestic life which a housekeeper may who will investigate too curiously into minutiae in warm, damp weather." Calvin Stowe's letters exhort her to improve her running of the household, with such helpful observations as: "In all respects in which both nature and an exceedingly defective or onesided education have made you imperfect, I recognize and admire in you an earnest and Christian-like purpose to amend." [31]

Stowe and the battle for Kansas-Nebraska

After the great moral tremor experienced by Northerners, including Harriet Beecher Stowe, as a result of the passing of the Fugitive Slave Act in 1850 came a whole series of public events which tended to harden attitudes on slavery on both sides of the Mason-Dixon line. It was, of course, the dispute which began in 1854, over whether the territories of Kansas and Nebraska should be settled as slave or nonslave states, that proved to be the great insoluble territorial issue between North and South. The motive of the great majority of northern Free Soilers was not a moral or humanitarian concern about the exploitation of black slaves. They mostly agreed with Abraham Lincoln, not yet a nationally known figure, that "the whole nation is interested that the best use shall be made of these Territories. We want them for the homes of white people. This they cannot be, to any considerable extent, if slavery shall be planted within them."[32] William Lloyd Garrison commented of the Free Soilers: "They went to make money ... I do not see that Kansas has given us any lessons of wisdom in regard to the management of the warfare against slavery."[33] Perceived self-interest was the major reason for the continuing growth in concern over slavery amongst large numbers of Northerners. It was the small farmers and artisans from the North who saw their hopes of settling in the new territories most threatened by the form of agricultural economy, large estates based on slave labor, which southern interests were most likely to introduce there.

There were, nevertheless, Northerners who articulated the struggle over slavery in Kansas in moral and religious terms. Most prominent of them was another member of Stowe's family, her brother, Henry Ward Beecher, a famous preacher like his father but more radical politically, who urged northern settlers to hurry to Kansas and, as their Christian duty, to use rifles ("Beecher's Bibles") to ensure that it became a free state. But proslavery settlers from the South had already established a strong foothold in Kansas and were just as self-righteous in their demand that Kansas be a slave state — and at least as willing to use arms.

Harriet Beecher Stowe later expressed her full support for the violent, confrontational stance adopted in Kansas by the settlers from New England, reading their actions in terms of her own moral and religious motives: "Then came the battle for Kansas-Nebraska fought with fire and blood, where a race of men, of whom John Brown was the immortal type [he led a raid on Ossawatomie and murdered five pro-slavery men], acted over again the courage, the perseverance and the military religious order of the old Covenanters of Scotland, and like them, redeemed the Ark of Liberty at the price of their own blood."[34] Violence, she evidently now believed, was justified at least to prevent the spread of slavery. For her, the struggle against slavery continued to be a moral struggle, but in responding to the new situation she found the terms of that struggle changing and she did not shy away from adopting those terms. Far from the attitudes of men in public life being softened under the influence of the "kindly, generous, peaceful and benevolent principles"[35] to which women could appeal, it would seem that Harriet Beecher Stowe and other northern women were increasingly adopting the bellicose rhetoric they had hitherto attributed exclusively to men. Harriet's position had, by this time, very little in common with that of her sister Catharine, and much more in common with Henry Ward Beecher.

This kind of ambivalence and shift undoubtedly has some of its origins in the puritan religious context within which Stowe lived. There was, in the period, a regular oscillation, in which the Beechers played a role, between a revivalist endeavor to gather in as many souls as possible for personal salvation through Christ (whose love Stowe and many other women writers of the period defined as "a *mother*'s love")[36] and fire-and-brimstone preaching about the imminence of the coming of the wrath of God the *Father* to punish sin. It has even been said of William Lloyd Garrison, the leading figure in the nonresistant wing of the abolitionist movement: "One could argue that Garrison was much more in favor of a vindictive war against the South than his public professions indicated. Certainly there was a constant and intense struggle within his puritan soul between hopes for utopian peace and dreams of a destructive purge of evil."[37] (Garrison's constant use of the metaphor of "warfare against slavery" offers some evidence for that argument.)

Events followed in rapid succession over the next four years: the savage beating in the Senate of the abolitionist senator, Charles Sumner, by a proslavery senator (1856); the emergence of the Republican Party in the presidential election of the same year with a platform clearly opposing the extension of slavery; the Dred Scott case in which the Supreme Court ruled that, in fact, the whole nation was constitutionally open to slavery (1856-57); and the failure of John Brown's raid on Harper's Ferry to bring about a slave insurrection (1859). During these years, popular opinion in much of the North was coming to see itself as being threatened by a southern "slave power conspiracy." As one historian has said: "The new abolitionists were riding the tiger born from the aspirations and resentments of a vast public of small farmers and artisans ... A deep and growing suspicion of the South, a traditional and endemic fear of competition from black slave labor, prepared northern settlers for conflict with southern settlers in the West."[38] Meanwhile many Southerners were coming to see themselves as threatened by a supposed northern plot to "vassalize" the South.

Slavery and the sentimental novel

Given that a rapid growth of antagonism between North and South (in which Stowe herself, as we have seen, participated) undoubtedly occurred in precisely the seven-year period following the publication of *Uncle Tom's Cabin* in volume form in 1852, should the novel be seen as having acted as an unsuccessful restraint on that antagonism, or, in some way, as having fueled it? It will be argued here that while the novel appeared to offer a restraining influence, there are many features in it which actually served to incite Northerners to adopt an antagonistic stance towards the South.

There were, it is perhaps surprising to discover, no significant precedents to *Uncle Tom's Cabin* of novels aiming to expose the nature of slavery. It might well be said Harriet Beecher Stowe's most innovative and provocative act, in writing *Uncle Tom's Cabin*, was to insert numerous familiar, heartrending elements from the widely loved tradition of the sentimental novel into a story about the one issue, slavery, over which there was likely to be the greatest disagreement between different groups of readers. These elements included: a family separated by misfortune (Eliza and George Harris), a mother saving her son with heroic courage (Eliza saving little Harry by fleeing across the frozen river), a loving family and domestic tranquillity (in Uncle Tom's and Aunt Chloe's cabin and the Halliday family household in the Quaker settlement), the death of a child with a strong religious faith (little Eva St. Clare), and the martyrdom of a devout Christian man (Uncle Tom).

The novelty of Stowe's handling of these elements lay in the fact that situations which were traditionally the domain of white characters, in the sentimental novel, now involved primarily black characters. The key device employed by Stowe to persuade her readers of the wickedness of slavery is her presentation of the distress or dilemma of slave characters in a way which invites the direct empathy of white readers, who are invited to imagine how they would feel if placed in the same situation. This passage relating to the escape of Eliza with her son Harry is typical: "If it were *your* Harry, mother, or your Willie, that were going to be torn from you by a brutal trader, to-morrow morning, — if you had seen the man, and heard that the papers were signed and delivered, and you had only from twelve o'clock till morning to make good your escape, how fast could you walk? ..." (*Uncle Tom's Cabin*, Chapter 6: 61-62).

The depth of the empathy achieved and its significance in the struggle against slavery has, I believe, been insufficiently recognized. Stowe perceived with extraordinary acuteness that the belief that the emotions of the heart should prevail over the cold intellect of the head and the conviction that the well-ordered, loving family offered the best model of social stability were ideological features, crucial to the appeal of sentimental novels, and underlying *both* the anti- and the proslavery positions.[39] It was by tapping these almost universally shared emotional reservoirs that she achieved overnight a degree of moral reframing, or reconceptualizing, of slavery in the minds of vast numbers of her readers in the North.

Stowe's exceptional shrewdness can be seen in her use of the sentimental devices of plot to systematically convey to her readers information about slavery to which most Northerners had previously been resistant. Built into the novel is a cataloguing of some of the specific brutalities of slavery: the breaking up of black families by the sale of individual family members; slaves being bought and sold as if they were nonhuman commodities; the flogging of slaves by slaveowners and overseers, or at a public whippinghouse; the murder of fugitive slaves by their owners or pursuers; the sexual violation and exploitation of female slaves by owners and traders; the suppression of education and religious teaching among slaves by slaveholders. *Uncle Tom's Cabin* was able to communicate unpalatable factual information about slavery to Northerners who had, before about 1851, in general refused to take such material in, by presenting it with the almost irresistible sugar-coating of the sentimental novel. (Some northern abolitionist leaders were critical of the novel at least in part because it exposed the extent to which the rhetoric used by abolitionists derived originally from the sentimental novel!) There is a striking contrast with Turgenev's *A Sportsman's Notebook*, which, it is generally agreed, conveyed little previously unacknowledged, factual information about the living conditions of serfs. The initial political importance of *Uncle Tom's Cabin* depended, then, on the widespread acceptance by northern readers that it told "the truth" about slavery in an emotionally charged medium.

Truth and lies in fiction

To most modern critics it no longer seems appropriate to apply the criterion of "truthfulness" to literary works of any kind. Modernism (let alone postmodernism!) in the arts, the recognition of the role played by representational conventions and of the ways in which those conventions operate within established ideological frameworks, all make the notion that a novel can present information that could be deemed "true" or "false" quite alien. As Wolfgang Iser has said, "fictional texts are not identical with real situations. They have no exact counterpart in reality. In this respect they could almost be called unsituated, in spite of the historical substratum which accompanies them."[40] Nevertheless, it is clear that readers have, at certain times, responded strongly and in large numbers to novels on the grounds of their supposed truthfulness in representing the living conditions or political situation of a real group of people — Upton Sinclair's *The Jungle*, Steinbeck's *The Grapes of Wrath*, Koestler's *Darkness at Noon*, Solzhenitsyn's novels about life in Soviet labor camps are some of the best-known examples. The manner in which each of these novels has worked in the world cannot be adequately described without reference to the criterion of truthfulness used by readers in responding to them. *Uncle Tom's Cabin* is such a novel.

The first responses of the novel's other main potential constituency of readers, the Southerners, were not as uniformly hostile as might be supposed. Thomas F. Gossett records some fascinating examples of proslavery southern readers who, seduced by the familiar sentimental features of the novel, initially responded warmly to its publication. One reviewer, for instance, stated that "it is a book of more than ordinary moral worth and is entitled to consideration," and that he did not believe "that the book would result in injury to the slaveholding interests of the country."[41] Gossett gives another example of a southern reader who was favorably impressed at first, but then decided he had been tricked by the novel and said he would burn it.[42] Many southern reviewers were evidently outraged at what they saw as the duplicity, the *underhand* nature, of Stowe's making slavery the subject of a sentimental novel.[43] But the eventual reaction of southern reviewers, and of the relatively small number of other Southerners who actually read *Uncle Tom's Cabin* (it was banned in many communities) was one of almost uniform hostility on the grounds, as one reviewer expressed it, that it presented "an exaggerated and distorted view of slavery — a view which presented the exception for the rule."[44] The question of the work's truthfulness about slavery was uppermost in the minds of Southerners, too, and was answered in the negative. In the illuminating words of the modern critic, Alice Crozier, southern readers were angered by the feeling that "the novel purported to be not fiction but a record of real life, and that, as such, it was a pack of lies."[45]

The notion that a work of fiction can *lie* accords even less with modern critical thinking than the idea of fictional works as significant sources of factual information. In any case, common sense suggests that lying is the uttering of a *fiction* with intent to deceive the listener into believing that it is an historical fact (for instance, "I've taken the money to the bank", when I've actually put it into my pocket). So how can a text which is acknowledged by both writer and readers to be fictional be said to lie? In my opening chapter I quoted Louis O. Mink's statement that "for fiction, there is no claim to be truthful *in any particular respect.*" And yet writers of literary fiction often *do* insert clues about which features of their text are to be read as historically factual. Writers of fiction can be accused of lying if it can be shown that they established, and maintained throughout the novel, expectations in the reader about the correspondence between certain features of the text (rather than the text as a whole) and historical reality, knowing this correspondence to be false.

Harriet Beecher Stowe explicitly vouched for the accuracy and typicality of *her* depiction of slavery in the "Concluding Remarks," declaring that "the separate incidents that compose the narrative are, to a very great extent authentic, occurring, many of them either under her own observation or that of her personal friends" (*Uncle Tom's Cabin*: 467). And, in making this statement, she was *not* being strictly truthful. In fact Stowe's direct experience of the slave states was minimal, being limited, it seems, to a single visit to the border state of Kentucky. Her main sources of information about slavery, apart from stories she heard in Cincinnati, were actually abolitionist papers and books, especially Theodore Dwight Weld's *American Slavery As It Is: Testimony of a Thousand Witnesses* (1839), but, given her desire to reach those audiences who had not previously been convinced by the abolitionists, she cleverly distanced herself from, and made few references to, abolitionist organizations in the book. So, for instance, she has Mrs. Shelby, when her slaveowning husband says she is talking like an abolitionist, answer: "'Abolitionist! if they knew all I know about slavery they *might* talk! We don't need them to tell us ...'" (*Uncle Tom's Cabin*, Chapter 5: 45). And some of the most effective passages condemning slavery are placed in the mouths of white Southerners. (It is true, too, that, even after the success of *Uncle Tom's Cabin*, Harriet Beecher Stowe always described herself as a writer who was also an abolitionist — to the occasional annoyance of women who had thrown themselves wholly into working for one of the abolitionist societies.)

Soon after the massive success of the novel, Stowe wrote a five-hundred page *Key to Uncle Tom's Cabin* (1853) whose title page, "Presenting the Original Facts and Documents Upon Which the Story is Founded, together with Corroborative Statements Verifying the Truth of the Work," slightly bends the truth, since the "corroborative statements" received after the publication of the novel greatly outnumber the "facts and documents" available to her in the writing of it.

Harriet Beecher Stowe: Uncle Tom's Cabin

New answers to new questions

The initial impact of *Uncle Tom's Cabin* in 1852 and 1853 needs therefore to be understood not only in terms of its having gotten under the moral and emotional guard of many Northerners to revive their waning sense of moral outrage over the Fugitive Slave Act, but also as having actively antagonized many Southerners. Moreover, as the months passed and it became evident that, despite Harriet Beecher Stowe's stated intention, the book was being viewed and used by Northerners as a weapon against the South (as well as against slavery), southern comment on it rose to an hysterical (and *blatantly* untruthful) pitch, attacking it for its "scenes of license and impurity ... ideas of loathsome depravity and habitual prostitution ... thinly veiled pictures of corruption."[46] These attacks were all the more effective because most of the Southerners who listened to them had *not* read the novel itself. The importance proslavery people attributed to *Uncle Tom's Cabin* as a weapon against them may be judged by the considerable number of (mainly) southern writers who produced anti-*Uncle Tom* novels designed to "set the record straight." (Thomas F. Gossett lists twenty-seven such novels published between 1853 and 1861.)[47] Rufus Choate, a proslavery lawyer and former senator, summed up the fears of the slaveholders when he said that *Uncle Tom's Cabin* would make "two millions of abolitionists."[48]

The crucial point to realize is that Stowe's novel did not just inflame northern readers against the slave states, it became, itself, an actual subject of dispute between Northerners and Southerners, in the course of which southern feeling, too, was extraordinarily inflamed. That southern anger was at least as much a response to northern (and foreign) praise of the novel as it was a direct response by Southerners to their reading of the novel.

As antagonism between North and South grew, for the variety of reasons I have already listed, over the five years or so after the publication of *Uncle Tom's Cabin*, the novel evidently remained present in the consciousness (individual and collective) of its northern readers. It will be the argument of the rest of this chapter that *Uncle Tom's Cabin* bears signs of its author's transitional state at the time of writing and that it is precisely this transitional, problematic quality about the novel which made it capable of acting as a catalyst in the complex process by which mass white opinion came, from its relatively fluid state in 1851, to solidify, by 1861, into the irreconcilably antagonistic blocs of North and South. I suggest that, as their reading of the political situation shifted,

The Power of the Story
▼ ▼ ▼

Northerners discovered, below the sentimental, loving surface of Stowe's novel, other elements which continued to "work" on them in politically important ways. As their militancy and their antagonism toward the South grew, they found features in *Uncle Tom's Cabin* (and in her next novel about slavery, *Dred*) which fed those attitudes. In the terms used by the reception theorist, Hans Robert Jauss, to account for shifts of interpretation of literary texts over time, the novel came to offer new answers to some of the new questions which were arising with increasing urgency in the minds of northern readers.

Mixed messages in a double plot

Discovery of a profound ambivalence in *Uncle Tom's Cabin* should not be too much of a surprise when it is remembered that the whole plot is structured around two contrary journeys, involving two contrary courses of action by slaves, both of of which appear to receive authorial approval. The narration of Uncle Tom's journey, from the Shelby plantation in Kentucky southward to his martyrdom, is intertwined with the narration of the journeys of George Harris, his wife Eliza, and their son Harry from the same plantation, northward to freedom. Uncle Tom has the chance to escape but chooses not to take it, while George Harris successfully takes his chance — and Stowe appears to express her warm approval of both responses. On the one hand, Uncle Tom is impelled by religious conviction and a sense of utter fidelity to his master and the estate to submit to being sold down the river to his eventual death: "'If I must be sold, or all the people on the place, and everything go to rack, why let me be sold. I s'ppose I can b'ar it as well as any on 'em ... Mas'r always found me on the spot, — he always will'" (*Uncle Tom's Cabin*, Chapter 5: 50). And at the moment of his death from the beatings of Legree, he can declare: "'*Heaven has come!* I've got the victory! — the Lord Jesus has given it to me! Glory be to his name'" (*Uncle Tom's Cabin*, Chapter 41: 445). Stowe's approval of his behavior is expressed in terms of her so organizing the story that his Christlike death brings about the conversion to Christianity of Sambo and the other slaves on Legree's plantation in Louisiana, and the immediate conviction in young George Shelby that "'from this hour, I will do *what one man can* to drive out this curse of slavery from my land'" (*Uncle Tom's Cabin*, Chapter 41: 448). On the other hand, George Harris's and Eliza's decisions to escape North after George is whipped and humiliated by his master and their son is to be sold by Mr. Shelby, are also given clear authorial approval. George is articulate and absolutely convincing in his reasoning: "'My master! and who made him my master? That's what I think of, — what right has he to me? I'm a man as much as he is. I'm a better man than he is. I know more about business than he does; I am a better manager than he is ...'" (*Uncle Tom's Cabin*, Chapter 3: 26).

The use of double plots, where one set of characters descended into misery and another set achieved happiness, was characteristic of the sentimental novel of the period, contributing to the major emotional rises and falls in the course of the story which are part of the attraction of the genre. Harriet Beecher Stowe's adoption of such a narrative strategy gave her novel an emotional dynamism that has been generally appreciated, but also permitted the development of moral and, eventually, sociopolitical complexities in the novel which have not been so widely recognized.

Commentators in this century, and postwar African-American critics in particular, have been preoccupied with the surface ambivalence expressed in these two kinds of journey, the question of whether the novel gives warmer approval to Uncle Tom's saintly acceptance of his martyrdom, or to George Harris's vigorous striving for liberty, as an appropriate black response to oppression. On the whole, they have tended to see Uncle Tom's submissiveness as the major statement about black responses to slavery in *Uncle Tom's Cabin*. After all, the novel's title has his name, not George's or Eliza's. James Baldwin, in particular, was infuriated by the fact that George Harris, the only male slave who fights for his freedom, is quite unrepresentative of slaves as a group, being (as Baldwin expresses it) "a mechanical genius, and ... moreover, sufficiently un-Negroid to pass through town, a fugitive from his master, disguised as a Spanish gentleman, attracting no attention whatever beyond admiration."[49]

These responses miss the point that *Uncle Tom's Cabin*, as Stowe in fact reminds us in many authorial asides, was a book addressed to white readers about the choices available to them on the issue of slavery, rather than a book about the choices slaves themselves might make. (Whatever angry slaveholders may have said, it was never a book addressed to slaves and remains almost unreadable for African-Americans now since it offers them no implied black reader's role to perform.) Indeed, by setting up Uncle Tom's martyrdom and George Harris's rapid disappearance to·Liberia as models of apparently contrary responses by slaves, when neither model posed any threat to northern whites, Stowe conveniently obscured the other possibilities, which would have alarmed northern white readers in 1852, of mass slave rebellion and an influx of former slaves to the North. This did not stop southern reviewers from accusing Stowe of writing the novel to foment revolt amongst the slaves, one declaring excitedly that: "Never until now did a female so far forget all the sweet and social instincts of her sex, as to do what Mrs Stowe has done — endeavor to whet the knife of domestic murder and shake over the head of every matron, maid and babe in the South, the blazing torch of midnight conflagration, the brutal and merciless instruments of death, that are struck to the heart or dash out the brains of the sleeping or the helpless, in the bursting out of a slave insurrection."[50] (In fact, her next novel about slavery, *Dred*, published in 1856, depicts preparations for a slave insurrection whose justification derives directly both from the moving personal experiences of the individual slaves and Biblical example. The acceptability of this to northern audiences, just four years later, indicates just how much more clearly the battle lines between slave states and free states were drawn.) In *Uncle Tom's Cabin*, Stowe led her white readers' imaginations away from such possibilities, no doubt sensing that at that time they would have harmed, not helped, the abolitionist cause.

"What can any individual do?"

Uncle Tom's Cabin was, then, a book addressed to whites about the choices confronting *them* over slavery. In her "Concluding Remarks" to the novel, Stowe responded to the question she supposed her (white) readers would be asking: "But, what can any individual do?" with the statement that "there is one thing that every individual can do, — they can see to it that *they feel right*" (*Uncle Tom's Cabin*: 472). Her apparent dependence here on the ultimate reliability of the individual reader's emotions and conscience disguises the extent to which, in the body of the novel, Stowe systematically transgresses the boundary between the private, domestic, traditionally feminine sphere and the public, institutional, traditionally masculine sphere. It will be my argument that readers who kept *Uncle Tom's Cabin* by them through the later 1850s, reexamining the twin journeys of Uncle Tom and George and Eliza, would have discovered there some much more specific answers to the moral and practical questions which confronted them during that period, and in terms not only of individual, but also collective, action.

When the twin journeys narrated in *Uncle Tom's Cabin* are examined in terms of the models they might offer for white action against slavery, the balance between the opposing models looks rather different.

Commentators have long recognized a saintly, even Christlike, quality in Uncle Tom's unwavering faith and his willingness to "turn the other cheek" until he is martyred. But several recent critics have pointed out that there are actually *two* martyrs in the novel, Uncle Tom and Little Eva, and have underlined the extent to which Uncle Tom plays a traditional heroine's, rather than hero's, role. Both possess unwavering faith and a saintly belief that their own deaths might contribute to the redemption of humanity. Little Eva declares of slavery: "'I can understand why Jesus *wanted* to die for us ... I've felt that I would be glad to die, if my dying could stop all this misery. I *would die* for them, Tom, if I could'" (*Uncle Tom's Cabin*, Chapter 24: 297). And she does. Tom and Eva, together, constitute one ideal type of human action.

In contrast to Tom's engaging, but distinctly archaic, religiosity, George Harris presents a persuasive, modern, rational secularity. A practical and passionate person, he has difficulty in curbing his bitter feelings toward those who have enslaved him. In contrast to the "feminine" Uncle Tom, Stowe depicts George Harris as an unambiguously "masculine" hero. (One Southern commentator, William Gilmore Simms, seizing on the evident attraction Stowe felt towards George Harris, referred slyly to the "most voluptuous portrait" she painted of him.)[51] His partner, Eliza, while she displays none of George's unchristian bitterness, is nevertheless equally passionate in her determination to save their son from being sold and equally resourceful in managing her and Harry's escape. Together they offer a contrary ideal of human behavior. George Shelby, the son of Tom's first owner, emerges at the end of the novel as a white version of the model offered by George Harris (his namesake), when, having witnessed Tom's death, he knocks Legree down and dedicates himself to doing "*what one man can*" to end slavery.

The death scenes of Tom and Eva were no doubt wonderfully effective at bringing great numbers of readers in the 1850s to tears, but it seems clear that neither is a figure with whom adult white readers would actually have *identified*. Little Eva is an angelic little being, one of those many child characters in novels of the period, whose meaningful deaths compensated readers for the inexplicable deaths of so many of their own infants, and Uncle Tom is a saintly black hero whom the white reader was invited to admire (even venerate) — but neither is a model to be *imitated*. Men have rarely seen martyrdom as an attractive option for themselves, but women, too, under the influence of feminist activists in the antislavery movement, like Angelina and Sarah Grimké, were coming to see the limitations of that domestic martyrdom which they were so often required to accept as their lot. And increasingly during the 1850s, Northerners of both sexes were convincing themselves that passivity to slave power was likely to lead them to a quite unproductive form of martyrdom. As the emotional heat over slavery rose in the North during the 1850s, so the qualities epitomized by Uncle Tom and Little Eva must have seemed increasingly archaic and irrelevant to northern readers, and the qualities of George and Eliza more modern and relevant. Given the feelings of the time, there is not the slightest doubt that Stowe made it easier for white readers to identify with George and Eliza by making them so light-skinned. (Here and elsewhere one sees Stowe, consciously or unconsciously, following her father's advice to the abolitionists "to make use of the current of human fears and passions and interests when they may be made to set in our favour instead of attempting to row upstream against them.") In the figure of George Harris (and then George Shelby), Stowe offers the most convincing answer in the novel to the question of how a *man* (whether white, black, or of mixed origin) can realistically be expected to behave in the modern world. In Eliza, she offers a model of modern womanhood which, even in the early 1850s, would likewise have been extraordinarily attractive. As models for *white* behavior, George and Eliza Harris, not Tom, are the central figures of the novel, a fact which has been neglected in recent discussion.

The disruption of traditional categories

If this argument is accepted, it is important to acknowledge the extent to which Stowe was disrupting prevailing ideological categories. Not only was she getting white readers to empathize with black characters, but her grouping of characters cut across both race lines *and* gender lines. Black Tom is associated with white Eva, black George Harris with black Eliza and white George Shelby. What is more, the passivity traditionally associated with both women and blacks is presented as archaic, even infantile, as a model for the behavior of people of either sex and any race. In this respect, Stowe was innovative to a degree and in a way which has not been recognized even by feminist commentators.

Equally innovative was Stowe's subtle disruption of the traditional dichotomy between the spheres of individual, personal morality (associated with women) and of public, institutional activity (associated with men). There are, it is true, numerous cues, not only in the "Concluding

Remarks" but scattered through the whole novel, directing the reader towards a reading of slavery, and opposition to slavery, in terms of individual, personal morality. Slaveholders, slavetraders and slavecatchers are depicted with a vivid, Dickensian grotesqueness as personally vicious or morally defective: Mr. Harris (George's master), Mr. Haley, Marks (Tom Loker's partner in slavecatching) and others. Virtuous characters, such as Uncle Tom, and Eva, are good despite their surroundings and as a direct consequence of their personal religious faith. Within this individual perspective, slavery is seen as the epitome of the unloving, unchristian life. Yet Stowe also ensures that the dialogue continually slips into commentary on public, institutional matters associated with slavery. It is, significantly, a woman, Mrs. Shelby, very early in the novel, who underlines the inadequacy of purely individual moral thinking about slavery: "'I was a fool to think I could make anything good out of such a deadly evil. It is a sin to hold a slave under laws like ours'" (*Uncle Tom's Cabin*, Chapter 5: 45). But it is Augustine St. Clare, himself a benevolent slaveholder, who articulates these arguments most fully: "'Talk of the *abuses* of slavery! Humbug! The *thing itself* is the essence of all abuse! And the only reason why the land don't sink under it, like Sodom and Gomorrah, is because it is *used* in a way infinitely better than it is ... he who goes the furthest and does the worst, only uses within limits the power that the law gives him'" (*Uncle Tom's Cabin*, Chapter 19: 242).

Stowe's swing from a traditionally Protestant concern with personal conscience and individual morality to a more modern, secular concern with social structures and political institutions was, it is true, certainly not unique in the period. In fact, as Raymond Williams suggests in an essay on Dickens's *Dombey and Son* (1848), this swing was being repeated in a general sense by male and female writers throughout the English-speaking world in that period:

> There is a kind of moral analysis in which society is a background against which the drama of personal virtues and vices is enacted. There is another kind — increasingly important in the development of nineteenth-century literature — in which society is the creator of virtues and vices; its active relationships and institutions at once generating and controlling, or failing to control, what in the earlier mode of analysis could be seen as faults of the soul.[52]

In this respect, too, *Uncle Tom's Cabin* is usefully identified as a transitional novel.

Uncle Tom's Cabin and the slave power conspiracy

It is through the structural device of pairing George and Eliza's journey towards liberty with Uncle Tom's journey towards death that Stowe broaches most forcefully the institutional questions relating to slavery. And on this level, the two journeys, far from standing in opposition to each other, constitute a joint commentary on that institution.

It is in the movement of Uncle Tom's journey that the reader is presented with the strongest evidence of the variety of dangers posed by slavery to a civilized society. Uncle Tom descends from an almost idyllic life on the estate of the Shelby family (and with his own family) in the border state of Kentucky, to the still benevolent, but disorganized, household of Augustine St. Clare in New Orleans, to the ghoulish, infernal life of Legree's plantation. His journey exemplifies the tendency of the institution of slavery to undergo continuous degradation: its respectable, benevolent manifestations slip inevitably (through chance, financial mishap, laziness, greed) into its most brutal forms. Slavery is represented as, *by necessity*, becoming always more corrupt and as tending always to corrupt more people, both white and black. In the course of this journey, the author repeatedly reminds readers of the pressure from the South for the wider acceptance of slavery. See, for instance, this comment on the slavetrader Haley: "The trader had arrived at that stage of Christian and political perfection which has been recommended by some preachers and politicians of the north, lately, in which he had completely overcome every humane weakness and prejudice. His heart was exactly where yours, sir, and mine could be brought, with proper effort and cultivation" (*Uncle Tom's Cabin*: 144).

Slavery threatens constantly to engulf the people and territory of the free states. Through the structural device of Uncle Tom's journey, Stowe was foreshadowing, in a vivid, personal way, the notion, which came so strongly to preoccupy Northerners in the mid-1850s, of "slave power."

Abolitionists had for many years employed the argument that slavery, if left unchecked, would eventually be used against white workers, too. It was an argument which came increasingly to persuade northern white farmers and artisans in the 1850s as they saw slave power encroaching on their territory. The abolitionist magazine, *The Emancipator*, declared, as early as 1839: "The struggle is between the antagonist principles of free and slave labor. They cannot much longer co-exist. One must prevail to the exclusion of the other. The laborers will either be free, or enslaved."[53] Abolitionists associated practices in the slave states with the grinding oppression to be found in the Old World, against which the United States had supposedly rebelled. Stowe's characters take up this argument on several occasions. Augustine St. Clare developed it most fully: "'The American planter is 'only doing, in another form, what the English aristocracy and capitalists are doing by the lower classes;' that is, I take it, *appropriating* them, body and bone, soul and spirit, to their use and convenience'" (*Uncle Tom's Cabin*, Chapter 19: 249).

Stowe is careful, it is true, to stress individual northern collusion in the practice of slavery (Legree and other vicious practitioners of slavery were born in the North) and the hypocrisy of the attitudes of many Northerners towards blacks. St. Clare's words to his northern cousin, Miss Ophelia, hit home: "'You loathe them as you would a snake or a toad, yet you are indignant at their wrongs. You would not have them abused; but you don't want to have anything to do with them yourselves'" (*Uncle Tom's Cabin*, Chapter 16: 195). Nevertheless, Stowe leaves no doubt that the roots of slavery are in the South, in an old, decaying and economically inefficient system, associated with aristocracy and the Old World, which contrasts with, and is capable of infecting, the democratic and properly American aspirations of the North. (Stowe, like many abolitionists, was quite blind to the new bondage, wage slavery, which northern industrial capitalists were imposing with increasing success on white factory workers. There are indications that she would have supported the abolitionist Samuel Gridley Howe who, in 1852, aligned himself with Massachusetts factory proprietors to oppose a law limiting factory workers to a ten-hour day, declaring [in terms which should suggest to the modern reader that there is nothing "new" about the so-called New Right] that it "emasculated people to be protected in this way. Let them get used to protecting themselves.")[54]

For the many northern whites who reread *Uncle Tom's Cabin* (alongside the more recently published *Dred*) in the late 1850s, and who increasingly came to believe that slave power would eventually threaten *their* freedom, emotional identification with George and Eliza Harris would have become not only easier but far deeper and more personally significant. It is in this sense, perhaps, that *Uncle Tom's Cabin* contributed most directly to the fusion of moral concern and perceived self-interest over slavery which occurred over those years in the North.

If Stowe did something, in *Uncle Tom's Cabin*, to fuel this source of resentment against the South amongst northern white readers, it was to be the statements of a number of Southerners in the mid-1850s which set it ablaze. Most infamous of these was the comment by George Fitzhugh of Virginia, in 1856, that "slavery is the natural and normal condition of the laboring man, whether white or black" which is said to have done more than any antislavery document to turn Northerners against slavery and the South.[55] Over the three years after 1854, the conviction grew among northern workers and small farmers that slavery and slavepower were indeed a serious threat to their interests. Harriet Beecher Stowe was in tune with, and brilliantly stirred, these fears amongst northern whites. Her novel *Dred* (published in 1856) contains several passages on the desperate plight of poor whites in the South, and pieces of dialogue in which slaveholders declare that "there ought to be a law passed to make 'em all slaves," or "there ought to be hunting-parties got up to chase them down and exterminate 'em just as we do rats." It is an indication of the rapidity with which anger over slave power advanced in the North that, by 1857, a nonabolitionist newspaper like the Cincinnati *Daily Commercial* could state: "There is such a thing as SLAVE POWER. It has marched over and annihilated the boundaries of the states. We are now one great homogeneous slaveholding community."[56] Stowe's foreshadowing of this march in *Uncle Tom's Cabin* was subtle but unmistakable.

The moral and constitutional arguments

If Uncle Tom's journey illustrates one kind of instability in the institution of slavery, its tendency to deteriorate and to suck an increasing number of people into its evil workings, George Harris's and the other slaves' journey of escape northward to Canada demonstrates two other aspects of the inherent instability of slavery: first, the immense and irresistible drive of the slaves for freedom, secondly the willingness of ordinary white people, when confronted with that drive, to assist slaves to freedom. While Uncle Tom's journey demonstrates the absolute necessity for slavery to be defeated, George Harris's offers evidence of a general kind about the means by which that defeat might be achieved.

Stowe, however, went much further than this in the sense that she encapsulated in the novel, for a mass white readership, debates on a number of moral and legal questions which were to become burning issues throughout the nation in the later years of the decade. These issues are broached both by the escaping slaves and, significantly, a series of white characters, John and Mary Bird, the Quakers, the old Dutch farmer Van Trompe, and others, who come to aid them in their flight. Although the issues are initially posed as private dilemmas, their public, institutional dimension quickly becomes evident.

The two main related questions which are explored concern the rightness of disobeying an unjust law and of using violence to defend life and freedom. Essentially three positions are set out, and some authorial support is implied for all of them. Uncle Tom, of course, occupies an absolutist position: he will not break the law by fleeing and, when given the opportunity by Cassy to kill his last owner, Legree, he absolutely will not contemplate it: "'Not for ten thousand worlds, Misse ... good never comes of wickedness ... The Lord hasn't called us to wrath. We must suffer and wait his time'" (*Uncle Tom's Cabin*, Chapter 38: 422-23). The Quakers who look after George and Eliza are equally clear that they *should* break the law to give assistance to escaping slaves but that they must use exclusively nonviolent means: "'for the wrath of man worketh not the righteousness of God'" (*Uncle Tom's Cabin*, Chapter 17: 207). The integrity of the different positions held by Uncle Tom and the Quakers is presented as self-evident. But Stowe also wrote a brilliantly persuasive argument (both as dialogue and as authorial comment) to justify a third position: George Harris's belief that he was right, not only to break the law, but to use violence to defend his, and his family's, freedom. Stowe provides George Harris with a powerful legalistic argument relating to the obligations of slaves: "'Mr Wilson, you have a country; but what country have *I*, or any one like me, born of slave mothers? What laws are there for us? We don't make them, we don't consent to them, — we have nothing to do with them; all they do for us is to crush us, and keep us down. Haven't I heard your Fourth-of-July speeches? Don't you tell us all, once a year, that governments derive their just power from the consent of the governed?'" (*Uncle Tom's Cabin*, Chapter 11: 125).

The related, but distinct, question of whether a white citizen should break laws which he or she believes to be morally obnoxious, that is, whether individuals have a general obligation to work within validly enacted laws (the question faced, in the novel, by the Quakers and others) was vigorously debated in the early 1850s — in relation to the Fugitive Slave Act, of course, but also in relation to the possible secession of the slave states. Strong arguments on both sides of the case could be derived from American tradition. The dominant line of argument, until the early 1840s at least, had been laid down in George Washington's 'Farewell Address' of 1796: "The constitution which at any time exists till changed by an authentic act of the whole people is sacredly obligatory upon all. The very idea of the power and right of the people to establish government presupposes the duty of every individual to obey the established government."[57] Even the abolitionists, up to the early 1850s, generally subscribed to this view. For instance, in 1836, William Lloyd Garrison and the Massachusetts Anti-Slavery Society condemned the mob rescue of two black women, alleged to be fugitives, from the Massachusetts Supreme Judicial Court.[58] An obvious practical attraction of this position for the abolitionists was that it tended to protect them against mobbings, lynchings, and other breakdowns in law and order promoted by their opponents.

The opposing line of argument, that any human law which contravenes moral law is void and should not be obeyed, had at least as long a history and was frequently advanced in the 1840s, most notably in 1849 by Henry David Thoreau in his *Essay on Civil Disobedience*: "If the injustice [of a law] ... is of such a nature that it requires you to be the agent of injustice to another, then, I say, break the law. Let your life be a counter-friction to stop the machine."[59] The issue came to a head, of course, in 1850 with the passing of the Fugitive Slave Act. Stowe's evident willingness, in the novel, to countenance northern whites' disobeying it by giving assistance to fleeing slaves drew disapproval from both sides. Southern readers could condemn her for her disrespect of the Constitution but, at the same time, they could see that the argument she presented might be used with only a little twisting to justify *their* eventual secession. Interestingly, too, many northern reviewers who praised the novel, including some abolitionists, rejected this argument within it.[60]

As for the related question of the use of violence against injustice, while Uncle Tom's and the Quakers' position is certainly presented as being admirable, Stowe again puts excellent arguments into the mouth of George Harris, as well as backing him with tongue-in-cheek authorial comment. When George faces his pursuers, brandishing a pair of pistols and crying out: "'We stand here as free under God's sky, as you are; and by the great God that made us, will fight for our liberty till we die'" (*Uncle Tom's Cabin*, 17: 215-16), he sounds like any number of earlier (and later) white American heroes. He fires and wounds Tom Loker, the slavecatcher (though, significantly, it is actually a white Quaker convert, Phineas Fletcher, who, momentarily forgetting his Quakerism, pushes him off the ledge). Stowe attached to this scene a commentary whose seductive power must have been irresistible to many white readers:

> If it had only been a Hungarian youth, now, bravely defending in some mountain fastness the retreat of fugitives escaping from Austria into

America, this would have been sublime heroism; but as it was a youth of African descent, defending the retreat of fugitives through America into Canada, of course we are too well instructed and patriotic to see any heroism in it; and if any of our readers do, they must do it on their own private responsibility (*Uncle Tom's Cabin*, Chapter 17: 216).

In taking up the issue of whether violence between citizens of the same nation could ever be justified, Stowe was focusing on one of the issues on which the abolitionist movement itself was strongly divided. William Lloyd Garrison and his associates consistently argued the pacifist line. As Bertram Wyatt-Brown says: "According to Garrison, all means of force led to oppression; the only weapon against evil was the testimony of nonresistance. He opposed institutions because these engines of coercion hindered the search for individual perfection."[61]

It was only by means of the moral reform of individuals that social reform could be obtained. Stowe gives some support for this position in *Uncle Tom's Cabin*, not only by depicting the Quaker community in which problems of potential conflict are resolved in terms of nonviolent, loving, personal responsibility, but also by portraying several slaveholders who undergo a complete change of heart, including the old Dutchman Van Trompe, Augustine St. Clare, and George Shelby. When Miss Ophelia asks Augustine St. Clare if their nation will ever voluntarily emancipate, he replies that he doesn't know, but adds: "'This is a day of great deeds. Heroism and disinterestedness are rising up, here and there in the earth. The Hungarian nobles set free millions of serfs, at an immense pecuniary loss; and, perhaps, among us may be found generous spirits who do not estimate honor and justice by dollars and cents'" (*Uncle Tom's Cabin*, Chapter 28: 337). The historian Dwight L. Dumond vouches for the fact that significant numbers of slaveholders in the 1830s and 1840s did free their slaves and leave the slave states because they found the moral atmosphere intolerable.[62]

Around 1852 a change of mood occurred, with a large section of the white abolitionist movement coming to accept the necessity of violence to end slavery. Stowe's references to Hungary give a clue as to one source of that change: American enthusiasm for the many uprisings which had occurred all over Europe during 1848 and 1849. Another source was the growing demand among black activists for the violent overthrow of slavery and the Fugitive Slave Act.[63]

Of course Stowe's treatment of justified violence is very tentative. George Harris uses his pistols only in self-defense when he and his family are on the verge of being captured. Just one shot is fired and Tom Loker is only wounded. The fugitives, themselves, rescue him from the gully into which he has fallen and carry him to a Quaker settlement, before continuing their flight. After some weeks of Quaker nursing, Loker rises from his bed a reformed character. This outcome is hardly a very severe test of the general moral argument about the use of violence to defend one's own rights or the rights of others. Even so, as the Garrisonians consistently argued (and Garrison's review of *Uncle Tom's Cabin* took Stowe to task on this)[64] once any degree of violence is held to be morally justified, there is no knowing where the argument may lead.

The fusion of maternal love and military fervor

In *Uncle Tom's Cabin*, Stowe quietly opened the door to the great issue which would arise in the dispute over Kansas and, later, in the Civil War itself, of whether, and in what circumstances, white citizens of the United States should take up arms against each other. The importance of her doing so can hardly be overestimated, since the convergence of the paths of the abolitionists and of the Free Soilers in the North in the late 1850s depended not only on the Free Soilers deciding that slavery was *worth* fighting over, but on the abolitionists (or many of them) deciding that *fighting* was the appropriate thing to do.

The essence of my argument about just how *Uncle Tom's Cabin* worked on mass white opinion in the United States between the time of its first publication and the beginning of the Civil War is easily summarized. Its initial major achievement was to draw large numbers of northern whites into a first emotional response to slavery, by inducing them to empathize with black fictional characters in situations resulting from the slavery laws. Southerners, who claimed that *Uncle Tom's Cabin* lied about slavery, developed a correspondingly strong emotional reaction against it, so that the novel itself became a serious additional subject of dispute between South and North. As dramatic events after 1854 posed new questions to northern whites, so they came to read through the soft sentimental surface of the novel, which had constituted its initial attraction, to the hard bedrock of its analysis of slavery as an institutional evil, of specifically southern origin, which would eventually pose a threat to northern whites. Empathy and concern for the sufferings of blacks grew into an increasingly sharp concern among northern whites for their own skins. The need for institutional action and the acceptability of violence to oppose slavery, subtly implied in *Uncle Tom's Cabin*, and then overtly declared in *Dred*, came to be widely accepted.

Within this broad argument there has also been a recurrent emphasis on the extent to which Stowe's mode of operation, in *Uncle Tom's Cabin*, substantially disrupted several of the dichotomies with which her contemporaries were preoccupied, not only the male/female and white/black dichotomies, but the rigid division of public from private, secular from religious, and aggressive from pacifist. This observation has considerable interest in the light of that strand of modern feminist thought, running from Simone De Beauvoir to Hélène Cixous which sees such dichotomies (or "binary oppositions") as one of the major tools of patriarchal oppression. Binary thought, according to Hélène Cixous, is a process by which the world is organized into conceptual pairs, such as nature/culture, light/dark, intellect/emotion, male/female, which always serve eventually to privilege the former (male) side, which is treated as the norm, as against the latter (female) side, which is treated as the deviant, what De Beauvoir called the "Other." To break down the traditional dichotomies should constitute a major challenge to patriarchy.

Stowe, however, did not commit herself to the wholesale destruction of dichotomous patterns of thought. Rather, she was participating in one of those massive redistributions of dichotomies which always occur around the beginning of a war, whereby the old oppositions are (for the duration of the war) largely suppressed in favour of the construction of that massive new ideological opposition between "Us" and the new "Other," i.e. the Enemy. Between 1854 and 1861, Stowe contributed substantially to the building, in the collective consciousness of northern whites, of that ideological dichotomy according to which the northern cause embodied all liberty, decency, and Christian righteousness, while the slave states embodied all that was foul, decadent, and satanic. (In more recent wars, women have been allowed, for the duration, to take over men's civilian jobs, racial minorities have been recruited into the armed forces to fight for "their" country, and the poor and oppressed have regularly been led to believe that they are defending "their" liberty and prosperity. Once the war is over, the old binary oppositions, whether of race, gender, or class, tend to reassert themselves, though perhaps without quite their former rigid grip.) Had that dichotomy not been established, the Civil War could not have occurred.

War, in which women are usually prohibited from taking a fighting role despite the fact that war's worst brutalities are so often directed against them, is regarded by many feminists as the ultimate manifestation of oppressive patriarchal power. So, does this mean that Stowe's contribution to the coming of the Civil War should be seen, after all, as a betrayal of women, or as the co-opting by patriarchy of her multiple, woman's powers? Stowe herself believed — and her statement about the encounter with Lincoln strongly suggests it — that she and her "sisters" had, on the contrary, gone some way to appropriate the patriarchal institution of war in the service of morality and liberty. Nevertheless, the cost for women like Stowe, who fused maternal Christian love with military fervor, is epitomized by the anguish, as well as the pride, with which she dispatched her second son, Frederick William, to the war, where he distinguished himself for heroism and was seriously injured at Gettysburg.[65]

The use and abuse of *Uncle Tom's Cabin*

Uncle Tom's Cabin, it has been suggested, was a mighty weapon in the struggle for the abolition of slavery. Yet when abolition came, blacks found that the liberty it gave them was only nominal, without land (unlike the Russian serfs), voting rights, or other kinds of economic and social power. The subsequent struggle by African-Americans to transform that nominal liberty into a real and full freedom has lasted for more than a century. All of the great energy of *Uncle Tom's Cabin* and its author had gone into achieving abolition. Neither of them had anything significant to offer black activists in the long struggle that followed. When northern whites returned to the novel after the Civil War, they found its sentimental charm enhanced by the glow they could feel from the fact that slavery no longer existed. They had banished the great evil to which *Uncle Tom's Cabin* referred and found the racial stereotypes to which they still remained attached largely unchallenged by it. The stereotypical portrayal of blacks, not only Uncle Tom's passivity, but the cute devilishness of Topsy and the clowning of Sam, became fixed in the minds not only of generations of whites, but, as Richard Yarborough has emphasized, of blacks, too.[66]

It needs to be remembered, however, that the postwar history of the reception of *Uncle Tom's Cabin*, the novel, becomes increasingly indistinguishable from that of the the grotesque, theatrical adaptations of the novel which circulated throughout the northern states. The cult of these versions in large part displaced the cult of the novel itself, and the statistics on the number of performances they received are almost as remarkable as those on the numbers of copies of the novel sold in the 1850s. By 1870 there were more than fifty acting companies touring the northern states in productions of *Uncle Tom's Cabin*; by the 1890s, five hundred. "Tommer shows" continued to be popular up to the 1930s. It is estimated that in total over a million performances of the various theatrical adaptations of Stowe's novel were given over a seventy-year period.[67] These productions varied from open-air performances involving only a few actors, doubling parts, to grand spectaculars in the big cities. Until early this century almost all productions involved only white actors, and those who "blacked up" to play the slave characters adopted the tricks of eyerolling, crooning, and softshoe shuffles traditional to the portrayal of blacks by whites on the stage. Stowe's novel was milked for all its melodramatic and comic potential with many extraordinary additions and distortions: Eliza and Harry were frequently chased by big dogs, Little Eva ascended to heaven suspended by a wire, Uncle Tom was whipped to death by Legree at center stage or, in some versions, saved from death at the very end. Uncle Tom, himself, was generally portrayed as old and feeble, sometimes, even, as a comic figure.[68] The flavor of the different productions obviously varied a good deal. In most there was a curious blend of pathos over Uncle Tom's plight and hilarity at the crude comic tricks of most of the other black characters. There is evidence that, in some cases, the beating of slave characters was carried out in such a way as to give pleasure to white audiences.[69]

All the moral seriousness and subtle ambivalence of Stowe were obliterated. Slavery was treated as a thing of the past and its abolition as a reason for self-congratulation by white Northerners. No hint was given that the blatant exploitation and repression of blacks still survived. The dramatic versions of *Uncle Tom's Cabin* served, almost without exception, to reinforce the most reactionary racial stereotypes about blacks and a sense of their utter powerlessness. The contemptuous "Uncle Tom" epithet used by blacks in the modern period probably derives its bitterness more from their response to the portrayal of Tom in the theatrical versions than from his portrayal in Stowe's novel, since for a long period most people (white and black) encountered *Uncle Tom's Cabin* not as a novel but in one (or several) of its stage adaptations.

It would be quite unreasonable to blame Stowe for the manner in which theatrical entrepreneurs mangled her work, since she neither authorized nor made a profit from the dramatic versions. Nevertheless, it has to be admitted that the populist character of her novel did somehow permit such a process to occur. All that was required was a reversal of the alchemy by which Stowe had transformed familiar and largely reactionary raw material into an intellectually demanding and politically challenging work.

NOTES TO CHAPTER 3

1. The greeting is recorded in slightly varying forms. See, for family recollections of the episode, Lyman Beecher Stowe, *Saints, Sinners and Beechers* (Indianapolis: Bobbs-Merrill, 1934): 205. For discussion of the possible interpretations of the greeting, see John R. Adams, *Harriet Beecher Stowe* (New York: Twayne, 1963): 8-9.

2. See, for instance, Thomas F. Gossett, *'Uncle Tom's Cabin' and American Culture*. (Dallas: Southern Methodist University Press, 1985): 311.

3. Gossett, *'Uncle Tom's Cabin' and American Culture*: 312.

4. Quoted in, for example, R. B. Nye and J. E. Morpurgo, *A History of the United States*, 2 vols. (Harmondsworth: Penguin, 1965), 2: 507.

5. Gossett, *'Uncle Tom's Cabin' and American Culture*: 314.

6. Reported in George F. Whicher, "Literature and Conflict," in *Literary History of the United States*, ed. Robert E. Spiller, Willard Thorp, Thomas H. Johnson, Henry Seidel Canby, Richard M. Ludwig, 3rd ed. (New York: Macmillan, 1963): 563.

7. Gossett, *'Uncle Tom's Cabin' and American Culture*: 184.

8. Adams, *Harriet Beecher Stowe*: 144.

9. James Ford Rhodes, *The History of the United State from the Compromise of 1850 to the Final Restoration of Home Rule at the South in 1877*, 8 vols. (New York: Harper, 1892), 1: 284-85.

10. Avery O. Craven, *The Coming of the Civil War*, 2nd ed. (Chicago: University of Chicago Press, 1957): 145.

11. Elizabeth Ammons, "Stowe's Dream of the Mother-Savior: *Uncle Tom's Cabin* and American Women Writers before the 1920s," in *New Essays on "Uncle Tom's Cabin"*, ed. Eric J. Sundquist (Cambridge: Cambridge University Press, 1986): 155.

12. Whicher, "Literature and Conflict": 563.

13. Whicher, "Literature and Conflict": 586.

14. Richard Yarborough, "Strategies of Black Characterization in *Uncle Tom's Cabin* and the Early Afro-American Novel," in *New Essays on "Uncle Tom's Cabin"*, ed. Eric J. Sundquist (Cambridge: Cambridge University Press, 1986): 47.

15. Yarborough, "Strategies of Black Characterization": 65.

16. James Baldwin, "Everybody's Protest Novel" (1949), in his *The Price of the Ticket: Collected Nonfiction, 1948-1985* (London: Michael Joseph, 1985): 28.

Harriet Beecher Stowe: Uncle Tom's Cabin

▼▼▼

17. Catharine Beecher, *An Essay on Slavery and Abolitionism with Reference to the Duty of American Females* (1837), quoted in Gossett, *'Uncle Tom's Cabin' and American Culture*: 43-44.

18. Quoted in Jean Fagan Yellin, "Doing it Herself: *Uncle Tom's Cabin* and Woman's Role in the Slavery Crisis," in *New Essays on "Uncle Tom's Cabin"*, ed. Eric J. Sundquist (Cambridge: Cambridge University Press, 1986): 88.

19. Quoted in Edward Wagenknecht, *Harriet Beecher Stowe: The Known and the Unknown* (New York: Oxford University Press, 1965): 181.

20. The standard edition is Harriet Beecher Stowe, *Uncle Tom's Cabin, or Life Among the Lowly*, ed. Kenneth S. Lynn (Cambridge, Mass.: Harvard University Press, 1962) but it seemed sensible to make my references to one of the paperback editions in which *Uncle Tom's Cabin* is most easily found today, the Signet Classic edition with an Afterword by John William Ward (New York: New American Library, 1981). Nevertheless, when quoting from the body of the novel, I shall cite chapter references as well as page references to help readers who have some other edition to locate the quotation.

21. Harriet Beecher Stowe, *Dred: A Tale of the Great Dismal Swamp* (London: Sampson, Low, Marston, 1856): 2.

22. Jane P. Tompkins, "Sentimental Power: *Uncle Tom's Cabin* and the Politics of Literary History," in ed. Elaine Showalter, *Feminist Criticism: Essays on Women, Literature and Theory* (London: Virago, 1986): 98.

23. Tompkins, "Sentimental Power": 96.

24. Gossett, *'Uncle Tom's Cabin' and American Culture*: 61.

25. Nye and Morpurgo, *A History of the United States*, 2: 435.

26. Nye and Morpurgo, *A History of the United States*, 2: 432.

27. Nye and Morpurgo, *A History of the United States*, 2: 435.

28. Quoted in Gossett, *'Uncle Tom's Cabin' and American Culture*: 23.

29. Gossett, *'Uncle Tom's Cabin' and American Culture*: 23.

30. Adams, *Harriet Beecher Stowe*: 45.

31. Quoted in Edmund Wilson, *Patriotic Gore: Studies in the Literature of the American Civil War* (New York: Oxford University Press, 1962): 17 and 26.

32. Nye and Morpurgo, *A History of the United States*, 2: 450.

33. Quoted in Bertram Wyatt-Brown, "William Lloyd Garrison and Antislavery Unity: A Reappraisal," in *Civil War History* 13 (1967): 19.

34. Gossett, *'Uncle Tom's Cabin' and American Culture*: 311.

35. Quoted in Yellin, "Doing it Herself: *Uncle Tom's Cabin* and Woman's Role in the Slavery Crisis": 87.

36. Ammons, "Stowe's Dream of the Mother-Savior": 188.

37. Wyatt-Brown, "William Lloyd Garrison and Antislavery Unity": 15.

38. Michael Fellman, "Rehearsal for the Civil War: Antislavery and Proslavery at the Fighting Point in Kansas, 1854-1856," in *Antislavery Reconsidered: New Perspectives on the Abolitionists*, ed. Lewis Perry and Michael Fellman (Baton Rouge and London: Louisiana State University Press, 1979): 289-90.

The Power of the Story
▼▼▼

39. On this point, see Ronald G. Walters, "The Boundaries of Abolitionism," in *Antislavery Reconsidered: New Perspectives on the Abolitionists*, ed. Lewis Perry and Michael Fellman (Baton Rouge and London: Louisiana State University Press, 1979): 21.

40. Quoted in Fokkema and Kunne-Ibsch, *Theories of Literature in the Twentieth Century*: 146

41. Quoted in Gossett, *'Uncle Tom's Cabin' and American Culture*: 185-86.

42. Gossett, *'Uncle Tom's Cabin' and American Culture*: 188.

43. See, for instance, Gossett, *'Uncle Tom's Cabin' and American Culture*: 195.

44. Gossett, *'Uncle Tom's Cabin' and American Culture*: 189.

45. Alice Crozier, *The Novels of Harriet Beecher Stowe* (New York: Oxford University Press, 1969): 4.

46. Gossett, *'Uncle Tom's Cabin' and American Culture*: 190.

47. Gossett, *'Uncle Tom's Cabin' and American Culture*: 430-31.

48. Gossett, *'Uncle Tom's Cabin' and American Culture*: 183.

49. Baldwin, "Everybody's Protest Novel": 30.

50. Gossett, *'Uncle Tom's Cabin' and American Culture*: 190.

51. Yarborough, "Strategies of Black Characterization": 59.

52. Raymond Williams, "Introduction" to Charles Dickens, *Dombey and Son* (Harmondsworth: Penguin, 1970): 16.

53. Quoted in Russell B. Nye, "Farsighted Reformers," in *The Abolitionists*, ed. Richard O. Curry (Hinsdale, Illinois: Dryden Press, 1973): 137.

54. Quoted in Jonathan A. Glickstein, "'Poverty Is Not Slavery': American Abolitionists and the Competitive Slave Market," in *Antislavery Reconsidered: New Perspectives on the Abolitionists*, ed. Lewis Perry and Michael Fellman (Baton Rouge and London: Louisiana State University Press, 1979): 217.

55. Quoted in Nye and Morpurgo, *A History of the United States*, 2: 416.

56. *Daily Commercial*, 12 March 1857, quoted by Russell B. Nye in ed. Curry, *The Abolitionists*: 135.

57. Quoted in, for instance, William M. Wiecek, "Latimer: Lawyers, Abolitionists, and the Problem of Unjust Laws," in *Antislavery Reconsidered: New Perspectives on the Abolitionists*, ed. Lewis Perry and Michael Fellman (Baton Rouge and London: Louisiana State University Press, 1979): 223.

58. Wiecek, "Latimer: Lawyers, Abolitionists, and the Problem of Unjust Laws": 225-226.

59. Henry David Thoreau, *Walden and Civil Disobedience*, ed. Owen Thomas (New York: W. W. Norton, 1966): 231.

60. Gossett, *'Uncle Tom's Cabin' and American Culture*: 179.

61. Wyatt-Brown, "William Lloyd Garrison and Antislavery Unity": 6.

62. Dwight L. Dumond, "Migrations to the Free States a Factor" in ed. Curry, *The Abolitionists*: 23.

63. Wyatt-Brown, "William Lloyd Garrison and Antislavery Unity": 13.

64. Quoted in Gossett, *'Uncle Tom's Cabin' and American Culture*: 170.

65. See Adams, *Harriet Beecher Stowe*: 74.

66. Yarborough, "Strategies of Black Characterization": 46.
67. For a full discussion of the "Tommer shows," see Gossett, *'Uncle Tom's Cabin' and American Culture*, Chapter 19.
68. See Edmund Wilson's account of the productions of the late-1870s as "half a minstrel show and half a circus" in his *Patriotic Gore*: 4.
69. Gossett, *'Uncle Tom's Cabin' and American Culture*: 270.

4. IGNAZIO SILONE:
"*Fontamara*" (1933)

▼ ▼ ▼

Fiction and fact

It is widely accepted that *Fontamara*, the first novel by the Italian writer, Ignazio Silone, exercised extraordinary influence as a document of anti-Fascist propaganda outside Italy in the late 1930s. The persuasive force of the novel in that period was recently recalled by Michael Foot, the veteran British Labour politician, who wrote that "ever since the murder of the socialist leader, Giacomo Matteotti, in 1924, no real excuse existed for those who could not publish or face the truth. But fiction can sometimes speak more strongly than fact. For some of us, *Fontamara* planted a more indelible impression than any other report from that scene of tyranny and terror."[1] *Fontamara*, it is clear, played a major role in discrediting Mussolini's regime in the eyes of a wide readership hitherto not reached, or not persuaded, by the reports from journalists in the less conservative press of the vacuousness of Fascist rhetoric and the viciousness of its practice. But just as remarkable as the specific political role that the novel played in that time and context, and much less noticed by literary historians, is the way in which *Fontamara* was subsequently to prove itself to be highly polyvalent, not merely in the sense that it came to be interpreted in different keys, but also in that it has engaged with political history in a number of different ways, as it has come to be read at several distinct moments and locations over almost sixty years.

Ignazio Silone wrote *Fontamara* in Switzerland during 1930 and 1931, mostly in a sanatorium, after eight years of clandestine anti-Fascist activity, inside and outside Italy, as an important official of the Italian Communist Party. Although an Italian edition was published in Paris in 1934, and a few copies did circulate among anti-Fascists in Italy, it could not be officially distributed in Mussolini's Italy. Thus, the first major reception of *Fontamara* was outside Italy and in translation. Between 1933, when it was first published in German in Switzerland, and 1935, it was translated into English, French, Spanish, Russian, and thirteen other languages.

Fontamara was one of the most widely reviewed, read and talked-about novels of the 1930s in North and South America, Europe and the Soviet Union.[2] It was praised and promoted by liberals and socialists in New York, Buenos Aires, London, Paris, Budapest, Copenhagen, Vienna, and Amsterdam, as well as having the rare distinction of receiving both official Soviet approval from Karl Radek at the Soviet Writers' Congress of 18 August 1934[3] (surprisingly, since Silone was by then an ex-communist) and warm recognition from the already exiled Trotsky, who wrote that *Fontamara* "deserves to have thousands of copies printed."[4]

Fontamara is the story of a desperately poor, remote, hilltop village in the Abruzzi region (which lies over the Appennine mountains east of Rome) whose centuries-long neglect by the authorities is disturbed when a rich local landowner and entrepreneur redirects the pitiful stream which supplies water to the villagers' vegetable plots to his own land further down the hillside. It is the summer of 1929. When the women of Fontamara take their protest to the local administration in the nearest large town their efforts are met with derision. It becomes evident to the reader, though not to the villagers who are years behind in their knowledge of political events, that "the Contractor" who has seized their water is invulnerable to protest since he is also the newly appointed Fascist *podestà* for the region. When the villagers interrupt a party given by the Contractor for the notables of the area to protest, they are informed that they willingly signed away their rights to the stream when they were visited by a local official with a petition whose content he did not reveal. As they threaten violence, the local lawyer, Don Circostanza, who has always claimed to be "the Friend of the People," emerges from the notables and proposes a formula which is supposed to help them: "'The podestà must be left three-quarters of the water of the stream, and the three-quarters of the remainder must be left to the people of Fontamara. Thus both parties will have three-quarters, that is, each will have a little more than half'" (*Fontamara*, 1938: 52).[5] The peasants (*cafoni*) are too naive to realize the flaw in this arrangement. When, later, the villagers are summoned to town for what they have been told is to be a discussion about the reallocation of farmland in the rich

Fucino plain, to which they want access, they find they have been tricked into participating in a Fascist rally.

Over the days that follow, the objections of the *cafoni* grow stronger — they burn down a fence the administration has erected to keep them off the common land on which they have always grazed their few animals. One day, while the men are out, working as day laborers in the valley below, a group of armed and masked blackshirts enter the village and rape all the women. When, finally, the male villagers return, not knowing what has happened, they are interrogated on their political beliefs. Their answers fail to satisfy the Fascist militiamen and an official note is made about this failure. The blackshirts eventually leave. One of the poorest but most independent of the *cafoni*, Berardo Viola, seeing no hope of making a good enough living at Fontamara to support Elvira, the woman he desires to marry, goes to Rome in search of work. While there, he comes across a young man, who looks "half-student, half-workman" — to the reader it is clear that he is a clandestine anti-Fascist activist — who offers him food in a café. They are arrested when a police search of the café reveals a bundle of subversive literature. In prison, the Mystery Man undertakes Berardo's political education. Berardo then tells the police the bundle of papers was his and the Mystery Man is released. The Mystery Man goes to Fontamara to tell the *cafoni* what has happened to Berardo and, after some resistance, convinces them to use the primitive printing device he has brought with him to start a peasant newspaper to recount all that has happened. Berardo dies under interrogation and the village is attacked by militia. Most of the villagers are killed, and this story is recounted by a father, mother and son who have supposedly escaped and come to Switzerland to find the author, a native of the area, who claims to have written it down for publication.

There can be little doubt that the precise dates of publication of *Fontamara*, late 1933 in German and 1934 in English, were crucial in determining the manner in which, and the political seriousness with which, it was read. In the early 1930s, many respected academics and politicians in Europe and America were still propagating the view that Mussolini had brought order and hope to Italians and must be valued as a bulwark against the spread of communism. Churchill, it will be remembered, had been favorably impressed by the atmosphere of Fascist Italy when he visited in 1927, commenting that "this country gives the impression of discipline, order, goodwill, smiling faces" and could still refer to Mussolini, in Parliament in 1933, as "the Roman genius" and "the greatest lawgiver among living men" (even if he rejected fascism as a model for Britain).[6] Gaetano Salvemini, the great Italian historian who had left Italy clandestinely in 1925, described the adulation with which Mussolini's claims for his own regime were still being treated by many Western politicians, journalists, and academics:

> Italy has become the Mecca of political scientists, economists and sociologists, who flock there to see with their own eyes the organization and working of the Fascist Corporative State. Daily papers, magazines, and learned periodicals, departments of political science, economics and sociology in great and small universities, flood the world with articles, essays, pamphlets and books, which already form a good-sized library, on the Fascist Corporative State, its institutions, its political aspects, its economic policies, and its social implications.[7]

So, P. M. Brown, professor of history at Princeton, was no isolated voice when, in 1931, he described the Italian Corporative State as "the most amazing creation of Fascism for the solution of the thorny problem of the relations of capital and labour" and "an extraordinary achievement, worthy of the closest study and admiration."[8]

Fontamara was published just months after Hitler came to power and many of those in America and Europe who had hitherto regarded Italian Fascism with outright approval, or at least tolerance, were coming to perceive a family relationship between the Italian phenomenon and its infinitely more pernicious German cousin. Graham Greene's review of *Fontamara* in the London *Spectator* in late 1934 was typical in commending the novel "to all those who believe that there are different brands of fascism and that the Italian trademark is any better than the swastika."[9]

"A little epic of peasant resistance"

The simple fact that goes almost unnoticed is that *Fontamara*'s power as anti-Fascist propaganda depended on its being understood by foreign readers in the 1930s (as it could not have been by Italian readers) as a literal, concrete, historically accurate account of recent events in a precise location in Italy. They interpreted it as a factual revelation of Fascist oppression and peasant resistance, which it neither was nor unambiguously claimed to be.

Almost all the early reviews and presentations of *Fontamara* assumed that it was to be read as literally factual. Clifton Fadiman, reviewing it in the *New Yorker* in 1934, was typical in stating that "*Fontamara* is a little epic of peasant resistance, based upon an actual event in recent

Italian history."[10] Graham Greene wrote: "*Fontamara* is the most moving account of Fascist barbarity I have yet read ... Only an old man, his wife and son escaped abroad to tell the story of how the Blackshirts came down on Fontamara. It should be read to its merciless end."[11] Thomas G. Bergin, writing in the *New York Times Book Review*, stated that "the propaganda, if it is such, is in the facts. The presentation is objective, impersonal, restrained."[12] An anonymous reviewer in the *Saturday Review of Literature*, claiming no special expertise on conditions in Italy, observed: "The stealing of the water ... the savage reprisals ... occupation by Fascist militiamen who rape all the girls ... a general massacre at the hands of government troops — if this is even fifty per cent true, Italy under Mussolini is worse off than Italy under the Austrians or the Lombards."[13] Karl Radek, in the Soviet Union, declared that "in *Fontamara* Silone has given us a sincere picture of the Italian villages"[14] and James Farrell, writing as late as 1939, continued to take the line that *Fontamara* presented readers with "concrete pictures of how human destinies unfold under the regime of Mussolini ... a re-creation of a direct sense of life in Mussolini's Italy."[15]

Interpreted in these terms, *Fontamara* led many of its readers outside Italy in the 1930s to the mistaken conclusion, which was highly significant from the propaganda point of view, that there existed in rural areas of (Southern) Italy a growing groundswell of active opposition to Fascism and that mass murder of peasant protesters taking part in that opposition was being undertaken by the Fascist authorities. In reality, neither was the case, and indeed many of the features of peasant existence described in *Fontamara*, including the aridity and the bareness of the landscape, the absence of birds, and the extreme ignorance and gullibility which Silone attributes to the peasants were not based on fact.[16] As for the supposedly complete alienation of the villagers from the political system in the first half of the novel (in Chapter 5, the male Fontamaresi are interrogated by Fascist thugs and appear not even to have heard of *il Duce*), there can be no doubt that Mussolini's publicity machine was powerful enough to ensure that, by 1929, every village in Italy had been pumped full of Fascist propaganda. There had, in fact, been considerable enthusiasm for Fascism in the Abruzzi from its earliest years, the population of the region having given the Fascists strong support in the election of 1924, and only a tiny number of contrary votes being recorded there in the plebiscite of 1929 compared with a substantial number in the regions of the North.[17] The level of anti-Fascist activity in the Abruzzi was very low, with tribunal records showing only four convictions for such activity during 1927 and 1928.[18] Moreover, there were no historical cases anywhere in Italy at that period, let alone in the Abruzzi, of whole villages moving from a position of indifference to the regime to one of comprehensive opposition and resistance, as is the case with Fontamara. Nor, in particular, were there any instances of peasant-produced, anti-Fascist news-sheets. (Such limited parallels with events in the period as can be established will be discussed later.) Most important of all, the level of repression to which the villagers are subjected had no historical parallels in the period around 1929. While squads of blackshirts humiliated, tortured, and imprisoned their opponents, murdering handfuls of them, nowhere in Italy had they resorted to the mass rape of women depicted in Chapter 5 or the mass murder depicted in the final chapter of *Fontamara*.

Manfred Durzak's argument that, when a literary text crosses national boundaries, the different "horizon of expectations" of the foreign audience may cause it to be read in a politically different way from that in which it is read by its home audience, has a rather special relevance here.[19] In the first place, the impossibility of the novel's being published in Italy meant that there was no previous reaction from a home audience to act as the norm. Secondly, foreign readers were encouraged to understand *Fontamara* as revealing previously unknown factual information about peasant resistance to Fascism and about massacres occurring in the repression of that resistance. This reading was supported by two sets of signals: both those planted in the text and by those from anti-Fascist critics and publicists.

The prewar edition includes a foreword which contains markers which led foreign readers, who lacked independent sources of information, to interpret the story as dealing with actual events in a precise geographical location. It begins: "What I am about to set down took place at Fontamara last summer. Picture Fontamara as the poorest, most primitive village of the Marsica, north of the reclaimed Lake of Fucino" (*Fontamara*, 1938: 5) and ends with the dateline "Zürich, Summer, 1930" (*Fontamara*, 1938: 10). There is a fairly accurate account of the draining of the Fucino lake in the nineteenth century and the improper acquisition by the Torlonia family of the rich agricultural plain that was left, which is linked to statements about the deteriorating plight of Fontamara and the other hill villages. This is followed by reference to "a series of events that took place in the space of a few months last year [that] shook Fontamara to its foundations. These events did not find their way into the press. It was only after some months had passed that rumors began to trickle out, in Italy and abroad" (*Fontamara*, 1938: 8). The story that follows purports to be a later confirmation and amplification of the rumors by three participants in the events, Giuvà, Matalé and their son. The narrator of the Foreword adds the comment that "some even took Fontamara as a symbol of a great part of Italy — Southern Italy" (*Fontamara*, 1938: 8).

Of course only a naive reader believes every claim to historical authenticity inserted in the foreword to a novel (the claim, for instance, that "the text that follows was found in an old trunk"). Fictional claims for authenticity are a well-established convention in the novel and only one instance of the wider convention of the "unreliable narrator." Silone's correspondence in the late 1930s expresses some embarrassment (not entirely genuine, perhaps, given both the strength of the signals just referred to and the usefulness of the novel as propaganda) at the tendency of foreign readers to interpret the story as both historically accurate in reference to a specific time and place, and generalizable to a large part of rural Italy. In a letter written to Gaetano Salvemini in late 1937, he regretted his misleading use of the "three quarters and three quarters" episode and declared that "Fontamara corresponds to the most backward village of the Marsica ... It's not my fault if foreigners, and even Italians, take Fontamara to be the average Italian village."[20]

Salvemini was, in fact, one of a number of anti-Fascist historians and journalists in the United States and elsewhere, many of them Italian and all of them knowledgeable enough about conditions in Italy to realize that *Fontamara* was not a strictly factual story, who nevertheless recognized the propaganda value of its being read as if it were. His attitude to *Fontamara* was, to say the least, ambivalent. In 1931, he had been sent a draft of *Fontamara* and had advised against publication in translation on the grounds that it would not be comprehensible to foreigners.[21] In a letter of 1936 or 1937, he wrote to a Mr. Aswell at the publishers, Harper, deploring the novel's exaggerations and propagandistic qualities.[22] Yet, in his public writings on Fascism, he referred to the novel as if it were a reliable source of information on the impact of Fascism on the Italian peasantry, noting in particular, for instance, in his *Under the Axe of Fascism* (1936), its value as an illustration of Mussolini's policy of forbidding the migration of agricultural workers who were starving in the country to find work in the cities. "Silone, describing with rare artistic power in his novel *Fontamara* the life of an Italian village under Fascist rule, gives an idea of this phase of Fascist economic policy."[23] Similarly, Carl T. Schmidt included *Fontamara* (and *Bread and Wine*,

1936) in a bibliography which is otherwise devoted entirely to scholarly and journalistic works, recommending them as "remarkable novels ... for description of life under Fascist rule."[24] Once the anti-Fascist publicists realized what effective propaganda *Fontamara* could be, they were willing to forget any reservations they had about its historical truthfulness. The political ends for which Salvemini and others appropriated the novel were, of course, ones which Silone broadly approved of — whereas the ends for which George Orwell's *1984*, for instance, was to be exploited would bear only a very remote resemblance to its author's intentions for it. The question of just how much of the power of *Fontamara* as anti-Fascist propaganda is to be attributed to the author, to the text independently of its author, and to the various intermediaries who shaped its political reception is not easily resolved.

There is a specific puzzle as to why *Fontamara* was equally acceptable to, and seized upon by, both liberal and socialist commentators in the 1930s. The answer, I suggest, is that, while both groups (in some cases ingenuously and in others not) interpreted the events recounted in *Fontamara* as historically factual, each nevertheless attributed a substantially different political sense to the work as a whole. Liberal commentators in the United States and Europe focused primarily on the depiction of the oppressive character of Italian Fascism, on the sufferings of the peasants, and, as Alberto Traldi has argued, on the political struggle as moral crusade.[25] They picked up on the explicit parallels between Berardo Viola, who chooses death for himself in the hope that this may lead to salvation for the peasants, and the figure of Christ. Berardo undergoes interrogation which aims to make him reveal the names of his (non-existent) accomplices. "Finally they brought him back to his cell, carrying him by the feet and shoulders, like Christ after He was taken down from the Cross" (*Fontamara*, 1938: 135). Before he dies, Berardo declares: "If I turn traitor, Fontamara will be damned for ever ... And if I die? ... I shall be the first peasant to die not for himself, but for the others" (*Fontamara*, 1938: 137). Most importantly, they read the end of the novel, with the massacre of the Fontamaresi, as being, even if a moral victory, an utter defeat in practical political terms. Graham Greene, for instance, referred in his review to the peasants' protest as a "useless, tragic revolt against the state."[26] Such readers did not see the novel as proposing that initiatives by peasants and workers were the means by which oppression might be defeated.

Socialist readers, both inside and outside the the Soviet Union, while also recognizing the propaganda value of the depiction of Fascist atrocities, were much more impressed by the representation of the various stages of the peasants' efforts to organize politically, the key role played by the Mystery Man as agitator amongst the peasants, and the hints that the party he represents must be the Italian Communist Party (he talks to Berardo in prison about Russia), as well as his insistence on the need for an alliance between peasants and workers. Specifically, they would have responded to the allusion in the title of the peasant newssheet, *What are we to do?*,[27] to Lenin's article of 1902 (whose title is usually translated into English as *What is to be done?*) recommending the setting up of a party newspaper on a national scale, around which would form the organization that would prepare the "nationwide uprising" that was to come. The massacre at the end of the novel must have been read by socialists as just one moment in a historical metanarrative which projected a great popular revolution (both national and international) in the not-too-distant future.

It is now evident, especially with the additional illumination provided by his later works (notably *Bread and Wine* [1936], whose protagonist is a clandestine activist racked by doubts) that the ambivalence of the novel's ending reflects the agonizing dilemma Silone was facing at the time of writing as a former activist at a high level in a communist movement he had grown disillusioned with and was in the process of abandoning. As George Woodcock, writing after the war, expressed it:

> *Fontamara* can be considered from two aspects. As a portrayal of the evils of Fascism it is confident and successful, both artistically and as a representation of factual truth. But as propaganda for a party or any definite course of action, it is virtually useless, because it is already impregnated with those doubts concerning the role of the revolutionary agitator which become so prominent in the later novels. Whether or not Silone intended it, the Mystery Man appears as a bringer of evil to the peasants, as a partner, however unwilling, with the Fascists in the perpetration of their final misery.[28]

But readers in the 1930s seem not generally to have perceived the ending to be ambivalent; rather, according to the horizon of expectations suggested by their own liberal or socialist convictions, they seem to have weighed in for one or other of the two alternative readings outlined above, with the former group seeing it as rather vaguely suggesting the need for a moral crusade against Fascism, the latter viewing it as an agenda for the building of a worker-peasant alliance.

Fontamara as wartime propaganda

The utilization of *Fontamara* by anti-Fascists outside Italy in the 1930s might be termed "opportunistic" in the sense that it involved the appropriation of a work which was already in the bookshops. A utilization of the novel of a much more willful kind occurred during the war, in 1942, when the British authorities arranged for a BBC broadcast to Italy of a dramatized version of *Fontamara* in Italian and also arranged for Jonathan Cape to publish a special edition of twenty thousand copies of the novel in Italian (without Silone's permission), some of which were distributed to Italian prisoners-of-war, others, after the Allied invasion of Italy in 1943, being dropped on German-occupied Italian territory, others again being distributed to Italian civilians, and soldiers fighting alongside the Allies, in liberated areas of the South.[29] (Only a tiny number of copies of *Fontamara* had hitherto reached Italy by clandestine means.) Governments which seek to utilize literary texts for political purposes characteristically assume that the political effect achieved will remain within limits which are strictly convenient to them. (See Chapter 5 for discussion of the regrets which the Soviet leader, Nikita Khrushchev, was to experience about having personally authorized the publication of Solzhenitsyn's *One Day in the Life of Ivan Denisovich*.) While the British authorities did not make a major error of judgement in this respect, it is clear that *Fontamara*, in part, thwarted their attempts to impose their own literal, concrete reading of the novel on Italian readers. (In Barthes's terms its "productivity" permitted it to evade the controlling power of the authorities.) Though a great number of Italians who came across *Fontamara* in that period vouch for the importance it had for them, it is evident that they read it, not as a plane-mirror reflection of real events in a remote rural area at a particular moment, but as a condensed, deformed image of the phenomenon of Fascism on a national scale and over the whole two decades of its existence (including the period *since* the novel's first publication).

Italians disillusioned with Fascism after 1942 who came across a copy of *Fontamara*, or heard the dramatization of it on the radio, responded to what Antonio Russi, who first read *Fontamara* in 1944, described as the demonstration in the novel that Fascism was "an organized trick."[30] Thus the mathematical tricks (not only the "three-quarters and three-quarters" but the "ten lusters" which the peasants are told is to be the duration of the diversion of the stream) played on the Fontamaresi by Don Circostanza would have been recognized as having precise parallels with the sleight-of-hand the Fascist regime had used to disguise wage-reductions, rent increases, and deteriorating unemployment statistics. Salvemini, in *Under the Axe of Fascism*, gives a vivid account of the way in which employers were encouraged to cut the wages of, for instance, women engaged in "finishing" in the woollen industry by instituting a new system of twenty-nine job classifications, each with its own wage rate. "It was easy for the employers to shift the women from the higher-paid to the lower-paid categories."[31] Not a wage reduction — just a reclassification! Similar devices were employed to allow, but disguise, excessive rent increases: "Having cut wages and salaries on the promise that a decrease in the cost of living would follow, Mussolini on June 14th 1927, decreed that rents could not exceed four times the prewar rate."[32] Carl T. Schmidt, in *The Corporate State in Action*, provides a description of the way in which employment statistics were made to look better by requiring jobs traditionally done by women in certain industries to be reallocated to men and then excluding female workers from the unemployment statistics.[33]

The varieties of verbal trickery to which the Fontamaresi are subjected likewise had recognizable parallels in Fascist practices at the national level. The prime example occurs when they are summoned to Avezzano for what they are told is to be a gathering to discuss the division of the rich agricultural land of the Fucino plain, where they are employed as day laborers. Eagerly they make the trek to town, only to discover that they are being used as unwitting supporters of a rally in praise of "the Government that doesn't rob the poor" (*Fontamara*, 1938: 57). When they eventually get to talk to a bureaucrat, they discover that the government has accepted the principle on which they have based their claim, "the Fucino to the people who cultivate it," but that this has been twisted to mean exactly the opposite of what they intended: "'The Fucino to the people who have the means to cultivate it, and the means to have it cultivated. In other words, the Fucino to the people who have sufficient capital. The Fucino must be freed from the wretched small tenant-farmers and handed over to the wealthy farmers. Those without great capital resources have no right to rent land at the Fucino" (*Fontamara*, 1938: 59). Such a specific and local verbal trick would have been recognizable to Italians in 1944 as an image in miniature of the whole range of rhetorical devices used by Mussolini and his ministers, especially in the early years of the regime, to legitimate the policy of giving freer rein to industrialists and landowners at the expense of the workers and peasants. So, for instance, Giuseppe Bottai, Minister for Corporations, perceived hidden benefits for workers in the wage cuts which were bringing their incomes down to the lowest levels in Europe. These wage cuts would "have valuable psychological and moral consequences by enforcing a more rigorous mode of living."[34] Another minor, but vivid, instance of such a device is the justification given in 1928 by Francesco Ercole, later to become Minister of National Education, for the increasing discrepancy between the lives of the rich and the poor, "The wealth of the few in whose hands capital is concentrated is also the wealth of the proletariat."[35]

It was by another kind of miniaturization that characters who assist the Contractor, who diverts the village's stream, in his exploitation of the peasants could be read as standing for whole social groups and even institutions under Fascism. The lawyer, Don Circostanza, "the Friend of the People," was recognizable as a caricature of the role played by a large number of the professional class, for instance those lawyers and accountants (appointed by the regime) who purported to represent the workers in wage negotiations under the corporative system. Schmidt noted that "the employers' delegation includes most of the important men of big business affairs, while the employees are represented largely by reliable accountants, engineers, professors, lawyers, doctors and politicians. Hardly any delegates come from the rank and file of workers."[36] The procedure in the Labour Court for wage negotiations was as follows: "The employers asked for a big reduction in wages; the union officials countered with a refusal or more often an offer of a smaller reduction; the Labour Court either confirmed the concessions of the union officials or compromised on a figure somewhere between those of the employers and those of the officials. As a result, the union officials proclaimed that the employers had been defeated and sang the praises of the Labour Court."[37]

Similarly, when the priest, Don Abbacchio, visits the Fontamaresi, supposedly as their spiritual protector, to warn them not to oppose the Contractor but to be patient and pray, he could be identified as a personification of the Church's betrayal of the people in signing the Concordat with the Fascist state in 1929. The Church thereby acknowledged the "legitimacy" of the Fascist state in exchange for the formal restoration of the temporal sovereignty of the Papacy over the Vatican City, an indemnity of 1,750 million lire in cash and bonds, and an enlarged influence over family life and education.[38]

It was, however, not just a miniaturized image of Fascism that *Fontamara* offered to Italians reading it in the later years of the war, but a deformed refraction of the historical data through a whole series of lenses and even, it might be said, a crystal ball. (A "political cartoon" was how a dissenting American reviewer had perceptively defined *Fontamara*,[39] though his compatriots had certainly not read it that way.) There were, it has already been stated, neither protests nor repression in the Abruzzi on the scale depicted in the novel during the period in which the action is set.[40] What Silone had done, in part, was transfer to the more backward and conservative hill villages of that southern region an exaggerated version of events which had actually occurred over several years in a few villages and small towns in the North, with a strong socialist tradition and a relatively educated population, who had maintained an organized opposition to Fascism into the late 1920s. For example: in 1926 several hundred men and women in Molinella, twenty miles from Bologna, attempted to form a de facto (non-Fascist) trade union, but were stopped by the local Fascists who beat nine of them up, with the collusion of the police;[41] and, in October of the same year, several hundred angry peasants gathered in the mountains near Bergamo, but dispersed again before clashing with the authorities.[42] Yet even in the North, there had been no mass murder of peasant protesters to resemble the scene depicted in *Fontamara*. Moreover, in depicting the production of the Fontamara newssheet, *What are we to do?*, Silone had offered not just a geographical relocation from North to South, but an attribution to the peasantry of a form of activism which had in fact only been undertaken by other, very different, social groups. There were a few clandestine newspapers in some of the cities of the North, printed by intellectuals and industrial workers. The major example was the Florentine paper *Non mollare* (*Don't give in*), whose editors, like the Fontamaresi, ran through several more conventional newspaper titles before hitting upon such a simple and direct one, and were ruthlessly pursued by the Fascist authorities.[43] The closest thing to a peasant newspaper in the late 1920s were the clandestine newssheets produced by trade unions in Piedmont and Lombardy, *La risaia* (*The rice field*) addressed to the rice-workers and *La difesa dei contadini* (*Peasants' defense*).[44]

Italians who encountered *Fontamara* for the first time between 1943 and 1945 must also have been overwhelmingly struck by the extent to which both the fears and the hopes expressed in the novel were now being realized all around them as the country was being fought over by Germans, Allies and partisans. On the one hand, the mass rape of the women and the final slaughter of villagers depicted in the novel had their awful echoes in, not only the punitive raids by the German occupying forces against villages suspected of harboring partisans, but also the atrocities against women committed by some of the Allied troops.[45] On the other hand, mass popular action (including peasant action) was now occurring on a large scale in the context of the resistance, particularly, by early 1944, in the Abruzzi and Umbria, and clandestine newspapers of many kinds were circulating in German-occupied regions.[46]

Fontamara could now be read as a prophecy in the process of being fulfilled. Far from being "useless, tragic," the novel's ending, for many Italian readers in that period, heralded a bright future still to be achieved. Geno Pampaloni, who read *Fontamara* (and *Bread and Wine*) as a member of a detachment of the Italian army of liberation in the Abruzzi in 1944, described his feelings and those of his comrades: "His books were passed feverishly from hand to hand in the regiment, like a secret anticipation of the liberty which seemed to be waiting for us beyond the war and the Appennines, like a first testimony of a new world and a new literature."[47] There is even some evidence that *Fontamara* played a directly empowering role in the land reforms in the Abruzzi and elsewhere in the period just after the war. Bruno Corbi, an Italian Communist Party activist and a leader of the peasant movement which led to the successful resolution in 1951 of the peasants' claims to the land of the Fucino, declared: "The Fucino peasants won; they left bodies on their lands, but they won dignity as men. I am certainly honored to be one of those who led those struggles, but I must acknowledge that a good part of the merit of that success should go to Silone who helped us to understand the reality around us and what had to be done."[48] (Under the leadership of Corbi — who attests that, until he read *Fontamara*, he knew more about the French and German peasantry than he did about the struggles of peasants in his own region of Italy — and others, a campaign of strikes, land occupations, and road blockages between 1946 and 1949 led to the expropriation of the land still held by the Torlonia estate, its distribution to former tenants, and the upgrading of all services in the region. The Fucino is now one of the most productive and prosperous agricultural areas in Italy.)[49] Independent peasant activism, especially when directed by a communist party, had certainly not been one of the outcomes desired or foreseen by the British authorities when they undertook the publication of an Italian edition of *Fontamara* in 1942.

I have been unable to trace any Italians who read *Fontamara* in British prisoner-of-war camps, so I can only speculate about the particular flavor it would have had in those circumstances. Until July 1943, prisoners with anti-Fascist sentiments were largely prevented from expressing them by Fascist punitive squads in the camps who would beat up and even kill offenders. Officers were mainly remarkable for "their ineptitude, their self-centeredness, their chameleon-like attitude."[50] As one prisoner expressed it: "If it hadn't been for our superiors, things wouldn't have been bad. You know what they are like. And that's the way they remained."[51] After July 1943 (with the removal of Mussolini by the Fascist Grand Council), and especially after September 1943 (with Italy's surrender to the Allies), anti-Fascist feeling came out into the open and attacks on some officers took place. In many camps, officers were then interned separately and, as Flavio Conti has remarked, this made it easier for the Allies to feed their propaganda to the mass of soldiers.[52] The stylistic simplicity of *Fontamara* would have made it particularly attractive to those private soldiers and noncommissioned officers who did read, and given the dearth of material in Italian in the camps, I have no doubt each copy was read by a large number of prisoners and the story retold to nonreaders, too. It seems likely that many soldiers (especially those of peasant origin) made quite direct parallels between the figures of the Impresario and Don Circostanza and their own officers. I am struck at this point by the validity of Hans Robert Jauss's statement that when a work is read by successive groups of readers it provides new "answers" to each generation as their experience causes them to approach it with new "questions" in mind, and by the fallacy in Luce d'Eramo's assertion (referring specifically to Silone's early work) that "the critic's task is to penetrate a work, forgetting everything else, otherwise one's judgement on a book would have to change according to whether it was read in prison or on holiday."[53]

The postwar reception by Italian critics

Many attempts have been made to analyze the reasons for the coolness with which Italian critics responded to *Fontamara* when it was first published in Italy in 1947, then in a revised version in 1949. Communist critics disapproved of Silone as an ex-communist, now visibly anticommunist. Catholic critics saw him as tainted by his experience in the communist movement and detected, too, Protestant leanings in his work (especially *Bread and Wine*) of which they were suspicious. In the jostling for position, both before and after the bitterly contested election of 1948, between intensely antagonistic rival groups, the Catholics, the Communist Party, and the lay parties, Silone's work satisfied none of them. Moreover, precisely because his novels had had such success in the

United States before the war (and perhaps because of their use as propaganda during the war) there was a tendency to regard his work as a product of his exile which the United States was trying to foist on Italians, along with so many other products both material and ideological — an accusation which was particularly unfair since he did not even visit the United States until much later. There is also the fact that, from 1945 to 1949, Silone was again visibly politically active, first in the PSIUP (the Italian socialist party as it emerged from the war), then as an independent socialist, then briefly in the PSU (the anti-communist group which split from the socialist party), all of these making it easy for critics to dismiss him as an activist rather than a novelist.

Luigi Russo encapsulated many of these prejudices in his dismissive comment, made in 1951, that "he gained renown abroad for reasons that have nothing to do with art and literature."[54] Italian critics had, and in many cases still have, difficulty in coming to terms with Silone's style, in which they saw neither the elegance and finesse of the traditional novelist, nor the striking experimentalism of some younger novelists, like Vittorini. As Emilio Cecchi expressed it: "The main defect, at least in my opinion, is in the somewhat conventional nature of the writing, or rather in its patient, solid character, which lays out, rather than bringing to life, presents its subject matter rather than identifying with it. I am referring to a lack of inner resonance."[55] And, while the ears of many critics were, in theory, open to hearing the voices of peasants, they had the strongest preconceptions about how those voices should sound.

Part of the problem lay in the fact that both their knowledge of the American response to *Fontamara* and the neorealist novels of Levi, Soldati, Pratolini, and others, which had their first publication in the late 1940s and early 1950s, led critics to expect a surface truthfulness which they did not find. As Carlo Falconi, writing in 1950, explained, "his stories are curiously counterproductive for Italian readers, who find in them the description of a Fascism they never knew nor experienced."[56] The modifications Silone made in the 1949 version, which considerably reduced the specific references to Fascism, exacerbated this reaction.[57] Most importantly, the cartoonlike condensation, deformation, and exaggeration which had such topical relevance to the relatively small number of Italians who came across *Fontamara* before 1945, eluded the Italian critics in the postwar period. (Political cartoons lose their force very quickly once the events and figures to which they refer have passed.) Italian critics after the war sought in vain the documentary accuracy that prewar, non-Italian readers believed they had found.

In recent years, the Italian literary establishment has theoretically acknowledged its early blindness to the merits of Silone's work, and in 1990 the Italian Communist Party declared his rehabilitation from the party's point of view. It has not, however, been noticed that an episode in Chapter 1 (when a Fascist official visits Fontamara with several blank sheets of paper which he presses all the men to sign) was almost certainly adapted from a personal experience Silone himself had had in the international communist movement and which he records as having contributed in a major way to his disillusionment with communism. The papers the Hon. Pelino brought: "constituted, in fact, a petition to the Government, a petition for which many signatures were necessary. It was true that he hadn't got the petition with him and that he didn't know what was in it. It would be written by his superiors. All he had to do was to collect the signatures, and all the peasants had to do was sign it" (*Fontamara*: 16).

The parallel with Silone's account of his participation in a meeting of the Executive of the Communist International in Moscow in 1927 seems inescapable:

> At the first sitting which we attended, I had the impression that we had arrived too late. We were in a small office in the Communist International Headquarters, the German Thälmann was presiding, and immediately began reading out a proposed resolution against Trotsky, to be presented at the full session. This resolution condemned, in the most violent terms, a document which Trotsky had addressed to the Political Office of the Russian Communist Party ... As no one else asked to speak, after consulting Togliatti, I made my apologies for having arrived late and so not having been able to see the document which was to be condemned. "To tell the truth," Thälmann declared candidly, "we haven't seen the document either."[58]

According to Silone, he was sent away with a Bulgarian to have the need for the condemnation of a document they had not read "explained" to him. He was unconvinced, and the following day still opposed the condemnation, which was then withdrawn. The delegates to the Executive meeting set off for home. Nevertheless, when Silone reached Berlin he learned from the newspapers that the Executive, of which he was a member, had supposedly rebuked Trotsky for the document.[59]

The popular reception of *Fontamara* in postwar Italy

The coolness of most Italian literary critics has not, however, prevented Silone from being throughout the last forty years one of the few truly popular Italian novelists, whose work, especially *Fontamara*, has reached a mass readership in Italy.[60] The mass of readers, unlike professional critics and academic readers, usually leave no written record of the manner in which they interpret the relatively small number of books they read, so some speculation is required in order to reconstruct the popular Italian response to the novel. The place to start, I suggest, is with the statement by the narrator of the foreword about the manner in which the story will be told. Storytelling, he says, is a traditional art of Fontamara:

> We learnt it when we were children, sitting on the doorstep, or round the fireplace in the long nights of winter, or by the handloom, listening to the old stories to the rhythm of the pedal.
> The art of story-telling, the art of putting one word after another, one sentence after another, explaining one thing at a time, without allusions or reservation, calling bread bread and wine wine, is just like the ancient art of weaving, the ancient art of putting one thread after another, cleanly, neatly, perseveringly, plainly for all to see. First you see the stem of the rose, then the calyx, then the petals. You can see from the beginning that it is going to be a rose, and for that reason townsfolk think our products coarse and crude. But have we ever gone to town to try to sell them? Have we ever asked townspeople to tell their story in our fashion? No, we have not. (*Fontamara*: 9-10).

To the prewar foreign reader, this statement seemed to guarantee the unadulterated, factual basis for the story: the story as chronicle. To the postwar Italian critic, on the other hand, it seemed like an admission in advance of the stylistic poverty, what Cecchi called "the poverty of inner resonance," of the work. What both groups missed is that this statement signals the closeness of *Fontamara* to the folktale tradition, with its extraordinary combination of surface flatness and complexity of historical and psychological reference. It is just the folktale qualities of *Fontamara* that have, I shall argue, made it seem so familiar, and so accessible, to a mass audience in Italy (and much the same qualities, I shall go on to suggest, which have made it meaningful to readers in a number of Third World countries).

Fontamara and folktale tradition

Many elements in *Fontamara* attach it to the folktale tradition. There is the fact that the story is told collectively, almost chorally, by three narrators — father, mother, and son — with no differentiation by person of storytelling style. There are numerous comic elements, including comic nicknames (Pontius Pilate, Marietta Sorcanera — a name equivalent in its connotations to "Marietta Blackpussy" who keeps the village bar and offers a welcoming bed to any spare men — General Baldissera, and so on) and funny stories, scattered, as happens with folktales, among episodes of great seriousness. A dream of one of the villagers, Michele Zompa, is recounted and given considerable significance, as often happens in traditional peasant narrative. On a more fundamental level, *Fontamara* belongs to the folktale tradition in its account of ordinary people in a life-and-death struggle with an oppressive, unreasonable, and, in part, mysterious power (which, in folktales, may take the form of an ogre, a dragon, or a tyrannical old king) related in a bald, matter-of-fact, and unemotional style. Claudio Varese was one of the very few Italian critics to perceive the folkloric quality of *Fontamara*, referring positively in his review of 1949 to the folktale-like deformation to be found in it and associating it with the paintings of Chagall.[61] It was, of course, just the same folktale-like features that so infuriated Giuseppe De Robertis, who described it as "a collection of anecdotes, stories, facts ... which the hand of the writer does not succeed in holding together ... since the art of representing and narrating is never held in high esteem by him ... Nothing happens on time; order and measure are lacking."[62] But, then, in the novel's foreword, Silone had anticipated just such a response from "townspeople."

Just as folktales flatten out any historical perspective, often retaining relics of practices (such as cannibalism and human sacrifice) and historical events (such as wars and floods) from much earlier ages, so *Fontamara* includes references to matters which occurred long before the 1920s. So, for instance, the ignorance of the Fontamaresi about the ten-year-old Fascist regime, unrealistic if understood as relating to the Abruzzesi of 1929, recalls the very real ignorance of the mass of illiterate southern peasants in the 1860s, who so completely failed to grasp what had occurred with Unification that some of them mispronounced the new term *l'Italia* as *la Talia*, believing it to be the name of the new king's wife.[63] And the role of Don Circostanza recalls the same period when peasants in the South, struggling to cope with the new order, were at the mercy of unscrupulous lawyers and notaries: "Don Circostanza, also known as the Friend of the People, had always made a show of special benevolence for the people of Fontamara; he was our patron and protector, and telling you about him would make a long story in itself. He had always been our defender, but also our ruin. All the lawsuits of the people of Fontamara passed through his hands, and for the past forty years most of the chickens and eggs produced at Fontamara had ended up in his kitchen" (*Fontamara*: 46). The narrator goes on to recount how Don Circostanza used to pay the Fontamaresi a small sum to notify him, rather than the proper authorities, of deaths in the village, so that he could continue to claim the votes at election time of those who had died.

Don Abbacchio's name has telling associations for any Italian who had attended high school, since it recalls Don Abbondio in Manzoni's *The Betrothed*, another priest who disregards the needs of his flock in deference to the demands of the big local landowner. The character also alludes to the role of the priesthood in southern Italy earlier in the century, when many village priests supported the interests of the landowning class against emerging peasant aspirations. Iris Origo recalls Silone's own memories of the period:

> When the first Peasants' Leagues were founded in the Abruzzi, in 1911 and 1912, their members could meet only in the village squares; but the parish priests would order the church bells to be rung so loud as to drown the speakers' voices. In Silone's own school, the bishop himself would address the boys on the theme of private property as a divine institution and of the sacrilegious attempt of the Peasants' Leagues to break up some of the neglected and untilled properties.[64]

In his depiction of peasant protest, too, Silone was making use of material from the thirty years after Unification (as well as earlier periods) when more or less spontaneous peasant uprisings in the South, against oppressive landowners, rising prices, and so on, were often brutally suppressed, sometimes with large-scale murder.[65] There are, moreover, relics of two distinct traditions of southern peasant activism to be found in the novel: on the one hand, the acts of sabotage (burning fences and blocking roads) undertaken by Berardo Viola early in the book belong to a long tradition of peasant banditry; on the other hand, the many religious stories and references (for example, the story of san Giuseppe da Copertino and his request on arriving in Paradise for a piece of white bread) derive from a popular tradition going back as far as the twelfth-century spiritual thinker, Gioacchino da Fiore, whose teachings concerning the imminence of God's kingdom and the abolition of coercion and laws, and their replacement with *caritas* (love), though they were declared heretical in 1471, have left traces in southern folk memory (especially in Abruzzo) to this day.[66]

There can be no suggestion that Italian readers have consciously identified *Fontamara* as a modern folktale, or that many Italians still live in the kind of isolated rural environment in which the traditional folktale was told. It is rather, as Luisa Passerini has argued in her article on the popular memory of Fascism,[67] that traditional patterns of thought and oral recollection, with all their inconsistencies and deformations of factual history by fantasy, live vigorously on in the mass of the population. (The mass panic in Italy at the beginning of the 1991 Gulf War offers a vivid illustration of this. The rush to the supermarkets, where all the pasta and canned tomatoes were bought up in a few days, reflects both an irrational fear that the war might pose an immediate threat to Italians in their own country *and* an equally irrational belief in the magical power of those food items to provide a talisman-like protection against the threat.) So, I suggest, the tendency in *Fontamara* for present reality and folk memory to merge into projections of possible best and worst scenarios for the future not only ties it to the folktale tradition but has made it seem "real" to nonprofessional readers in Italy as it has not to professional critics and intellectuals.

It is not transparently obvious what the political implications are of the link between *Fontamara* and traditional folktales, a link which I hypothesize to exist in the popular response to the novel. There is a good deal of debate about whether folktales perform an entirely conservative, acculturating social function, reconciling individuals to traditional social roles and structures, or whether they also perform an oppositional, subversive function. In many respects they appear escapist: they serve to socialize young males in the audience into stereotypically adventurous and aggressive roles, young women into passive, domestic, decorative roles; the lack (of food, a wife, a successor to the throne ...) or threat (from an ogre, monster, witch ...) with which they begin is removed by a quick-witted hero who, by following the instructions of helpers and with the use of magic, passes the tests (relics no doubt of rites of passage) which he (or less often, she) finds in his path; and, finally, the tale ends with the restoration of traditional order and authority — the countryside is rid of the ogre or the stepmother is banished, the young couple marries, a new king is put in place etc.[68] At the same time, some critics (for instance, Marie Maclean)[69] argue that traditional storytelling is also a means by which the weak, especially women, may briefly exploit, and subversively widen, gaps in the control of the dominant power, by recording, even if in deformed fashion, an act of oppression they have suffered, speculating on worst and best scenarios for its outcome, disrupting the official political and historical narrative imposed by the authorities, and (in Dario Fo's words) using the comic to "dismantle the structures of power."[70]

The Power of the Story
▼ ▼ ▼

Vivid examples of such tactical, oppositional storytelling are to be found in the interchanges between the villagers and a local official in Chapter 1 of *Fontamara*. In the course of the Hon. Pelino's attempts to persuade the men of the village to sign his mysterious piece of paper (which is later discovered to assign the use of the water of their stream to the Contractor), Michele Zompa recounts his apparently irrelevant dream concerning a concession which the Pope asked Christ to make to the peasants following the signing of the Concordat: not a share of the Fucino land, not dispensation from paying taxes, not a good harvest, because all of these, in their various ways, might disadvantage the rich:

> "So on the night of the conciliation Christ and the Pope came flying over the Fucino and all the villages of the Marsica. Christ went in front, with a large bag on His shoulders, and behind Him came the Pope, who had permission to take from it whatever might benefit the *cafoni*. In every village the holy Visitors saw the same thing, and what else was there for them to see? The *cafoni* were grumbling, cursing, squabbling and worrying, not knowing which way to turn for food or clothing. And the Pope was afflicted in his heart at what he saw. So he took from the bag a whole cloud of a new kind of lice and released them over the houses of the poor saying: 'Take them, my beloved children, and scratch yourselves. Thus in your idle moments you will have something to distract your thoughts from sin'" (*Fontamara*: 20-21).

The Hon. Pelino becomes angry at what he (rightly) regards as a subversive tale, threatening Zompa with the wrath of the authorities. The peasant responds with his equally subversive image of the structure of power in the world, which places God at the top of the ladder, Prince Torlonia on the second rung down, his guards in third place, his dogs in fourth place, then nothing, then nothing, then nothing and, below all this nothing, the *cafoni*. When pressed by the Hon. Pelino, he distributes "the [Fascist] authorities" among the prince's guards and dogs. The Fascist official trembles with rage and makes a fool of himself by rushing off on his bicycle. (Luisa Passerini notes that while the Fascist Ministry of the Interior painstakingly recorded "jokes, graffiti, rhymes, shouts of drunken men, complaints by women about prices at the market" in their archives, it dismissed them as expressions of discontent "of an apolitical kind, ones which could not be transformed into organized protest and directly challenge the dictatorship."[71] She makes the important point that anti-Fascist historians have subsequently also underestimated the oppositional significance of such acts.)

Other parts of the story of the Fontamaresi's misfortunes are narrated in a way which leaves the reader uncertain about whether the villagers are more naive or cunning. When the fence around the common land appropriated by the Contractor is burnt down, the villagers speculate about the reason for it: "'The wood was too dry,' Berardo explained. 'It caught fire in the sun.' 'You mean the moon. It caught fire at night,' I pointed out." (This last comment belongs to the father, who is narrating this part of the story.) When it burns down a second time in the presence of an armed communal roadsweeper who has been sent to guard it, the story is recounted as follows: "He distinctly saw flames coming out of the ground and burning down the whole fence in a few minutes. As is obligatory in the case of every miracle, he immediately described the incident to Don Abbacchio, and then to everyone else who would listen. Don Abbacchio decided that the fire was unquestionably of supernatural origin and therefore the work of the devil, whereupon we decided that the devil was not so black as he was painted" (*Fontamara*: 96).

The narrative form of *Fontamara* constantly implies that, at an intuitive level, the peasants understand more than anyone gives them credit for. (The anti-Fascist newspaper *Non mollare* recorded the opinion of some simple peasant women near Siena who commented, when they saw workers marching past in a "spontaneous" Fascist rally in 1925, that they supposed they were "prisoners of war."[72] The women were more right than wrong!)

If, as I am suggesting, *Fontamara* has appealed to a mass readership in Italy because readers have sensed its relation to traditional folk narrative, it must also be observed that there is an important respect in which the novel modifies and brings seriously into question elements which are regarded as essential to the traditional folktale. Certainly, when the male Fontamaresi are subjected to interrogation by the Fascists (Chapter 5), the passage has much in common with the tests and puzzles found in folktales. But when the peasants are asked such questions as "'Long live who?'" (to which the reader knows the required answer must be "*il Duce*") they do not know how to reply, trying such responses as: "'Our Lady of Loreto,'" (the long dead) "'Queen Margherita,'" "'the legitimate government'" and finally, in desperation, "'the illegitimate government.'" Failing to satisfy their interrogators, they are recorded as, respectively, "refractory", "constitutionalist", "perfidious," and "scoundrel." They utterly fail the test (as they have already failed to protect the women of the village against the Fascists' sexual assaults). Similarly, while they are assisted by a mysterious helper (the Mystery Man) and given an object with seemingly magical powers (the box with the printing materials), the helper and his magic object in fact lead the villagers to their destruction. There is no simplistic, fairytale ending. The young hero (Berardo) and the beautiful heroine (Elvira), far from marrying and living happily ever after, die. Rather than the oppressor being defeated and the traditional social order being restored, they are seen to be one and the same. In the short term at least, the oppositional tactics of the weak are seen to count for nothing. And the ending contains none of the consolatory, conservative features of the traditional folktale ending. *Fontamara*, I am therefore suggesting, lays bare the conservatism of traditional folktales and practices, and poses in radical form a series of vital questions to peasants and workers: What are the possibilities and what are the dangers of different kinds of resistance to oppression? What is the role of the masses, in particular peasants, including women, in resistance? What is the role of a party organization? And what sort of relationship is possible between peasants and city-dwelling industrial workers? The power exercised by those who ask uncomfortable questions is a very important one.

The Third World reception of *Fontamara*

Fontamara was translated into seventeen languages in the few years following its first appearance. Since the Second World War, it has been translated into Turkish, Afrikaans, Japanese, Arabic, Kannada (the language of the southern Indian state of Mysore), and Bengali. A new Spanish translation (the fourth) has become available in South America. Indeed, perhaps the most remarkable feature of the history of the reception of *Fontamara* is the extent to which it has, over the last thirty years, been taken up in countries of the Third World, in Asia, in Africa and, especially, in Latin America by liberals and political activists who, with no particular interest in Fascism in Italy in the 1930s, see it as having relevance to the oppression of peasants in their own colonial or postcolonial countries. J. Sarkis Najjar wrote, in 1965, of the Arabic translation just published in Lebanon: "What interest could the Arab reader find in *Fontamara*? ... The Arab reader will find so many points of contact with what we experienced not long ago, during, and even after, Turkish rule. And so many readers will be moved as they read these pages by the Italian author and discover points of similarity with their own present life."[73]

The capacity *Fontamara* has shown in recent years to be interpreted as illuminating processes of repression and resistance common to peasants in many countries derives in part from the revisions Silone made to the Italian text of 1949, on which most later translations have been based. Not only did he reduce the specifically Fascist references but he added signals in the Foreword which invited an internationalist reading, including the comment that: "Poor peasants, who make the soil productive and suffer from hunger — fellaheen, coolies, peons, mujiks, cafoni — are alike all over the world: they form a nation, a race, a church of their own, but two poor men identical in every respect have never yet been seen"(*Fontamara*: 1).

Readers in countries as far apart as India and Brazil have apparently had little difficulty in detaching *Fontamara* from its Italian background and finding the political and economic processes it depicts to be familiar. Guido Piovene cites as evidence for the fact that *Fontamara* is known in the most surprising places his experience when visiting a Navajo reservation in the United States. As soon as he mentioned that he was Italian, his guide indicated that he knew Silone's work.[74] While it is inevitably true that *Fontamara* has not reached a mass audience in the Third World, those activists who have read it have evidently found it illuminating of their own situation and so, to use the term employed by Paulo Freire, the Brazilian social activist, empowering. In this context, *Fontamara* has been appropriated for purposes of which Silone would have wholly approved.

Fontamara is now best known in Central and South America.[75] The reasons for this, I believe, relate both to political and literary developments in that region. *Fontamara* places peasants, rather than industrial workers, in the center of the political stage, as Latin American revolutionary theorists have done, and underlines the need for individuals to emerge from the indigenous masses as an heroic focus for revolt. Silone's portrait of Berardo Viola anticipates Che Guevara's description of the dead guerilla hero, Camilo Cienfuegos: "He did not have culture from books; he had the natural intelligence of the people who had chosen him out of thousands for a privileged position on account of the audacity of his blows, his tenacity, intelligence and unequalled devotion. Camilo practised loyalty like a religion."[76] Similarly, Berardo's discussion of the value of sabotage, and the importance of choosing targets for sabotage which do the greatest damage to the system which oppresses the poor while putting the smallest number of workers out of a job, precisely anticipates Che Guevara's writings and speeches on the same topic. When the other villagers talk of sabotage against the Contractor, which he previously advocated, Berardo now argues on the other side: "'If you burn down the Contractor's property, do you suppose we shall be able to live on the ashes next winter? If the workmen now employed at the Contractor's cement works and brickworks and tannery lose their jobs, do you suppose the people of Fontamara will benefit?'" (*Fontamara*: 142).

This is not just Berardo running away from a fight: he is also beginning the very necessary debate about the effects of sabotage to be developed by Guevara in later years: "It is ridiculous to carry out sabotage against a soft drinks factory, but it is absolutely correct and advisable to carry out sabotage against a power plant. In the first case, a certain number of workers are put out of a job but nothing is done to alter the rhythm of industrial life; in the second place, there will again be displaced workers, but this is entirely justified by the paralysis of the life of the region."[77]

In a more general sense, Silone's interweaving of Marxist and Christian threads in *Fontamara* (and in his other works) foreshadowed in a remarkable way the emergence in the early 1970s of the Liberation Theology of Gustavo Gutiérrez, Leonardo Boff, and others, which emphasizes both the historical role of the Church as a pillar of the established order and the possibility for the future of an alliance with the oppressed (and perhaps socialist parties) to promote revolutionary, egalitarian change.[78] In terms of literary form, its folkloric deformations anticipate the "magical realism" of so much modern Latin American fiction, including that of García Márquez.

Polish, Croatian, and Indian "readings' of *Fontamara*

Curiously, it emerges that the two most radical instances of the international migration and interpretation of *Fontamara* occurred, not in the postwar period on the basis of the revised edition of 1949, but in the 1930s on the basis of the original edition. Both instances raise extremely interesting theoretical issues.

The first of these occurred in Eastern Europe in the mid-1930s, when permission was sought from the censors in both Poland and Croatia for the publication of translations of *Fontamara*. Permission was refused by the authorities in both countries on the astonishingly self-incriminating grounds that the work in question was clearly a work written to expose outrages in their respective countries, dressed up as the work of an Italian author![79] This, it seems to me, is one of the most vivid illustrations of Barthes's assertion of the constantly elusive, and so subversive, nature of literature as it confronts monolithic power.

Ignazio Silone: "Fontamara"
▼ ▼ ▼

The second instance relates to the Indian reception of *Fontamara*. Silone's novel was translated into the Kannada language (in 1950) and into Bengali (in 1957) but a "translation" of a rather different sort had already reached India in 1938. This was Raja Rao's novel *Kanthapura*, very closely modelled on *Fontamara*, but set in an Indian village. (Rao, who came from the southern state of Mysore — where Kannada is spoken — came across *Fontamara* in France in the mid-thirties and was directly inspired to write his own work.) In this novel, written in English and very widely circulated both among educated Indians and the British, the events and characters of *Fontamara* have been "translated" into a remote village of Mysore in the same period as the action of the Italian novel. Fascist oppression has become the oppression of the British Raj; the Fucino Valley has become the Skeffington Coffee Plantation on which the "coolies" are mercilessly exploited; the Contractor has become the British sahib who runs the plantation; Don Circostanza and Don Abbacchio merge in the figure of Bhatta, the village's leading Brahmin who gobbles and belches his way through the feasts offered to him by the villagers and regularly betrays them to the authorities; the divisions between the villagers have become divisions of caste; the three narrators have become one, an old woman in exile recalling the dramatic story of the village. The novel ends, as *Fontamara* does, with the destruction of the village by the authorities, the murder of many of its inhabitants, and the relocation of the survivors to other areas.

Raja Rao's achievement in "translating" some of the deepest features of the Italian novel into an Indian setting is remarkable. The novel's foreword refers to the way in which he has aimed to integrate *sthala-purana* (the legendary history of the village) with contemporary history, so that "the past mingles with the present." It refers, in words which closely echo those of Silone's Foreword, to the problem of rendering a local story in a language which is alien to the villagers. In Silone's words: "The Italian language cripples and deforms our thoughts, and cannot help giving them a banal and insipid twist, the flavor of a translation ... Even though we tell the story in a borrowed tongue, the manner of telling it will be our own" (*Fontamara*, 1938: 10). In Raja Rao's words: "The telling has not been easy. One has to convey in a language that is not one's own the spirit that is one's own."[80] Indian commentators underline the extent to which, despite being written in English, "the style of narration in this novel is typically Kannada."[81] They emphasize, as I have done in discussing *Fontamara*, that *Kanthapura* conveys both a real sense of village life and an image in miniature of the whole nation and that "time past and time present are both projected into time future."[82]

The Power of the Story
▼ ▼ ▼

Indian critics and the one Italian critic, Silvia Albertazzi, who has written about the link between *Fontamara* and *Kanthapura*, insist, however, on the importance of the differences between the two novels. The central character of *Kanthapura*, young Moorthy, is, in a sense, a blend of Silone's Berardo and the Mystery Man. He is a villager who has gone to study in the city, become fascinated by Gandhian philosophy, and returned to his village to teach it to the other villagers. Significantly, he survives the massacre and returns to the city to work with Nehru. M. K. Naik contrasts the two novels in these terms: "*Fontamara* is a story of the exploitation of the poor by the rich, as seen through the eyes of an anti-Fascist and socialist of the 1930s. Its message is purely political and social. *Kanthapura* is an account of the renaissance of Indian spiritual life under the impact of the independence movement. Its message is essentially spiritual and cultural."[83] Silvia Albertazzi similarly insists that "the revolt of the Fontamaresi remains a gesture of anger 'against,' without organization and desperate, while the inhabitants of Kanthapura achieve a true political and religious consciousness."[84] Both commentators, I suggest, undervalue the complexity of *Fontamara* and miss its religious thread, which Latin American readers (and some Italian critics in works with titles such as *L'inquietudine e l'utopia: il racconto umano e cristiano di Ignazio Silone*)[85] have discerned. (Specifically, it should be mentioned here that the title of the peasant newssheet in *Fontamara*, as well as recalling an article of Lenin's, may actually be thought to echo the title of Tolstoy's work preaching Christian pacificism, *What is to be done?*)

In a more general sense, I believe, such comparisons overlook the dialectical nature of the intertextual relationship between the two novels. I have argued, with Hans Robert Jauss, that a literary text which is read over a long period of time by different groups of readers, offers each group a different answer, according to the different questions they bring to their reading of it. Raja Rao, however, read *Fontamara* as itself posing a series of political and philosophical questions to which he, in *Kanthapura*, strove to respond. The questions he identified (which relate closely to those posed by Liberation theologians) concerned: the role of peasants (and particularly women) in resistance; the relevance of religion to political action; and the form which peasant activism should take. Raja Rao's answers are loud and clear: peasants can be central to a radical political movement; women must be free to form their own groups and participate fully in public protests; religious belief and practice must be the core of political action; and non-violent passive resistance is the means to be employed. His novel leaves no doubt in its ending that such peasant action will eventually triumph. Yet full credit needs to be given to *Fontamara* not only for posing the questions, but for having offered the narrative model, opened up the literary space, which permitted Raja Rao to write a novel which itself came to play a significant role in a struggle taking place in another country several thousand miles away. This is another of the many kinds of power which the polyvalent literary text is capable of exercising.

NOTES TO CHAPTER 4

1. Introduction to Silone, *Fontamara*, trans. Eric Mosbacher (London: J. M. Dent, 1985): iv. Now the most readily available English translation of the revised 1949 version.

2. The extent of the fame achieved by *Fontamara* within a few years of its first publication in German in 1933 has been well documented by Luce d'Eramo in *L'opera di Ignazio Silone: saggio critico e guida bibliografica* (Milan: Mondadori, 1971) and, more recently, Alberto Traldi in *Fascism and Fiction: A Survey of Italian Fiction on Fascism* (Metuchen and London: Scarecrow Press, 1987). Professor Traldi kindly gave me a copy of his dissertation, "Realism and Nonrealism in Ignazio Silone's *Fontamara*" (Ph.D diss., Columbia University, 1973) an invaluable (and unpublished) piece of work from which I gratefully quote here.

3. Published in *Rundschau* (Basel) 6 September 1934.

4. Published in Italian translation by A. Marver and E. Lo Gatto in *Il Punto* (Rome) 8 March 1958.

5. In discussing the prewar reception of *Fontamara*, I quote from one of the most widely read translations of the time, the translation into English by Gwenda David and Eric Mosbacher (Harmondsworth: Penguin, 1938). This translation was first published in 1934.

6. Martin Gilbert, *Winston Churchill: 1922-1939* (London: Heinemann, 1976): 224 and 457.

7. *Under the Axe of Fascism* (London: Gollancz, 1936): 10.

8. Article in *Current History* (May 1931): 163.

9. Graham Greene, "Fontamara," *Spectator*, 2 November 1934: 692.

10. *New Yorker*, 22 September 1934: 101.

11. Greene, "Fontamara": 692.

12. *New York Times Book Review*, 23 September 1934: 6.

13. *Saturday Review of Literature*, 22 September 1934: 125.

14. *Rundschau* (Basel) 6 September 1934.

15. James T. Farrell, "Ignazio Silone," *Southern Review* 4, no 4 (Spring 1939): 775.
16. See Alberto Traldi, "Realism and Nonrealism" for a full discussion.
17. Renzo De Felice, *Mussolini il fascista: l'organizzazione dello Stato fascista 1925-1929* (Turin: Einaudi, 1968): 438.
18. De Felice, *Mussolini il fascista*: 470.
19. See Chapter 1.
20. Letter of 2 November 1937, quoted in Iris Origo, *Bisogno di testimoniare. Quattro vite: Lauro de Bosis, Ruth Draper, Gaetano Salvemini, Ignazio Silone e un saggio sulla biografia* (Milan: Longanesi, 1985): 225.
21. Letter of 2 October 1931, quoted in Luce d'Eramo, *Ignazio Silone*: 16.
22. In Origo, *Bisogno di testimoniare*: 226.
23. Salvemini, *Under the Axe of Fascism*: 276.
24. Carl T. Schmidt, *The Corporate State in Action: Italy Under Fascism* (London: Gollancz, 1939): 160.
25. Traldi, "Realism and Nonrealism": 148.
26. *Spectator*, 2 November 1934: 692.
27. The Italian title in the pre-war version, *Che dobbiamo fare?* (literally *What should we do?*) was shortened in the 1949 version to *Che fare?* (*What is to be done?*). Eric Mosbacher makes no change between his two English versions of the novel. For a detailed study of Silone's sources for this title, see Judy Rawson, "'Che fare?': Silone and the Russian 'Chto Delat'?' Tradition," *The Modern Language Review* 76 no. 3 (July 1981): 556-565.
28. George Woodcock, "Ignazio Silone," in his *The Writer and Politics* (London: Porcupine Press, 1948): 162.
29. Silone is regularly quoted as saying that this edition was "full of errors," but an examination of it (there is a copy in the London University Senate Library) reveals that this is not the case. The reference to *Fontamara* having been dropped behind the German lines is to be found in Walter Allen, "Ignazio Silone," *London Magazine*, January 1955: 58.
30. See his article on Silone in *Gli anni della antialienazione: 1943-1949* (Milan: Mursia, 1966): 103-113.
31. Salvemini, *Under the Axe of Fascism*: 222.
32. Salvemini, *Under the Axe of Fascism*: 208-9.
33. Schmidt, *The Corporate State*: 113.
34. Giuseppe Bottai in *Il sole*, 1 January 1931, quoted in Schmidt, *The Corporate State*: 108.
35. Quoted by William Elwin, *Fascism at Work* (London: Martin Hopkinson, 1934): 195.
36. See Schmidt, *The Corporate State*: 89.
37. Salvemini, *Under the Axe of Fascism*: 235.
38. See, for instance, Schmidt, *The Corporate State*: 95.
39. John Chamberlain in *The New York Times*, 19 September 1934: 17.
40. Valuable accounts of the forms of protest and the response of the regime in the region are to be found in the survey article by Luigi Ponziani, "Dopoguerra e fascismo in Abruzzo. Orientamenti storiografici," in *Italia contemporanea* 164 (September 1986):

93-103 and the autobiographical memoir by Nando Amiconi, *Il comunista e il capomanipolo* (Milan: Vangelista, 1977).
41. See, for instance, Salvemini, *Under the Axe of Fascism*: 41-43.
42. See Adriano dal Pont, Alfonso Leonetti, Massimo Massara, *Giornali fuori legge: la stampa clandestina antifascista 1922-43* (Rome: Associazione Nazionale Perseguitati Politici Italiani Antifascisti, 1964): 270.
43. See *Non mollare (1925): Riproduzione fotografica dei numeri usciti. Tre saggi storici di Ernesto Rossi, Piero Calamandrei, Gaetano Salvemini* ed. C. Francovich (Florence: Nuova Italia, 1955, 2nd ed. 1968), especially: 73 for an account of the editors' search for a title.
44. See Adriano dal Pont et al., *Giornali fuori legge*: 134.
45. Most notoriously, the mass rape of Italian women by French Moroccan troops in late 1944.
46. See for instance: Roberto Battaglia and Giuseppe Garritano, *La resistenza italiana: lineamenti di storia* (Rome: Editori Riuniti, 1974): 88.
47. Geno Pampaloni, "L'opera narrativa di Ignazio Silone," in *Il ponte* 5 (January 1949): 49.
48. Interview on West German television, 27 October 1969.
49. See Silone's own account of these changes in his article "Avezzano e la Marsica: un West italiano," in *Tuttitalia: Enciclopedia dell'Italia Antica e Moderna*, volume on Abruzzo Molise (Florence: Sadea Sansoni, 1965): 231-34.
50. Flavio Conti, *I prigionieri di guerra italiani 1940-1945* (Bologna: Il Mulino, 1986): 421.
51. Conti, *I prigionieri di guerra italiani*: 421.
52. Conti, *I prigionieri di guerra italiani*: 423.
53. Jauss's argument is discussed in Chapter 1; Luce d'Eramo, *Ignazio Silone*: 242.
54. Luigi Russo, *I narratori: 1850-1950* (Milan: Principato, 1951): 378.
55. Emilio Cecchi, *Di giorno in giorno* (Milan: Garzanti, 1954): 347.
56. Carlo Falconi, "La letteratura ispirata al Marxismo," *Humanitas* 5 (May 1950): 515.
57. For a detailed comparison of the two versions, see Giuseppe Farinelli, "*Fontamara* di Silone nella prospettiva delle varianti," *Testo* 5, no. 6-7 (1984): 33-48.
58. Silone, *Uscita di sicurezza* (Milan: Mondadori, 1965): 112.
59. Despite the Italian literary establishment's recent, belated praise of Silone, I was struck, while collecting material for this chapter in Italy, by the regularity with which Italian academics I met lost interest in my research when they discovered that Silone was the subject of it. In fact there is still no copy of *Fontamara* or Luce d'Eramo's fundamental critical work on Silone in the libraries of the University of Bologna, either the central University Library or the library of the Department of Italian Literature.
60. See both Antonio Russi, *Gli anni della antialienazione*: 113 and Elio Guerriero, *L'inquietudine e l'utopia: il racconto umano e cristiano di Ignazio Silone* (Milan: Jaca, 1979).
61. Claudio Varese, "Ignazio Silone," in *Lo Spettatore italiano* 2 (1949): 169-174.
62. Giuseppe De Robertis, *Tempo*, 11 June 1949: 14.
63. Denis Mack Smith, *A History of Sicily: Modern Sicily* (London: Chatto and Windus, 1968): 441.

64. Iris Origo, "Ignazio Silone: A Study in Integrity," *Atlantic Monthly* 219 (1967): 87.
65. Denis Mack Smith, *Italy: a Modern History* (Ann Arbor: University of Michigan Press, 1969): 73.
66. See Elio Guerriero, *L'inquietudine e l'utopia*.
67. Luisa Passerini, "Oral Memory of Fascism" in *Rethinking Italian Fascism: Capitalism, Populism and Culture*, ed. David Forgacs (London: Lawrence and Wishart, 1986): 185-196
68. For instance, Jack Zipes, *Breaking the Magic Spell: Radical Theories of Folk and Fairy Tales* (Austin: University of Texas, 1979); see also Michael Hanne, "Peasant Storytelling Meets Literary Theory: The Case of *La finta nonna*," *The Italianist* 12 (1992): 42-58.
69. Marie Maclean, "Oppositional Practices in Women's Traditional Narrative," *New Literary History* 19 (1987-8): 37-55.
70. In an interview for a Swedish television program, date unknown.
71. Passerini, "Oral Memory of Fascism": 186-7.
72. *Non mollare*, no. 12, April 1925.
73. J. Sarkis Najjar, "La traduzione araba di *Fontamara*," *Levante* (Rome), January 1965.
74. Quoted by Origo, *Bisogno di testimoniare*: 232.
75. On the reception of Silone in Latin America, see Marzia Terenzi Vicentini, "Silone sulle tracce di Celestino," *Revista de Letras* (Brazil) 12 (1969): 155-165; Ney Guimaraes, "Ignacio Silone - Escritor social," *Cla: revista de cultura* (Fortalezar Ceará, Brazil) (August 1948) 4: 58-61; Alma Novella Marani, *Narrativa y testimonio: Ignazio Silone* (Buenos Aires: Nova, 1967).
76. Che Guevara, *Reminiscences of the Cuban Revolutionary War*, trans. Victoria Ortiz (London: Allen and Unwin, 1968): 240.
77. *Guerrilla Warfare* (Lincoln and London: University of Nebraska Press, 1985): 62.
78. See for instance Philip Berryman, *Liberation Theology* (Philadelphia: Temple University Press: 1987).
79. Willy Eichler, "Silone: Poet, Socialist and Political Thinker" in *Socialist Commentary* (October 1943): 87.
80. *Kanthapura* (Delhi: Hind Pocket Books, 1971): 5.
81. Shiva Niranjan, "Philosophy into Fiction: A Study of the Thematic Aspects of Raja Rao's Novels," in *Response: Recent Revelations of Indian Fiction in English*, ed. Hari Mohan Prasad (Bareilly: Prakash Book Depot, 1983): 98.
82. Ramesh K. Srivastava, "Raja Rao's *Kanthapura*: a Village Revitalized," in his *Six Indian Novelists in English* (Amritsar: Guru Nanak Dev University, 1987): 15.
83. M. K. Naik, *Raja Rao* (New York: Twayne, 1972): 76.
84. Silvia Albertazzi, *Il tempio e il villaggio* (Bologna: Patron, 1978). I am most grateful to Dr. Albertazzi for having first made me aware of the link between Silone and Raja Rao.
85. Elio Guerriero, *L'inquietudine e l'utopia*.

5. ALEXANDER SOLZHENITSYN:
One Day in the Life of Ivan Denisovich (1962)

▼ ▼ ▼

The book to mark a new era?

"There are three atom bombs in the world," declared Veniamin Teush, a friend of Solzhenitsyn, after reading the typescript of his *One Day in the Life of Ivan Denisovich* a year before its publication in the Soviet Union. "Kennedy has one, Khrushchev has another, and you have the third."[1] If it were ever published, he predicted, Soviet life, indeed the world, would never be the same again. And when, in November 1962, *One Day* was published in the Soviet Union, the depth of the public response and, most importantly, the reviews carried by most Soviet newspapers suggested that, with its publication, a new era had, in fact, begun. With headlines such as "Thus It Was But Will Never Be Again" and "This Must Not Happen Again,"[2] they declared that the revelations that it contained about the labor camps and the absurd judicial processes which had condemned innocent people to live in them for years, and in many cases to die in them, would ensure that such things could never recur. Changes were taking place in the Soviet Union, they agreed, which would be irreversible. An indication of the unprecedented public interest in Solzhenitsyn's story can be gained from the eloquent letter he received in mid-1963 from a reader in the Ukraine, Mark Ivanovich Kononenko: "In Kharkov I have seen all kinds of queues — for the film *Tarzan*, butter, women's drawers, chicken giblets and horse-meat sausage. But I cannot remember a queue as long as the one for your book in the libraries ... I waited six months and to no avail. By chance I got hold of it for forty-eight hours."[3] *One Day* reached every region and very nearly every social group in the Soviet Union. Its reception may well have outstripped even that of *Uncle Tom's Cabin* in the United States of the 1850s in terms of the proportion of the country's population who knew of its existence.

Six years later, however, in late 1968, it must have seemed all too evident that those early commentators had been overoptimistic and had exaggerated the story's liberating force. Khrushchev had fallen and, under Brezhnev, Stalinism was reasserting itself, even if in attenuated form. The experiment in democratization of government in Czechoslovakia had just been crushed by Soviet troops. The Soviet labor camps for political prisoners, though they had been greatly reduced in number after Stalin's death, had continued to exist throughout the Khrushchev years, despite the official acclaim given to *One Day*, and were again being used extensively. After a very few years of officially sanctioned glory, Solzhenitsyn was being hounded by the KGB, prevented from publishing either *Cancer Ward* or *The First Circle* in his own country, and copies of *One Day* were being withdrawn from libraries or put in their reserve collections.[4] Moreover, within this longer timeframe, it could be seen that the publication of *One Day* had occurred relatively late in the process of de-Stalinization.

Khrushchev had initiated de-Stalinization in 1956 with his "secret speech" to the Twentieth Congress of the Soviet Communist Party denouncing the brutality and injustices of the Stalin years: "Arbitrary behavior by one person encouraged and permitted arbitrariness in others. Mass arrests and deportations of many thousands of people, execution without trial and without normal investigation created conditions of insecurity, fear and even desperation."[5] While the text of that speech had not been fully publicized in the Soviet Union, it had been widely circulated amongst Party members, setting in motion an authorized critical debate on many aspects of the Stalin era. So, over the years that followed, there had been official attacks on many of Stalin's policies, defined as consequences of the so-called "cult of personality": his disastrous agricultural policies, the pact with Hitler and the Soviet Union's unpreparedness for war with Germany, and some of the kinds of persecution carried out under his rule. This debate had culminated in Khrushchev's comprehensive public denunciation of Stalin at the Twenty-Second Party Congress in 1961 and the subsequent removal of his remains from the Lenin Mausoleum in Red Square.

Khrushchev personally authorized the publication of *One Day* in 1962, as part of his struggle with the surviving Stalinists in the Presidium, using it as an instrument to defend himself against their increasing attacks. This and the other tactics he employed more and more desperately throughout 1963 and 1964 failed to save him. So, by the late 1960s, it must have seemed painfully obvious that the publication of

One Day had been less a causally contributing factor than a late symptom, a dying gasp, in the relaxation of the oppressive features of the Soviet regime that took place under Khrushchev's leadership. Solzhenitsyn was looking more and more like a pawn who, having been moved by the losing player in the leadership game, might very soon be permanently removed from the board.

Writing now, thirty years later, the question of his role in political change has a dramatically different aspect. Not only did the Soviet regime under Gorbachev, with the policies of *glasnost* (more open government) and *perestroika* (economic reform), discard its most oppressive features, but the Soviet Union itself has been dissolved. Solzhenitsyn, who was forced into exile in the West in 1974, has seen his novels since *One Day*, which were previously banned in the Soviet Union, finally (May 1989) cleared for publication, *Gulag Archipelago* awarded (December 1990) the State literature prize, and himself finally invited back to live in Russia. (As of October 1993 he is still talking of returning and of the advisory role he might play, without yet saying when that will be.) Indeed the whole debate about the causes of the collapse of the old Soviet system, unforeseen as it was by most specialists, remains remarkably open. Two of the major questions to be discussed by historians concern the way in which the Khrushchev years are to be written into the longer narrative of the history of the Soviet Union since the death of Stalin, and the role of writers and intellectuals after 1960 in undermining the legitimacy of the regime. These two questions intersect in the case of Solzhenitsyn's *One Day*. To state the issue of this chapter simply: is there a sense in which *One Day* not only engaged significantly with the leadership struggles occurring at the time of its publication, but also entered the nation's memory as a permanent symbol of mass resistance, thus playing its part in weakening the fabric of the system?

Preserving the nation's lost history

The initial significance of the publication of *One Day* lay, of course, in its being read, as *Uncle Tom's Cabin* and *Fontamara* had been, as a truthful account of a subject on which information had previously been suppressed. The release of information and comment in the years after 1956 about the brutalities of the Stalin era had been spasmodic and patchy. Despite the revelations that had been permitted on many topics, no previous work, fictional or nonfictional, had dealt in detail with the painful

The Power of the Story
▼ ▼ ▼

question of the labor camps for political prisoners. While it was very much part of Khrushchev's intention in approving publication of *One Day*, in November 1962, that it should be seen as telling the truth about the camps under Stalin, he completely failed to foresee the extent to which it would open the door to public discussion not only on this topic but on a host of related topics which it did not suit the leadership to have discussed. In so doing, he unleashed a tiger which neither he nor his successors in the leadership were going to be able to control.

In the less than seventy pages of which the Russian text consists, the reader is drawn into intense participation in the details, the physical privation, the cold, the hunger, but equally the moments of hope and satisfaction, in a single day of a carpenter of peasant origin, Ivan Denisovich Shukhov. In the first few pages of the novel, the narrative voice asks: "How can you expect a man who's warm to understand one who's cold?" (*One Day*: 23).[6] Yet Solzhenitsyn's remarkable achievement is to make it almost inevitable that readers who have not been in labor camps will experience at least the illusion of understanding those who have.

It is winter 1951. Shukhov, who has already been in labour camps for eight years, has another two years to serve. Fighting on the northwest front in 1942, he was briefly captured by the Germans, escaped, and, reaching his own lines again, was accused absurdly of spying for the enemy. This is the story of one day in his life in a prison camp in northern Kazakhstan. He wakes with a fever, aching and hoping he will not be sent out to work that day. The narrative traces his every action during the ninety minutes before his team sets off into the snow to its construction job, the march to the site, the day's labor and the satisfaction he gains from it, the return to camp, the extra plate of kasha he obtains at dinner, and the biscuit, sugar, and sausage he is given by a prisoner who has received a food parcel that day. With all the privations of camp existence, "Shukhov went to sleep fully content ... A day without a dark cloud. Almost a happy day" (*One Day*: 142-143). So strong has the reader's involvement in the protagonist's daily struggle to survive become that it seems entirely appropriate that near the end of the book, as Shukhov's column of prisoners races to avoid being the last group back, the narrative shifts for a few pages from the third person — "They forgot to talk; they forgot to think; everyone in the column was obsessed by one idea: to get back first" — to the first person plural: "It was easier for *us* now, *we* were running down the middle of the street. And *our* escort had less to stumble over at the sides. This was where *we* ought to gain ground" (*One Day.* 142-143, my italics). For the reader, as for the prisoners, the camp has, in some sense, become "home."[7]

Solzhenitsyn wrote the first draft of *One Day* in May and June 1959, revised it later the same year, and further revised and shortened it during 1961. Released from prison in 1953 and from exile in Kazakhstan in 1956, he was living a quiet and apparently conformist provincial life in Ryazan, one hundred miles south-east of Moscow. Reunited with Natalia Reshetovskaya, from whom he had been divorced during his time in prison, he was teaching part-time in the local school while she taught chemistry at an agricultural institute. His existence was in fact, however, passionately devoted to writing, though he had no expectation that his work could be published in his lifetime. The manuscript of *The First Circle* was already in its third draft when he started work on *One Day*. Solzhenitsyn was certain that neither of these works would be acceptable to the censors and had no intention of seeking publication for them in *samizdat* (clandestinely circulated) form or abroad. It was not just a matter of his being understandably fearful that he might find himself in prison again (he had seen the attacks on Boris Pasternak for allowing *Doctor Zhivago* to be published in Italy in 1957) but of his being little preoccupied with the leverage for immediate change that clandestine or foreign publication might offer, and more concerned always with the long historical perspective.

The Twenty-Second Party Congress of October 1961, at which Khrushchev made his dramatic promise to erect a monument in Moscow "to the memory of the comrades who fell victims to arbitrary power"[8] caused Solzhenitsyn to wonder whether publication in the Soviet Union was, after all, an unattainable dream. Alexander Tvardovsky, a member of the Central Committee and editor-in-chief of the cultural magazine *Novy Mir* (whose title means "New World") speaking after Khrushchev, specifically appealed to Soviet writers to represent "the labors and ordeals of our people in a manner that is totally truthful and faithful to life, without varnishing and without cunningly smoothing out all contradictions."[9]

Solzhenitsyn discussed these developments at length with the small number of friends who knew he was writing and, finally, arranged in November 1961 for an intermediary to take his manuscript, its author's identity concealed by a pseudonym, to an editor in the prose section of *Novy Mir*, Anna Berzer. She, excited by what she read, decided to bypass the conservative head of her own section and give it directly to Tvardovsky. He, overwhelmed by the strength of the story and determined to publish it, circulated it to other Moscow intellectuals, who, with very few exceptions, added weight to his belief that it should and could be published. Just as Berzer had been obliged to bypass her senior to get the manuscript to Tvardovsky, he was sure that, if he submitted it in the usual way to Glavlit, the censoring body, it would be rejected out of hand, so he made the extraordinary decision to bypass Glavlit and arrange for it to reach Khrushchev himself through his private secretary, Vladimir Lebedev, in early September 1962. At his boss's Black Sea holiday villa, Lebedev read extracts from the story aloud to Khrushchev, who called Mikoyan in to listen. Their response was immediately and strongly positive: as well as seeing advantage to himself in his struggle with the hard-liners in the Party if it were published, Khrushchev was apparently moved to tears by hearing *One Day*. Political opportunism and emotional involvement perfectly coincided.

This whole episode, including the maneuvers of Berzer and Tvardovsky, is a useful reminder of the existence of vast numbers of small whirlpools of power within what appears from the outside to be a unified flow of power downward through an authoritarian political system. The point is even better illustrated by what followed Khrushchev's expression of enthusiasm for the work. Whilst Tsar Alexander, supposedly the omnipotent autocrat in his own empire, could in practice not change a law in that empire without first persuading the bureaucracy, First Secretary Khrushchev could not even personally authorize publication of a story he wanted to see in print. As Zhores Medvedev has pointed out, while he had the right to prohibit any publication, even if it had been passed by Glavlit, he did not have the right, on his own, to authorize publication of material which had not been passed by the censoring body. Only the Presidium, or the Secretariat of the Central Committee, had that right.[10]

Novy Mir had to get twenty-three copies of *One Day* printed overnight so that all the members of the Presidium had the chance to read it. The question was discussed at one, or possibly two, meetings of that body in the middle of October 1962 and Khrushchev apparently had something of a struggle gaining approval for publication. Opposition came especially from two hard-liners, Frol Kuslov and Mikhail Suslov, who are supposed to have objected to the unfavorable portrayal of camp guards.[11] When faced by the silence of many members, Khrushchev is reported to have said, "There's a Stalinist in each of you; there's even some of the Stalinist in me. We must root out this evil."[12] The significance Khrushchev gave to the publication of *One Day* is best indicated by a remark he made once approval had been given: "This isn't a campaign, it's a policy."[13]

The notion that a world leader could use a work of narrative fiction to make policy, or at least express it, is so extraordinary as to require detailed examination. There is, moreover, the question of just *what* policy Khrushchev saw publication of *One Day* as altering or initiating.

It seemed to many commentators, especially those outside the Soviet Union, that it represented some kind of breakthrough toward a general freedom for Soviet writers to determine what and how they would write. Philip Rahv, reviewing *One Day* in *The New York Review of Books* in January 1963, stated that "No one, not even the most astute Kremlinologist among us, could possibly have foreseen that the party-hierarchs would be prevailed upon to permit the publication of a work so devastating in its implications."[14] It is said that, when other members of the Presidium suggested that certain sections of *One Day* be cut, Khrushchev stated that "no one had the right to alter the author's version."[15] Nevertheless, it seems clear that a general liberalizing policy in the arts was not in Khrushchev's mind. As far as censorship of written material was concerned, the most he would have been contemplating was a decentralization of responsibility for it from Glavlit to Party-approved general editors of magazines and publishing houses like Tvardovsky.[16] Just how little he believed in open slather in the cultural field was vividly demonstrated shortly after publication of *One Day*, when he visited an exhibition of abstract and modernist paintings at the Manezh Gallery and made a vituperative attack on them as "simply anti-Soviet," "amoral," "painted by jackasses." He declared that "we are going to maintain a strict policy in the arts."[17] While it seems that the arch-conservatives in his entourage deliberately steeered the Soviet leader into viewing paintings they knew he would hate,[18] it is hardly likely that this last comment was provoked just by this experience. Cultural works would still be required to serve Party interests, but Khrushchev and others within the leadership were shifting their conceptions both of how they might do so and, indeed, of what Party interests were.

There is an extraordinary sense in which antagonists operating within the same power system often share some fundamental notions. In the speech Solzhenitsyn prepared in acceptance of the Nobel Prize (but which he did not deliver personally) he wrote, in terms alien to Western readers, of literary fiction as an alternative version of history: "literature becomes the living memory of a nation. Thus it preserves the nation's lost history."[19] Khrushchev, evidence suggests, also saw *One Day* as rewriting Soviet history, though not of course in the profoundly subversive manner in which Solzhenitsyn viewed it. He had long been aware in his own rough intuitive way that, in order both to initiate new policy and to consolidate his own leadership, he had to promote a retelling of the narrative of events from the October Revolution in 1917 through the Stalin years and the Second World War to his own time. From the moment of the Twentieth Congress in 1956, Khrushchev had taken every opportunity not only to redefine the Stalin years as a deviation from the path set by Lenin but to emphasize the directness with which the true path led to him and his present policies. Nancy Whittier Heer, an American historian of Soviet affairs, describes *One Day* as having been not only a "tidal wave" that "in one stroke opened up the whole hideous history of the Siberian concentration camps to public discussion" but "a turning point in Soviet historiography [which] can only be compared to Khrushchev's secret speech in 1956."[20] I shall suggest that Khrushchev himself sought to use *One Day* (and a number of other literary works which had been permitted publication in the preceding few months) opportunistically as tentative contributions to the official rewriting of Soviet history.

The advantages for an authoritarian regime in maintaining a unified, officially sanctioned body of historians whose task it is to tell the history of their nation according to a broad single narrative scheme approved by the leadership are obvious. As Heer expressed it, "he who controls the record of the past legitimates his authority to command the present and define the future."[21] Marxism-Leninism, of course, has its own overarching narrative, whose later stages, projecting into the future, refer to the revolutionary role of the vanguard of the Party, the dictatorship of the proletariat and, eventually, a classless society. Historians have always been seen by the Soviet leadership as playing a central role in demonstrating the consistency of the nation's history since the October Revolution with the principles inherent in that grand narrative. When, however, the regime's policies and structures have shifted radically and a redefinition of the basis of its legitimacy is required, the disadvantages for the leadership of such a monolithic approach to history become paramount. How is the massive structure to be partially dismantled to permit the necessary remodeling without completely destroying public confidence in it? It was fascinating to see Mikhail Gorbachev struggling with the historical record of the Stalin era in a way which closely recalls Khrushchev's own difficulties with the subject. In the major address he gave in November 1987, on the seventieth anniversary of the revolution, his attempt to redistribute the weight of the official narrative was painfully unconvincing: "To stay faithful to historical truth, we have to see both Stalin's indisputable contribution to the struggle for socialism, to the defence of its gains, as well as the gross political mistakes and the abuses committed by him and his circle, for which our people paid a heavy price and which had grave consequences for society."[22] Over the following four years the problem for Gorbachev and others seeking radical reform without the wholesale abandonment of socialism became how to ditch Stalin completely without also discarding Lenin: an aspiration which, in the short term at least, has failed.

One Day was not the first, though it was certainly the most outstanding, literary work authorized for publication in 1962 to criticize aspects of Stalin's rule. In April, *Izvestia* had published a story by Em. Kazakevich, *Enemies*, depicting Lenin's tolerant treatment of his Menshevik opponent, Martov, which, to Soviet readers, at once suggested unfavorable comparison with Stalin's brutal treatment of those socialists he defined as "enemies of the Party." And in its March, April, and May numbers, *Novy Mir* had published a novella by Iury Bondarev, *Silence*, set in the immediate postwar years, which depicted midnight arrests, false denunciations, and the generalized fear experienced by loyal Soviet citizens. (Early reviews of *Silence* were generally negative, but, no doubt on the initiative of the leadership, the tone of later reviews became enthusiastic, describing the work as "honest" and "powerful.") On 14 October, *Pravda* (evidently with Khrushchev's full authorization) published Yevtushenko's poem "Stalin's Heirs," remarkable for its implication that Stalinism had survived Khrushchev's discrediting of Stalin:

> As long as Stalin's heirs exist on earth
> It will seem to me
>   that Stalin is still in the mausoleum.[23]

A number of reasons can be identified for the leadership's choice of literary works, and *One Day* in particular, as first steps in the rewriting of Soviet history. In the first place, the specificity of the fictional narrative seemed enormously advantageous: the fact that, on the surface at least, Solzhenitsyn's story did not claim to recount more than a single day in the life of one man in one camp; that indeed, being a fictional text, it did not make any particular claim to truthfulness. To fill the gap in the historical record as it related to the labor camps would have required an amount of investigation and of work in assembling the material that would not only have taken much longer than the leadership could afford but have involved a political upheaval that would have been highly undesirable from its point of view. Preferable for the moment was a fictional narrative which could hint at, imply the existence of, the wider phenomenon, without having to indicate either the vast numbers of people unjustly imprisoned and killed in the camps or the individuals in the government structures responsible for the organization of the camps, as a work of investigative journalism or history would be required to do. A brief, vivid story such as *One Day* would reach a vast audience very rapidly, whereas a drily academic account of the labor camps by historians fearful for their own skins in case of a leadership change would have none of the same immediate public relations value. It was assumed, moreover, that an ostensibly fictional work would be less disturbing to its readers than, say, a factual memoir such as Evgenia Ginzburg's recollections of imprisonment, *Into the Whirlwind*, which circulated only in *samizdat*. While fictional works draw readers into the world they create, they may also distance them from the most awful features of that world, making it more tolerable. Moreover, Khrushchev's insistence (only rhetorical, of course) on the relative autonomy of the literary author meant that, while the convergence of the fictional work with the Party line could at one moment be portrayed as an independent confirmation of that line, if political circumstances changed, the leadership could disclaim responsibility for the work, and even deny its validity, in a way that would not be possible with an overtly historical work. An advantage of the unstable position of the literary work is that it can be used to try out ideas which may subsequently either be integrated into history or discarded. Nancy Whittier Heer contrasts "the more exposed and defenseless position of belles lettres" with "the relatively greater integrity and lesser malleability of Soviet history."[24]

There are, however, very specific features of *One Day* which "seduced" Khrushchev and his allies within the leadership into the mistaken belief that they could use it as a tactical instrument without damage to themselves. In the first place, they had no difficulty in reading Solzhenitsyn's story as belonging to the tradition of socialist realism. *One Day* is not, after all, a modernist work. Indeed, as late as 1969, György Lukács was happy to refer to it as "a significant step in the renewal of the great traditions of the socialist realism of the nineteen-twenties."[25] Solzhenitsyn's choice of Ivan Denisovich Shukhov, a tradesman of peasant origin, not an intellectual, as his protagonist is crucial. Not only was he adhering to the conventions of socialist realism in choosing a positive worker-hero, but Shukhov's character must have appeared at first sight quite unthreatening to Khrushchev, himself no intellectual. Shukhov makes no claims to political or historical insight; he does not understand the discussion he hears between two film enthusiasts about the work of Eisenstein; he even shares the belief of people from his village that God crumbles up the old moon into stars and makes a new moon each month. He is described as "a man of timid nature" (*One Day*: 24). He is, nevertheless, one of the most skilled of the prisoners in managing his existence: gaining an extra slice of bread where he can, involving himself fully in the work he is forced to do, neither getting too upset about the things that go against him nor building false hopes that his lot will improve. Most moving is his refusal, even in the appalling conditions of the camp, to allow his personal dignity to slip. However cold it is, he always takes off his cap to eat; he will not betray or steal from another prisoner; he will not take or give a bribe; when he is given food by a fellow prisoner, he passes some of it on to a young prisoner he feels sorry for. Crucial, too, no doubt, was Solzhenitsyn's choice of a relatively "good" day, his decision to avoid representing the worst atrocities of the camps. (He had, in his own words, "lightened" the originally very dark tone of the first draft before the question of its being acceptable for publication even arose.)[26] There is no doubt that Lebedev's choice of passages to read to Khrushchev helped, too, especially his emphasis on Shukhov's conscientious attitude to his work in building the wall at the generating station. It is clear that Khrushchev and his associates read the story supposing Solzhenitsyn to be a sincere socialist, disillusioned with Stalinism, convinced of the capacity of working people to withstand adversity and looking to a restoration of Leninist principles in the Soviet Union.

Specifically useful to Khrushchev was the way in which the story, while relating only one day in the life of one prisoner, refers to the experiences of the various members of Shukhov's team including a wide range of the absurd grounds on which Stalin's paranoid security system imprisoned people: Tiurin is condemned merely for being the son of a *kulak* (well-to-do farmer), Buinovsky because a British naval officer, to whose ship he was assigned for a time during the war, later sent him a present; Senka Klevshin, "a quiet luckless fellow," because, having been captured by the Germans during the war and sent to Buchenwald, he must, in the eyes of the security system, be a spy. (In fact there is only one prisoner in the camp, among the hundreds of supposed spies, whom the other prisoners believe to have been a "real spy" [*One Day*: 97]). Young Alyosha, like a number of his fellow prisoners, is in the camp for his unyielding, public affirmation of his Baptist faith.

There was a level on which Khrushchev and his associates were doubtless happy that the camp should be seen by readers as, not just representative of the (undefined, in the story) number of other labor camps in existence under Stalin, but a metaphor for some of the other deformations which his rule had brought about. So they would not have been too concerned to see a critic named Drutse, in an article published within weeks of the appearance of *One Day*, declaring, "Are we not struck by the austere landscape of this story because we, too, as often as not scanned the skies with morbidly strained eyes? Did we not also lay bricks, each in his own wall?. ... And didn't we also look back on each day, just like Ivan Denisovich, and with a logic inscrutable to common sense rejoice inwardly, 'Oh well, the day didn't go too badly'...?"[27] Or, as Lukács was to express it in his 1964 essay: "Although the camps epitomize one extreme of the Stalin era, the author has made his skilful grey monochrome of camp life into a symbol of everyday life under Stalin."[28]

The major, and in part mistaken, assumption behind Khrushchev's authorization of the publication of *One Day* was that he would be able to limit its explosive impact to those targets he wanted destroyed, leaving those he did not want damaged (including himself and his supporters) untouched. In particular, he assumed that readers could be persuaded to interpret the story as being wholly about a period which had been definitively consigned to the past.[29]

The first reception of *One Day*

Efforts by Khrushchev's supporters to control the reception of *One Day* began before the November issue of *Novy Mir* hit the streets. Copies of the typescript of *One Day* were "stolen" from Tvardovsky's safe during October and early November 1962, no doubt with official approval and for distribution to key political and literary figures with the idea of stacking the first reviews and other public reactions in favour of the work and of appropriating for the current leadership the work's extraordinary power. Anticipation built up to such an extent that other periodicals felt some jealousy at having been upstaged by *Novy Mir*. *Izvestia* rushed to publish its own poor-quality labor camp story in early November, just a few days before *One Day* came out.[30] Solzhenitsyn's story, in a curious way, made stories about the camps officially fashionable for a short time. In a state subject to rigid censorship, authorization of publication of a work may be no less an exercise of asymmetric power than prohibition.

Tvardovsky insisted in his Preface on the gulf between the Khrushchev era and the Stalin era represented in *One Day*: "Although these events are so recent in point of time, they seem very remote to us. But, whatever the past was like, we in the present must not be indifferent to it. Only by going into it fully, courageously and truthfully can we guarantee a complete and irrevocable break with all those things that cast a shadow over the past."[31]

The first Soviet reviews almost all stressed, likewise, both the truthfulness of this fictional work and the idea that factual information about the evils of the past should make it possible to avoid those evils in the future. "Let the Full Truth Be Told" was the title of the review in *Trud*,[32] "In the Name of Truth, in the Name of Life" in *Pravda*.[33] Other papers carried headlines such as "About the Past in the Name of the Future."[34] (The fact that these were, in most cases, the same newspapers which had played an active part in the suppression of information on the camps could hardly have escaped any of their readers.) Tvardovsky had promoted such a cathartic reading of *One Day* in the Preface: "The effect of this novel, which is so unusual for its honesty and harrowing truth, is to unburden our minds of things so far unspoken, but which had to be said."[35]

Most of the first reviewers emphasized the consistency of *One Day* with current Party policy. Vladimir Ermilov, for instance, declared in *Pravda*: "There can be no doubt that the fight against the consequences of Stalin's personality cult, taken up by the Party and the Soviet people since the Twentieth and Twenty-Second congresses of the CPSU, will continue to facilitate the appearance of works of art outstanding for their ever-increasing value … The possibility of telling the truth has been affirmed by the Party and the people.[36] And Konstantin Simonov wrote in *Izvestia*, "I believe that Alexander Solzhenitsyn, in his story, has shown himself a true helper of the Party in a sacred and vital cause — the struggle against the personality cult and its consequences."[37]

Khrushchev sought both to endorse and to take credit for the publication of *One Day* on two major occasions before the end of 1962. In late November he told delegates to a plenary session of the Central Committee of the Communist Party in the Kremlin that *One Day* was an extremely important work which they should all read (thousands of copies of it having been placed on the bookstalls outside the meeting room) and then, on 17 December, he presented Solzhenitsyn personally to a meeting of Party leaders with four hundred writers, artists, and intellectuals at the Pioneer Palace in Moscow. Reviewers almost all followed his lead. The *Literaturnaya Gazeta* was typical in praising *One Day* as "a purifying pain" and stated: "Old, healed wounds do not pain.

But a wound that still bleeds must be healed and not cravenly hidden from sight. And there is only one cure — truth. The Party summons us along this path of truth."[38]

It is not easy, now, to reconstruct Solzhenitsyn's state of mind at the moment of publication. It seems that he experienced a mixture of delight at having, against all his earlier expectations, achieved publication for his work, and apprehension at thus being made vulnerable to future persecution. As for being called "a true helper of the Party" and what he may have hoped for from Khrushchev and the de-Stalinization process, his later account of this period, in the first four essays in *The Oak and the Calf*, is not an entirely reliable guide. It should be remembered that Solzhenitsyn underwent a long personal, intellectual, and political journey from being an active member of Komsomol during his university years, in his own words "enthralled" by Marxism-Leninism, to being an effective officer in the Soviet army during the war, increasingly disgusted with Stalin and Stalinism but still very much an idealistic socialist, to the increasing political disillusionment of his prison years, to the complete antagonism to both socialism and American-style democracy which he began displaying in the 1970s.[39] Certainly, by 1967, when he came to write the early parts of *The Oak and the Calf*, having witnessed the fall of Khrushchev and the end of de-Stalinization and finding himself personally harassed by the authorities, he was entirely cynical about the capacity of the Soviet state to reform itself. It seems highly likely, though, that, however great his disillusionment with what he had seen of socialist practice, in late 1962, at the time of publication of *One Day*, he allowed that disillusionment to slip and came to wonder whether the Soviet system might, after all, be capable of genuine and lasting reform under Khrushchev or his successors and whether his literary works might play a part in such a process. He was not quite as far along the track towards wholesale abandonment of the socialist ideal as, five years later, he was to suggest. In seeking publication he was surrendering one kind of power (the untested potential of the guerilla fighter waiting, hidden in the hills) for another (the capacity of the prominent, respected figure to influence both government policy and public opinion).

It is an indication of his utter confidence in the integrity of his work that he seems to have had no concerns about the possibility of the Party's successfully appropriating *One Day* to a conservative agenda. Nevertheless, a number of commentators in the West sympathetic to Solzhenitsyn and hostile to the Soviet regime were visibly concerned in the years immediately following that he might be regarded as having dirtied his hands as a writer by allowing *One Day* to engage so directly with the internal politics of the time. See, for instance, Max Hayward's unconvincing attempt to detach the work from the moment of its publication: "It is ironic that this work, which must be judged primarily for its lasting worth as a work of literature in the grand Russian tradition, should have appeared as the result of a squalid political intrigue."[40]

The compromises Solzhenitsyn made personally both before and after publication were in fact minimal. Under pressure from Tvardovsky and other members of the editorial board, he had made a few, not many, changes to the text of *One Day* before it reached Khrushchev to make it more palatable to him and the Party, while successfully resisting the demand for changes that he felt would "destroy the harmony of my story or go against my conscience."[41] He did accept membership in the Soviet Writers' Union, without which it would have been very difficult for him to be a full-time professional writer, when it was offered to him soon after publication of *One Day*.

On the other hand, he strictly avoided interviews with journalists, Soviet or Western. This is significant for several reasons. In the first place it meant that he resisted the opportunity, or temptation, to try to steer the reception of his own work. Specifically, he refused either to endorse or deny the limited, cathartic reading recommended by the leadership. By leaving open the question of his personal political position, he allowed the literary text's own openness to begin working in the world. Of this period, he later wrote (and on this I think we should believe him): "I did not realize the extent of my newly won strength, or, therefore, the degree of audacity with which I could now behave. The force of inertia kept me cautious and secretive. ... I was in a hurry to stop before I was stopped, to take cover again and pretend that I had nothing further in mind."[42]

So, for the moment, he avoided trying to nudge internal political change along through public statements. The one effort he did make in this direction came at the beginning of 1964 when he sought meetings with a number of bodies responsible both for the legislation by which citizens were sent to prison on political grounds and for the running of the camps. His attempts to obtain, at least, an improvement in conditions for the hundreds of thousands of such people still imprisoned under Khrushchev were met with a polite refusal.

The massiveness and depth of the public response to *One Day* has already been referred to. By early 1963, a million-and-a-half copies had been printed in magazine and book form, almost every one of which passed through dozens of hands. *One Day* reached every region and every social group in the Soviet Union.

The brevity and apparent simplicity of the story, the use of a tradesman of peasant origin as protagonist, indeed many of the very features which had pleased Khrushchev, made it entirely accessible to a very wide readership. (Some of the intellectuals who read the work in advance of publication were disparaging about the fact that Solzhenitsyn had not used an intellectual as his central figure: if they had had their way, *One Day* would doubtless have been a very much less popular work.)

The economy and vividness with which Solzhenitsyn sketched the contrasting personalities of the prisoners on Shukhov's work team have often been noted. The reader gains an acute sense of the dynamics of the team and its hierarchy, which descends from the team leader, Tiurin, who is respected by prisoners and guards for his competence and authority, to the lowest of them all, Fetiukov, despised by everyone, as he slobbers beside any prisoner with a cigarette, begging for a drag on it, and "the sort who when he was looking after someone else's bowl took the potatoes from it" (*One Day*: 17). Status in the team is defined in terms of a combination of factors, including length of imprisonment, social origins, personal courage, and work skills. So Buinovsky, an ex-naval commander and a recent arrival, is respected for his courage and education, but mocked a little for his lack of physical strength and the difficulty he is having in adjusting to his new circumstances. Kilgas and Shukhov, both skilled tradesmen, gain respect, and an extra allowance of bread, for their contribution to the day's work.

Essential, too, to the work's popular appeal was the fact that the team is a microcosm of the great range of nationalities represented in the Soviet Union. In addition to those characters already mentioned, who, apart from Kilgas, a Latvian, would all have been Russians, there is Gopchik "a Ukrainian lad of about sixteen, pink as a sucking-pig" (*One Day*: 47) and young Tsezar, a filmmaker, who was "a hotch-potch of nationalities: Greek, Jew, Gipsy — you couldn't make out which" (*One Day*: 28) and two Estonians — one a fisherman, the other having spent his childhood in Sweden — who share everything, consult each other on every matter, talk exclusively in their own language and hang on to each other "so closely that you'd think one would suffocate unless he breathed the same air as the other" (*One Day*: 44). Shukhov has contact outside the team with a Moldavian (the only "real" spy in the camp) and a

Hungarian. Solzhenitsyn skilfully indicates some national characteristics (a newly arrived West Ukrainian crosses himself whereas the Russians have "forgotten which hand to cross themselves with" [*One Day*: 16]) without ever falling into, or allowing Shukhov to fall into, national stereotypes. If one Latvian is represented as avaricious and cunning (the one from whom Shukhov buys tobacco) another (Kilgas) is depicted as generous and funny. Readers of any social origin or nationality within the Soviet Union could readily identify with one or another of the characters. (As George Gibian has observed, *One Day* is a much less exclusively *Russian* novel than almost all of Solzhenitsyn's later works.)[43]

Much more evident in the original text than in the necessarily flatter translations of *One Day* is the stylistic device which added to its attractiveness for a mass audience, whereby the story is narrated in the third person in a language which reflects both the speech of the peasant protagonist and the peculiar slang of the labor camps, a language with an occasionally playful, obscene quality.[44] Alongside the contemporary freshness of the language there are, as James M. Curtis has demonstrated, features deriving from Tolstoy in the characterization and narrative technique.[45] There can be little doubt however that Solzhenitsyn's choice of language and style, as well as of his choice of protagonist, greatly enhanced the popular appeal of his book.

The novel takes on its own momentum

Within a fairly short time, it became evident that the reception of *One Day* had slipped right out of Khrushchev's control. In the first place, its publication generated the production and circulation of a great number of other accounts of camp life, including both factual memoirs and fictional accounts, many of which depicted the treatment of prisoners, and the camps as a whole, in a much less favorable light than *One Day*. Not surprisingly, it was the hundreds of thousands of former prisoners of such camps for whom the book meant most. The effect on them of seeing something of their experiences recounted publicly for the first time was extraordinary. Many wrote to Solzhenitsyn to testify to the accuracy of his depiction of camp life. As one, P. R. Martynyuk, said, "I worked on the White Sea and Volga-Moscow canals, and by a miracle stayed alive. What is described in the story is a tiny part of what I personally saw and lived through."[46] They were overwhelmed by the feeling that, at last, their suffering was being publicly acknowledged, and by the changes this brought about in their neighbors' attitudes to them. As G. Benediktova wrote: "Just a little sympathy for those who perished is beginning to penetrate such people, and the cold indifference is beginning to give way to warmth" and, in I. Dobryak's words, "this story has opened the eyes of many people to whom we were a mystery."[47] It was as if *One Day* prompted former prisoners to find a voice they did not know they had. They jostled to remind the world of the presentness, for them, of their experience in the camps; many prisoners were prompted to record their experiences and show what they wrote to their friends or mail it to the literary journals.[48] The capacity of one literary text to generate others, any of which may have its own political significance, is a recurrent theme throughout these case studies. Already, in a speech in March 1963, Khrushchev was complaining about the number of other works on the camps in circulation.

Secondly, publication of *One Day* led to a widespread expectation that investigation and removal from office of those responsible for the labor camps would follow. The letters written to Solzhenitsyn by ordinary readers in the eighteen months after November 1962, on this and other issues, indicate the degree to which his story had opened the floodgates of discussion. N. I. Ryabinin must have been speaking for a vast number of thoughtful readers when he wrote: "Those ... who exercised this tyranny, in the majority of cases did so in full consciousness of what they were doing. And they are still walking around, although they should long ago have been dispatched to the other world."[49] This expectation was quite unrealistic since most of the the current members of the Presidium, including Khrushchev, who had been Stalin's "viceroy" in the purge of the Ukraine in 1938-39, would have belonged to this category. This unhealthy (as it seemed, equally, to Khrushchev and his Stalinist adversaries) public fascination with the question of the involvement of members of the current leadership and senior bureaucrats in the purges of the 1930s led him to undertake what has since come to be known (in the United States rather than the Soviet Union!) as "an exercise in damage limitation." In his speech of March 1963, delivered to a gathering of writers, Khrushchev found it necessary to "clarify" the role of senior members of the Party in Stalin's most repressive measures: "Did the leading cadres of the Party know about the arrests of people at the time? Yes, they knew. But did they know that people were being arrested who were in no way guilty? No, they did not know. They believed Stalin and did not admit the thought that repression could be applied against honest people devoted to our cause."[50]

Alexander Solzhenitsyn's: One Day in the Life of Ivan Denisovich

▼ ▼ ▼

A third problematic question raised in the public mind by *One Day* was the question of the continued existence of penal camps for political prisoners. I. G. Pisarev wrote to Solzhenitsyn asking, "One thing I do not understand — did you want to say *that* no longer exists or that what there was before still remains?"[51] And a joint letter from prisoners in a camp still in existence stated: "For us now it is considerably worse … In December 1962 out of 300 men in our camp there were 190 suffering from malnutrition."[52]

In other respects, too, by no means all readers were convinced that there had been as clear a break with the past as the official reading suggested. For many, indeed, *One Day* seemed to reflect, depressingly, their *present* existence. Olga Chavchavadze made clear just how it made her feel about her life when she wrote to the author: "After reading it, the only thing left to do is to knock a nail into the wall, tie a knot and hang oneself." Another reader informed him that "my neighbor read it, started drinking and drank for a week."[53] This was hardly the "unburdening" effect Tvardovsky had foreseen.

The extent to which the novel tended, despite the intentions of Tvardovsky, Khrushchev, and the liberal faction within the leadership, to profoundly undermine the whole socialist narrative, is epitomized by the words of yet another reader who corresponded with Solzhenitsyn: "When reading this story one is forced to consider the question — how could it come about, that the people were in power and that the people permitted such oppression?"[54] It was just that kind of grand question which the leadership could not afford to have people asking, since it cast doubt on the Party's own grand narrative. Specifically, it undermined the leadership's claims that, firstly, the "personality cult" around Stalin had not infected the whole socialist enterprise in the Soviet Union, and secondly, that the failings of that era had not lasted into the post-Stalin period. A population can, by and large, actively express discontent about its situation only when it has the terms of reference, the concepts, with which to do so. *One Day*, it appears, provided those terms of reference for many of its first readers. Using devices which have something in common with those employed by Silone in *Fontamara* thirty years before, Solzhenitsyn captured in a popularly accessible, miniaturized form a sense of the prison-like qualities of the society in which they were still living.

The divergence between the reassurances given by Tvardovsky and other liberals within the Communist Party about the "positive," limited impact, from the perspective of the Party and the current leadership, to be expected from the publication of *One Day*, and the responses of many readers, devastating in their far-reaching criticisms of that leadership, shows that, in approving the publication of *One Day*, Khrushchev had released a creature to which he would subsequently attribute some of the blame for his downfall.[55]

"A stew that will attract flies like a carcass"

The reception of *One Day* was further complicated by the volatility of both the internal political situation in the Soviet Union (to which some reference has already been made) and its external relations. As well as provoking the antagonism of the old hard-liners with the rhetoric of de-Stalinization, Khrushchev had raised wider discontent with his handling of the economy, especially of agriculture. He had annoyed the KGB by reforming its structure and reducing its numbers and status. Finally, at the very Central Committee meeting in late November 1962 at which he praised *One Day*, he proposed major administrative changes in the Party, greatly alarming the conservatives. (This juxtaposition may well have exacerbated the subsequent split in the reception of the story between liberals and conservatives in the Party.)

Meanwhile, the international backdrop to the publication of *One Day* could hardly have been more dramatic. Khrushchev's policies in the area of foreign relations had swung spectacularly from efforts at détente in the late 1950s to a revival of Cold War tension with the United States in 1961, when he threatened to restrict use of the Berlin air corridors. In the summer of 1962 he wound the tension up to a breaking point by quietly installing Soviet nuclear missiles in Cuba. The Cuban missile crisis reached its height in October at the very time when *Novy Mir* was preparing to publish *One Day*. In fact Khrushchev finally agreed to dismantle the missiles on 28 October (a moment which few people alive at the time and aware of the risk of nuclear war will ever forget), a decision which fell midway between the meeting of the Presidium at which approval was given for publication and the appearance of the November issue of *Novy Mir*. While this sequence of events was largely coincidental, in the sense that Khrushchev could not have known at the time he pressed for publication that he was going to have to back down on the missiles, it did mean that by mid-November Khrushchev was all the more on the defensive and all the more in need of the support for his position, which he hoped to derive from the appearance of Solzhenitsyn's story. More important still, perhaps, reminders to the Party and the population at large of some of the appalling deficiencies of his predecessor were as good a way as any of distracting attention from his own failings.

As Khrushchev's control over the Party itself waned in the following eighteen months, so the official status of *One Day* and Solzhenitsyn shifted radically. Publication of *One Day*, which had been treated as a small personal triumph for Khrushchev and certainly an effective weapon against the neo-Stalinists, came increasingly to be spoken of as yet another of his blunders and, indeed, a weapon for the conservatives to use against him. The antagonism of leading conservatives drew support from that sizeable group of readers who had at some time worked as guards or officials in a labor camp. The letters written to Solzhenitsyn by readers provide evidence of a substantial minority interpretation, which not only deviated from that proposed by Khrushchev and the majority of Soviet reviewers, but which resisted numerous signs within the text itself. A number of such readers wrote to defend the camps and criticize the behavior of Ivan Denisovich Shukhov. A. F. Zakharova, for instance, stated: "When he had washed the floor he threw the sopping cloth behind the stove and poured the dirty water on to the path used by the authorities. This shows how he respects communists and looks after socialist property. ... All he hopes for is the sick-bay. After all he is in a corrective labour camp, even if he is innocent, so he ought to set an example to the others, like a good Soviet citizen, and show how to fire the others with enthusiasm and not go to pieces."[56]

Another reader wrote to say that: "The principal character of the story, Shukhov, is shown negatively, like all the others, who, as the story shows, disorganized life in the camp." More damning still, "you feel neither sympathy nor respect for Shukhov, nor do you feel any particular anger at injustice done to him."[57] The relative openness of the literary text allowed such readers, whose personal role in the existence of the camps encouraged them to continue to subscribe to the Stalinist "story", to read *One Day* as, in some sense, justifying the existence of the camps and the way in which they were run.

The translations of *One Day* published abroad in the early months of 1963 and the reception given to those translations by foreign commentators posed further problems for Khrushchev and, eventually, for Solzhenitsyn. Given that the translations were of a work which had already been given authorized domestic publication, they had a very different significance from the translations of, say, *Doctor Zhivago* or the satirical stories of Andrei Sinyavsky and Yuli Daniel, published in the West, under assumed names. On the one hand, of course, the regime could reasonably take credit abroad for having permitted publication, for having initiated discussion of the camps, and for the change of policy that implied. On the other hand, it could not even attempt to predetermine the work's reception abroad, as it tried to do at home. In particular, the distinction between conditions under Stalin and conditions under Khrushchev was one which hostile commentators in the West could easily blur, since the mass of readers did not have the personal experience of the two eras which the Soviet public had on which to make a judgement. Khrushchev was already aware of this danger and showing concern at the implications of his having promoted *One Day* when, in March 1963, he declared: "Take my word for it, this is a very dangerous theme. It's the kind of 'stew' that will attract flies like a carcass, enormous fat flies; all sorts of bourgeois scum from abroad will come crawling all over it."[58] Nevertheless the key to which way the story "worked" on public opinion in the West lay, to a considerable extent, in the hands of the Soviet leadership. If Khrushchev had been able to maintain the momentum of de-Stalinization (and perhaps if he had avoided the adventurism in foreign policy to which he was prone) *One Day* could have fluttered abroad as a proud banner of Soviet liberalization. Once it became clear that the momentum was lost, *One Day* remained as an unequivocal symbol of the failings of Soviet socialism. Indeed much of the rest of this chapter will be concerned with the clumsy manner in which the Soviet authorities in effect handed Solzhenitsyn over to the West as a weapon to be used against them.

Solzhenitsyn under attack

While Khrushchev himself came under increasing attack from conservative factions within the Party throughout 1963, the position of *One Day* and Solzhenitsyn seemed, for the moment at least, unassailable. This was due in part, no doubt, to the explicit endorsement they had received from the leadership, but in large part, too, to the unprecedented enthusiasm with which a vast public was seeking out and devouring *One Day*. The feverish circulation of copies of *One Day* over the following year and discussion of its implications could not have been interrupted without provoking massive discontent. It was evident to all factions within the Party that, given that the cat had been let out of the bag, it was better not to go through the undignified process of trying to catch it and stuff it back in again. The only thing to do was to ensure that it did not breed and strenuous efforts were made to limit the number of works about life in the prisons and camps gaining publication.

Throughout 1963, it was still not feasible for the conservatives to attack *One Day* directly, but disparaging comments were made about two short stories Solzhenitsyn published during the year. Interestingly, however, a number of "anti-*One Day*" stories written by supporters of the conservative faction were published. They were designed to show the positive side of camp life in rather the same way as the "anti-*Uncle Tom's Cabin*" novels of the 1850s in the United States depicted slavery in a favorable light. As in the case of the American novel, this signals both the political importance attributed to the original story and a belief in the possibility of using fiction as a counterweapon.

It was an indication of the decline of both Khrushchev's and, consequently, Solzhenitsyn's standing with the Party that, when it came to the awarding of the Lenin Prize for literature in April 1964, the conservatives were able to maneuver *One Day*, obviously the outstanding work, off the short list. Particularly ominous were the way in which this was done (at the last moment, Sergei Pavlov, the hard-line chairman of the central committee of Komsomol, made the slanderous claim, which he later, but too late to repair the damage, withdrew, that Solzhenitsyn had surrendered to the Germans during the war) and the way in which it was announced (on the day of the final ballot *Pravda* published an editorial stating that *One Day* was unsuitable for the prize since it failed to meet the high standards set by previous winners, lacked the necessary Party spirit, and did not observe the "best traditions of the Russian literary language.")[59] In the months that followed, there were outright attacks on *One Day* in a number of literary journals and it became increasingly evident that Tvardovsky, despite his personal enthusiasm for the novel, was not going to be able to publish *The First Circle*. Any idea of submitting it directly to Khrushchev was dropped, since the leader's goodwill towards Solzhenitsyn had long since evaporated. In October, Khrushchev fell from power, and with him, though this was not entirely clear for another three or four years, the possibility of Solzhenitsyn's publishing officially again in his own country. Within months, the KGB seized typescript copies not only of *The First Circle* but of a number of shorter works.

From this point on, the story of Solzhenitsyn's involvement in the shifts of national and international power took on a very different character. As it gradually became clear that he would be prevented from publishing another major fictional work in his own country, his direct engagement with the Soviet system came to take place exclusively through other means: the circulation of his literary works in *samizdat*, the writing of open letters to official bodies and newspapers which he also circulated in *samizdat*, and the publication of his major literary works abroad — all actions he had previously eschewed. It was these actions which led to his being awarded the Nobel Prize in 1970 and to his eventual expulsion from the Soviet Union and exile in 1974.

This decade of his life is often referred to by commentators in David-and-Goliath terms as an epic struggle between the little individual, mustering what weapons he could, and the monstrous forces of the whole Soviet system. These are certainly the terms in which Solzhenitsyn himself narrates the story in *The Oak and the Calf* (1975): he is the calf who tries to uproot, and nearly triumphs over, the massive oak. Indeed, now, twenty years later, it might be suggested that he inflicted wounds during that period which contributed in a major way to the eventual felling of the mighty tree. Since my prime concern in this study is the political role of literary texts, I shall paint the decade from 1964 to 1974 and, then, the period of Solzhenitsyn's exile, with very broad strokes, aiming to capture no more than a general impression of the mechanisms of power within which the writer came to operate.

Samizdat and publication abroad

After Khrushchev's death, Solzhenitsyn long retained a power base in the Soviet Union which derived both from the endorsement which Khrushchev and virtually the whole political and literary establishment had given to *One Day*, and the claim that he could reasonably make to have reached a mass audience with that story and to be in a position to represent them (as well as the memory of the millions who had died in the camps) in continuing to focus public attention on the indefensible repressions to which the regime had committed itself over a thirty-year period. In other words, it was of the greatest importance that David had, initially at least, lured Goliath into allowing him to use his sling freely. (This must be one of the nicest pieces of evidence for Ross Chambers' argument that the seductive power of narrative tends to work against coercion.) Given the greater size and intellectual complexity of *The First Circle* and *Cancer Ward*, it is quite likely that, if they had been published in the Soviet Union, neither would actually have attracted the mass readership of *One Day*. Solzhenitsyn paradoxically gained a strategic advantage in his struggle with the authorities during this period from the fact that his mass support hinged on a single, readily accessible fictional text. It was said of *One Day* at the time of its publication that it depicted Shukhov in one-to-one combat with Stalin, in which, on the moral level, Shukhov won. For some years, Solzhenitsyn, who in reality was no simple peasant at all, appeared to a mass public as another Shukhov standing up for them against the authorities. The rough clothing and simple lifestyle he preferred worked to his advantage. And the slanderous mud (lies about his family, his racial origins, his school days, his war record, his behavior on being arrested and in prison, the supposed luxury and sexual permissiveness of his life now that he was famous, etc.) which the authorities slung at him took longer to stick than with most other intellectuals whom they sought to discredit. Nevertheless there is evidence that, at the time of his expulsion in 1974, a majority of people "on the street" had eventually come to view him as a traitor to his country.[60]

The issues of power associated with *samizdat* are quite complex. The works first circulated in *samizdat* in the late 1950s had been the writings of earlier Russian authors like Bulgakov and Mandelstam which had attracted official disfavor and been banned. By the early 1960s, a few works by Western authors and some controversial new works by Soviet writers had been added to the list and the *samizdat* phenomenon had become semirespectable, in the sense that most intellectuals, including Party members, had *samizdat* copies of certain works in their possession, and no attempt was made by the authorities to root out the practice. It represented an illegal, somewhat subversive, but more or less tolerated, means of circulating alternative ideas. The proportion of the reading population it reached was inevitably tiny, but among that group it had the significance of forbidden fruit (as opposed to the "canned fruit" of works which had been through the censorship process).

Another type of subversion, the publication abroad of works by living Russian authors which had not been approved for publication in the Soviet Union, was regarded with much greater hostility by the authorities. The authors, if they could be traced, were savagely persecuted, whether the work itself merely seemed somewhat nostalgic for prerevolutionary life (as was the case with *Doctor Zhivago*) or attacked, by satire or direct polemic, some aspect of the Soviet system. Mikhail Naritsa found himself committed to a mental asylum for three years for allowing *Unsung Song* to be published in Frankfurt in 1960 under a pseudonym. Yuli Daniel and Andrei Sinyavsky were publishing work in the West in the same period but their identity was not traced until 1965, when they were arrested, tried and convicted. The significance of the publication abroad of such works was threefold. In the first place, their influence was considerable on Western intellectuals, especially those on the Left who were regarded by the Soviet regime as their best public relations agents in the West. (Solzhenitsyn was scathing about what he saw as the selective blindness of intellectuals like Jean-Paul Sartre who highlighted human rights abuses in Greece while ignoring them in the Soviet Union.)[61] The reception of such works in the West was subsequently reflected back to the Soviet Union by Western radio broadcasts, whose importance to Soviet intellectuals grew during the 1960s and early 1970s. After about 1972, the publication of works by Soviet authors exposing human rights abuses — and the way in which the Soviet authorities treated those authors — led to repercussions on the policy of détente which President Nixon was pursuing. Unauthorized publication abroad was regarded by the authorities as akin to revealing state secrets to an enemy.

Solzhenitsyn was opposed to both *samizdat* circulation of his works and foreign publication (referring to Sinyavsky and Daniel's choice of the latter as "literary schizophrenia")[62] as long as he saw any hope of their being published at home. He first slid towards *samizdat* out of fear that all copies of a manuscript might be seized and destroyed by the KGB. Thus he secretly deposited copies at the houses of several friends in different cities. In this way his works came to be read by more than just the people to whom he entrusted them. He first committed himself to *samizdat* proper in 1964, more or less in a fit of pique, when his *Miniature Stories* (a series of very brief sketches, almost prose poems) were turned down by *Novy Mir*. This soon turned out also to be his first (unintentional) venture into unauthorized foreign publication, as an émigré magazine in Frankfurt, *Grani*, got hold of a copy and published it without his permission. Such an occurrence was made more likely both by the Soviet Union's refusal to sign world copyright agreements and the existence of émigré organizations hostile to the Soviet regime eager to publish works which they regarded as damaging to it. Publication of *Miniature Stories* abroad not only provoked hostility from the authorities but antagonized Tvardovsky, who felt personally betrayed.

The first manuscript he deliberately sent abroad was that of *The First Circle*, just after Khrushchev's fall in 1964 and, again it seems, primarily to safeguard it against destruction, rather than seeking publication.

To publish a work abroad first was to guarantee that it would not be accepted for publication in the Soviet Union. Only in 1968, when all hope of such publication had evaporated, did he finally complete negotiations for its foreign publication. It was also in 1968 that the KGB, not knowing what Solzhenitsyn was planning with *The First Circle*, took the extraordinary step of sending a typescript of *Cancer Ward* to the West, wanting it to be published without Solzhenitsyn's consent to prevent *Novy Mir* (or anyone else) from publishing it in the Soviet Union. Conversely, when there had been a rumor the previous year that the same novel was about to be published in London without his approval, some of the editors of *Novy Mir* were able to use this as an argument in favor of *their* committing themselves to immediate publication, though this did not, in fact, eventuate.[63] (This illustrates again how the mechanisms of power, oppressive or not, operate indirectly even in the most authoritarian state.) Another twist in the labyrinth is to be found in the debate which occurred among sympathetic western intellectuals about whether foreign publication would help or harm the author. As an American specialist on Soviet literature, Katherine Feuer, declared: "How tragic if, accustomed to operating in a free society, [western publishers] have misjudged the situation and are playing into the hands of Solzhenitsyn's enemies, while thinking to serve freedom and literature."[64] It was widely feared that publication would lead to Solzhenitsyn's arrest and even, perhaps, his death. Solzhenitsyn has always claimed that he did not authorize publication: "*Cancer Ward* was precisely the book I had never tried to pass to the West. I had had offers, there were ways, but somehow I had always refused without really knowing why," he wrote in 1971.[65] Michael Scammell argues that it is highly likely that he did in fact give his permission.[66] Nevertheless, he had to make it seem that publication had occurred against his wishes.

"You are, needless to say, not against Soviet rule"

Solzhenitsyn has tended to attribute his success in resisting harassment by the Soviet authorities over the period 1964 to 1974 primarily to his switching from a defensive to an offensive posture, whereby, rather than keeping silent about his works and avoiding interviews, he would fire off letters to newspapers or the Writers' Union or make speeches, always ensuring a hundred or more further copies were distributed in *samizdat* so that his words would not simply be ignored and lost. He would certainly have been influenced in this by the example of another writer,

Valeri Tarsis, who had published two stories, "The Bluebottle" and "Red and Black," abroad in 1962. Instead of concealing his identity, Tarsis publicly claimed authorship of his work and challenged the KGB either to bring him to trial or have him "accidentally" killed. Judging rightly that, in either case, the uproar in the West would be too great, he remained free for another year, at which time the authorities permitted him to emigrate. While there is a good deal of truth in Solzhenitsyn's claim about attack being the best form of defense, other features both of his literary works and of his other utterances in this period contributed greatly to reducing his vulnerability.

With extraordinary consistency, Solzhenitsyn retained, in *The First Circle*, *Cancer Ward*, and his public statements through, at the least 1970, considerable ambiguity about the degree of his opposition to the Soviet regime. Certainly his focus on the evils of the Stalin era, and the labor camps in particular, was sufficient to provoke the greatest hostility in the leadership and the dominant faction within the Party, but he continued to give liberals in the Party the impression that he was criticizing the system from a socialist position, attacking it for its failure to fully implement Leninist principles, when, as the private letter he wrote to Andrei Sakharov in 1969 makes clear, he had come to believe that Stalinism was implicit in Leninism.[67] Though, by the mid-1960s, he had undoubtedly become cynical about the whole Soviet experiment, he continued to impress old associates within the Party like Tvardovsky with the sense that he was one of them. Tvardovsky and some other members of the editorial board of *Novy Mir* considered both *The First Circle* and *Cancer Ward* for publication between 1964 and 1968, attempting to gain agreement with Solzhenitsyn on the removal of episodes that caused them concern, and with hostile figures in the bureaucracy to have the novels accepted. It was only after long delays and a great deal of effort on their part that, as the political climate became more and more hostile, Tvardovsky accepted defeat. When, in 1966, the board of *Novy Mir* was discussing with Solzhenitsyn the changes its members believed would have to be made to the text of *Cancer Ward* to make its publication possible, Tvardovsky declared: "No one is asking you to make concessions on matters of principle. You are, needless to say, not against Soviet rule, or else we should not even be talking to you!"[68] Although, to many readers of *Cancer Ward* in the West and to a proportion of those in the Soviet Union who came to read it in *samizdat*, it seemed crystal-clear that cancer was a metaphor for socialism itself, Solzhenitsyn could convincingly dismiss the suggestion, as he did at a branch meeting of the Writers' Union in late 1966: "Some speakers have said that there was a cancerous growth in our society. Yes, there was. But that wasn't what I had in mind. When I called the book *Cancer Ward*, it was the sickness I had in mind, and the struggle against this sickness. ... That was why I quite calmly employed this title, that and no more."[69] It is sometimes expedient for a novelist to make only rather modest claims for a fictional work which may in reality insinuate a more grandly subversive significance into the minds of at least some of its readers.

The comments of Lukács in his 1969 essay on Solzhenitsyn are particularly interesting in this regard. The great critic had, to be sure, distanced himself from the Soviet leadership over many issues, most notably the invasion of Czechoslovakia, by this point — otherwise he would not have been writing appreciatively about the newly published *The First Circle* and *Cancer Ward*— but he was no less of a socialist for that. While Lukács perceived some limitations to Solzhenitsyn's commitment to communism (he "criticizes the Stalinist period from a plebeian and not from a communist point of view"),[70] he had no difficulty in seeing his novels as having brought about "the re-birth of socialist realism and its new growth into a significant world literature."[71] In particular, he defended Solzhenitsyn against "persistent opponents" who "read into his works far-fetched political ideas" and "compare his novels with the biased and ignorant politically intended babble of Stalin's daughter" declaring that "their criticism can readily be rejected as slander."[72]

The open letters Solzhenitsyn specialized in between 1966 and 1969 likewise maintained a certain reserve in their attacks on the regime, implying that it failed to live up to socialist ideals, that it was opposing him without justification and that his critical position was from within socialism. This involved a certain duplicity on his part, which he only dropped once he was in exile.

Political ambiguity of a rather different kind served as a further source of protection to Solzhenitsyn during the late 1960s and early 1970s. This concerned his attitude to the West. Unlike many dissidents of the period, his resistance to the attractions of capitalism and Western-style democratic government was real and ran very deep. As he expressed it in a section of the *The Oak and the Calf* written in 1967, but not, at that time, intended for publication: "I put no hopes in the West — indeed, no Russian ever should. If we ever become free it will only be by our own efforts. If the twentieth century has any lesson for mankind, it is we who will teach the West, not the West us. Excessive ease and prosperity have weakened their will and their reason."[73]

He had no great interest in politics and culture outside the Soviet Union except in that they impinged on his own country and knew rather little about foreign literature. He allowed his anti-Western sentiments to emerge in ways and to degrees which satisfied not only liberal members of the Party in his own country but intellectuals on the Left in the West. So, for instance, in a letter to foreign publishers in 1968 he was specifically disparaging about what he saw as the poor quality of the translations of *One Day* which he ascribed to twin motives, typical of the West: greed and the desire for a propaganda advantage.[74] At the same time, his distance from Western values made the support he received from Western intellectuals and media outlets of many political colors all the more telling.

Solzhenitsyn and the dissident movement

Solzhenitsyn has been criticized, and I believe justly so, for another feature of his strategy in these years: the distance he kept from the emerging dissident movement. I have referred already to his disagreements with Sakharov in the late 1960s. As author of *One Day* and, subsequently, in asserting publicly his inalienable right to publish *Cancer Ward* and *The First Circle*, he had perhaps done more than anyone to open up the space in which the Democratic Movement (or Human Rights Movement) came into existence, yet, for various reasons, he refused to ally himself with the emerging dissident group. The immediate origins of the Democratic Movement are to be found in the demonstration by two hundred people in December 1965, demanding an open trial for Daniel and Synyavsky. Solzhenitsyn did not participate in the demonstration and, though he followed the trial avidly, he apparently begrudged the amount of publicity given to the trial by Western media, feeling that it distracted attention from the KGB's confiscation of his manuscript of *The First Circle*.[75] Most significantly, he refused to sign the letter protesting the imprisonment of Daniel and Synyavsky, which was addressed to the Twenty-Third Congress of the Communist Party in 1966 by sixty-three Moscow writers. Solzhenitsyn told the signatories that he disapproved of writers who sought fame abroad. When Natalia Gorbanevskaya, Pavel Litvinov and others published, unofficially, in April 1968, the first issue of their *Chronicle of Current Events*, detailing infringements of human rights by the authorities and the attempts to resist them by groups and individuals, Solzhenitsyn, again, made contact with them, but avoided joining them, partly because they were admirers of of the Czech reform movement and saw democratic communism of that type as the model to follow in the Soviet Union. The reason he gave for not joining the Democratic Movement was that, in his view, many of its members were slavishly attached to Western ideas. When the Soviet Union invaded Czechoslovakia in August 1968, he was deeply shocked, contemplated circulating a public statement deploring it, but eventually refrained. He consistently refused to join in collective letter-writing or to fight on any grounds but his own. After being awarded the Nobel Prize in 1970, he did accept Sakharov's pressing invitation to join the Committee for Human Rights, but appears soon to have regretted the move and took very little part in its activities. One must conclude that, out of an excessive concern for his personal independence and his role as a creative writer, Solzhenitsyn missed the opportunity to play the part he might have played in the movement which was to become the great progressive force in the Soviet Union throughout the 1970s and early 1980s.

The Nobel Prize

The power plays surrounding the awarding of the Nobel Prize to Solzhenitsyn were, likewise, quite complex. Solzhenitsyn took the unusual step, for an eventual prizewinner, of campaigning vigorously on his own behalf throughout 1970, seeing it not only as his due, but as a lever he could use in his struggle with the regime. (He had, apparently, been in contention for it in 1969.) The Nobel Committee had played an inconsistent game in its relations with the Soviet government over the previous decade or so, firmly antagonizing it in 1958 with the award to Pasternak but offering a feeble pacifying gesture in 1965 by awarding the Prize to Mikhail Sholokhov (author — though doubts were later cast even on that — of *Quiet Flows the Don*) whose main work had been produced more than thirty years before and who had taken on the role of Party hack in his later years. By the late 1960s, Solzhenitsyn had made full use of publication in the West, despite his previous disapproval of other writers who sought this route, and would hardly have been eligible for the prize if he had not done so. The Nobel Committee was acknowledging the greatness of all his published works, from *One Day* to *Cancer Ward*, in the context of the obstacles raised to publication by the authorities of his own country. It was not primarily playing power-politics as it had done in the case of Pasternak (whose novel was not of the caliber of his less controversial poetry) and, in a contrary way, Sholokhov. It became clear, at the time of the Nobel ceremony, that the committee (and the Swedish government) were bending over backward not to offer a platform to anti-Soviet statements. Therefore, the last sentence of Solzhenitsyn's letter explaining his absence was not read out ("let none at this festive table forget that political prisoners are on hunger-strike this very day in defence of rights that have been curtailed or trampled underfoot"),[76] an exhibition of his works set up near the ceremony was removed and, when he declined to attend, the committee refused to make the award to him in a public ceremony in Moscow. The prize naturally increased both the difficulty for the Soviet authorities in attempting to silence him and the likelihood of his eventual expulsion. Indeed, his main reason for not attempting to attend the ceremony was not so much that he did not believe the authorities would allow it, but that, once out of the country, he feared he would not be allowed back in. (A personal factor in this was his relationship with a new partner, Natalia Svetlova, later to be his wife, and his recent discovery that she was pregnant.) The award of the prize had two effects: it provoked the Soviet authorities into a knee-jerk denigration of the prize-winner, which made them look foolish, and it also gave Western governments an opportunity to seek to appropriate the value of his work, whether he liked it or not.

Solzhenitsyn's Nobel lecture, which came out in early 1972, gave him the opportunity to express in a concise, generalized form (rather than a merely topical, propagandist way) his ideas about the social and political functions of literature. This statement of his conception of literature, with its insistence on the truthfulness of literature, its capacity to defeat the lies of history and conventional wisdom and to convey the concentrated experience of one people, without distortion, to another, who may thereby avoid making the same errors, appears at first sight extraordinarily old-fashioned, an anachronism in the second half of the twentieth century. On the other hand, it must be recognized not only that Solzhenitsyn's own work (including, most notably of all perhaps, his then unpublished *The Gulag Archipelago*) can be said to have done just what he claimed, but that, on the theoretical level, his statement corresponds extraordinarily closely to Barthes's claim, which I referred to earlier, that literature has the capacity to evade power. The evidently archaic quality of Solzhenitsyn's thought curiously intersects with the apparently innovative quality in

Barthes's. At the same time, it should be acknowledged that, by the early 1970s, the dissidents within the Democratic Movement could reasonably have made equally grand claims for the power of their forms of nonliterary truthfulness as Solzhenitsyn did for literature.

Expulsion and exile

Solzhenitsyn had known for five or six years before his expulsion from his homeland in 1974 that such an outcome was likely. Whereas some dissidents, who had a strong attachment to the West, actually looked forward to expulsion, it was, for him, one of the severest punishments imaginable. At the same time, it was in a curious sense a victory, an indication of the size of the threat the Soviet leadership saw him as posing to them and of their impotence to silence him or dispose of him in an even more brutal way.

The immediate origins of the expulsion lay in the publication of the first volume of *The Gulag Archipelago,* in Paris, in the final days of 1973. He had contemplated its publication on several occasions since 1969, but delays in getting it translated and political circumstances had, each time, convinced him to delay publication abroad even in Russian. Harassment of Solzhenitsyn and his associates had been growing in strength since the publication abroad in 1971 of his novel, *August 1914*. At the beginning of 1972, a new tactic against Solzhenitsyn was used for the first time: the sponsoring by the Soviet authorities of supposedly independent articles written by foreign journalists (German and Finnish) who purported to find in Solzhenitsyn's wealthy pre-Revolution ancestry an explanation for his supposed lifelong hostility to the Soviet system and to show that *August 1914* should be read as an allegorical depiction of the Nazi-Soviet conflict of thirty years later, in which the author's sympathies were wholly with German discipline and against Russian inefficiency. Throughout 1972 and 1973, however, official harassment of Solzhenitsyn (and of Andrei Sakharov also) was constrained by the desire to pursue détente, which was dependent on the Soviet Union's not being seen to take its persecution of world-renowned figures beyond a certain point. However, in September 1973, covert activities against Solzhenitsyn reached a new peak. The KGB picked up a former secretary to Solzhenitsyn, Elizaveta Voronskaya, who, under the greatest duress, revealed the whereabouts of a buried copy of *The Gulag Archipelago.* (She died shortly afterward, almost certainly by suicide.) In great agitation and distress, Solzhenitsyn gave instructions for the book to be published abroad in Russian as soon as possible.

The Gulag Archipelago is different from all of Solzhenitsyn's preceding work not only in that it depicts (in its full version) the labor-camp system in a closely documented, factual (though still clearly literary) manner over the whole period from 1918 to the time of his writing it, but despite his authorship it is a visibly *collective* work, containing testimony from over two hundred former prisoners. The imaginatively oblique, the apparently localized qualities of his fictional works from *One Day* to *The First Circle* are cast off, for a full frontal assault on one of the most brutal continuing features of the Soviet system. The reader cannot but see in *The Gulag Archipelago* a devastating critique of the whole Soviet system from Lenin to Brezhnev.

It took less than two months, until mid-February 1974, for the Soviet authorities to decide to expel him. In so doing, they represented him to the Soviet public as a traitor to his country who was being handed over to his supposed foreign employers. It appears that this propaganda, strikingly inaccurate since Solzhenitsyn had few affinities with capitalism as an economic system, with liberal democracy as a political system, or even with Western literary culture, was widely believed in the Soviet Union. Only a tiny number of intellectuals had read, in *samizdat* his fictional and other works since *One Day*; the mass of the population did not have sufficient evidence for disbelieving the official view. The mass support which Solzhenitsyn had maintained through much of the 1960s had eventually been eroded by the continuous trickle of hostile publicity which the official media had been releasing over the twelve years since the publication of *One Day*.

Given that his removal to the West was not something he had sought, it can be viewed as the last major hostile act, the last great act of oppressive power against him by the Soviet authorities. At the same time, of course, it was an admission of their inability either to tolerate or to control his ongoing presence within the country, an admission of his power to defy them. And in a further paradox, while it granted *him* a greater freedom than he had ever previously had to express his views, in certain respects it removed his capacity to irritate (whether as tumor or as pearl!) within the body of his own nation. In the minds of his readers and listeners outside the Soviet Union (and the few inside) there would be, from this point onward, a reduced urgency, a duller edge to his words, precisely because, in writing and speaking, he was no longer putting his life at risk.

There is a degree to which the Soviet authorities succeeded in marginalizing him as a voice of protest by expelling him. And, as Solzhenitsyn would soon discover, the direct political influence of the creative writer in relatively open societies is far less than in many closed societies.

In terms of international relations, the moment of Solzhenitsyn's expulsion was quite a delicate one. Negotiations on détente between the Soviet Union and the United States were coming to their conclusion and it seemed for a while that public outrage in the West over the human rights issues surrounding the expulsion might make it too difficult for the United States to sign. There was considerable debate about the extent to which détente implied not only a reduction in the risk of nuclear war but a tolerance of human rights abuses in the Soviet Union. It quickly became evident, however, that Nixon and Kissinger were as anxious as the Soviet leadership that the Solzhenitsyn issue should not get in the way of their impending visit to Moscow to sign the agreement with Brezhnev. "Our human, moral and critical concern for Mr Solzhenitsyn and people of similar convictions should [not] affect the day-to-day conduct of our foreign policy," Kissinger is reported as saying the day the writer was expelled.[77] And so détente was not interrupted.

Commentator in exile

The story of Solzhenitsyn's engagement with world political changes from the time of his expulsion in 1974 to the present is, in a sense, rather anti-climactic. While several of the things he had longed to see in the Soviet Union — including the collapse of the communist system, growing Russian nationalism, and increasing interest in religion — have indeed come about, he did not accurately predict the way in which they were to occur, nor, for the moment at least, does it appear likely that they will deliver the benefits which he hoped for.

Solzhenitsyn's greatest influence over this period remains linked to the publication in translation between 1974 and 1978 of the three volumes of *The Gulag Archipelago*, which is widely agreed to have played a major part not only in discrediting the Soviet system among Western liberals but in undermining support for the communist parties of France and Italy. It conveyed, more comprehensively than any other text, historical or fictional, the enormity of the offenses against humanity committed in the Soviet Union, with greater or lesser intensity, continuously throughout all the years since 1917. Moreover, in *The Gulag Archipelago* and in interviews and articles through the mid-1970s, Solzhenitsyn rightly reminded the West of its direct complicity in certain moments of those atrocities, including its (particularly Britain's) compliance with the Soviet Union's demand at the end of the Second World War that between one and two million Russians and Ukrainians living in Germany, Austria, and Yugoslavia be returned to the Soviet Union to face certain persecution. He was considerably less effective (though perhaps no less accurate) in pointing out, in the period immediately after his arrival in the West, the morally dubious grounds on which détente was occurring, and especially the willingness of Western governments, for short-term political reasons, to play down the most oppressive actions of the current Soviet leadership. Salutary, too, were his observations to Western intellectuals on the left of the inconsistency with which they condemned oppression in Spain under Franco or Chile under Pinochet while, frequently, remaining silent about the vastly greater oppressions of the Soviet system. A dramatic (though hardly typical!) indication of his occasional persuasive force was the resignation from the British Labour Party of the former Foreign Secretary George Brown in 1976 following an interview for British television in which Solzhenitsyn attacked that party for the moral inconsistencies of its former policies toward the Soviet Union.[78]

To Solzhenitsyn's credit, he has been scrupulous in exile in avoiding the temptation (not very strong given his independent nature!) to accept the traditionally polarized nature of the debate about the relation between the Soviet Union and the West. His rejection of the Soviet system has not meant an enthusiastic embracing of capitalism and the American version of democracy. He has been as willing to underline the decadence and corruption of life in the West as he ever was to point to the inhumanities of Soviet life. He has also remained consistent, since his *Letter to the Soviet Leaders* of 1974, in his skepticism about the capacity of revolution of any color to fulfill the hopes of its idealistic supporters.

Nevertheless there are numerous respects in which Solzhenitsyn has proved himself, once the constraints on his freedom of expression were removed, to be an unreliable and, eventually, an ineffective commentator on world affairs. There have even been occasions when it has seemed that the Soviet authorities might after all have been rather astute in expelling him, since his political influence has diminished as readers, both in the West and in the Soviet Union, have come to know what he really thinks on many issues (though, in 1978, the historian of Russian literature, Deming Brown, made the point that "it is quite possible that Solzhenitsyn's voice is now heard more extensively in his native land than before his departure, through clandestine circulation of foreign editions of his works and through foreign radio broadcasts of his views.")[79] His capacity to alienate actual and potential supporters has been remarkable.

In the first place, in his memoir of the period 1962 to 1974, *The Oak and the Calf*, first published in translation in 1979, and in interviews and writings since, he has shown a most unfortunate tendency to promote an image of himself as the only serious battler against oppression in the Soviet Union, consistently disparaging other Soviet intellectuals. Tvardovsky is depicted as a drunk and a coward and given no credit for his personal courage in pushing back the limits of what could be published during the 1960s. Voluntary exiles are heavily criticized and many former friends of Solzhenitsyn, who risked so much to help him, are attacked for one supposed weakness or another. Most seriously, perhaps, the influence of intellectuals who worked by other means than his, especially in the Democratic Movement, is seriously undervalued. Not surprisingly, Solzhenitsyn antagonized many dissidents remaining in the Soviet Union and their supporters in the West. It was by a rather similar process, his repeated accusation that historians of the Soviet Union in the West were uniformly submissive to Soviet propaganda, that he invited attack from another group of potential allies.

Equally unfortunate, on another level, has been his willingness to pontificate on matters about which he is inadequately informed. Not only the barriers of censorship in the Soviet Union but personal inclination had greatly limited his knowledge of Western history and culture. These limitations have become only too obvious in the inaccuracies which have peppered his many pronouncements on the moral and political state of the West.

Eventually, however, it is the inaccuracy of his broad vision of world affairs that has become so evident. The key document here is his *Letter to the Soviet Leaders* of 1974.[80] In it he referred to the West as being "on its knees," in a state of political and moral collapse, daily conceding ground to a Soviet Union which was "at the peak of staggering successes" and in a period of major expansion. There is a curious sense in which Solzhenitsyn seems to have been deluded by the very Soviet propaganda toward which he showed such skepticism. He has regularly underestimated, on the one hand, the extreme fragility of the Soviet economy and political system, and on the other hand, the infinite adaptability of capitalism, its capacity to alter its form and location, the near-global penetration of the multinationals and the stylistic diversity of political systems associated with capitalism, from the North American (which he despises) to the Swiss (which he admires). He is also blind to the roles played by countries in the Third World in the evolution of international power relations. He has propagated an apocalyptic vision of relations between the West and the Soviet Union which has, in the long run, neither attracted many followers nor been confirmed by events. To quote Deming Brown again, "whereas his literary work is tempered by robust mental health and freedom from neurosis, a sense of measure, and intellectual humility ... the same cannot be said ... of his recent speeches and articles in the West, which, to many observers, seem didactic to the point of arrogance."[81] For many commentators, the moment when, in 1987, after more than a decade of diatribes about the corruption and decadence of the West, Solzhenitsyn chose to send his son Ermolai to the exclusive British school, Eton, confirmed their worst suspicions.

Solzhenitsyn has turned out to be, like many creative writers who have taken up a political position before him, infinitely less persuasive at proposing political arrangements for the future than at opposing the status quo. Just as Harriet Beecher Stowe fell into recommending the dispatch of former slaves to Liberia, so Solzhenitsyn has promoted formulae for the revival of Russia which appear to almost all commentators to be irretrievably reactionary, in fact very much like a Slavophile of the 1850s. He increasingly demonstrates a nostalgia not just for pre-Revolutionary Russia but for the period before the schism which took place in the Orthodox Church in the seventeenth century! (Similarly, he blames all the ills that he perceives in the West on the secular rationalism which he sees as having come to dominate Western thought in the Renaissance and Enlightenment.)[82] His most optimistic vision of Russia's future is of a theocentric state, curiously both authoritarian and decentralized on the model of the Soviets of the 1920s. On the basis of personal taste, rather than the ecological vision of an environmentalist or the political vision of an anarchist, he advocates that Russians abandon material progress, the use of cars, the development of heavy industry, for the development of small-scale, rural communities in its remoter territories. On different occasions he has referred to Swiss-style direct democracy and the Israeli religious state[83] as models for the Russia of the future, without apparently noticing the intimate dependence of both nations on capitalism and the Western powers for their prosperity (on the one hand) and survival (on the other). Unkind (but not entirely unfair) critics have referred to him as "the Russian Ayatollah."[84]

There are several different ways in which it would be possible to account for the anticlimactic role of Solzhenitsyn as a political commentator in exile. In the first place, the fact that he is longer required, as he was when he was still living in the Soviet Union, to duck and weave, in constant fear for his own life, to choose his moment for striking unexpected blows against the monolithic regime, has greatly reduced the gladiatorial appeal of his writings and statements. Secondly, the point has been well made by Ilya Zilberberg, another writer born in the Soviet Union, who left (under different circumstances) in 1971, that, while Solzhenitsyn served as a wonderful teacher to the younger generation in the Soviet Union, paving the way for the Democratic Movement, for instance, through his struggles and writings, he was nevertheless tragically infected by the system against which he fought: "You have liberated us representatives of 'the present' more quickly and successfully than you have liberated yourself."[85] Eventually, however, one returns to the observation already made in relation to Balzac, that political narrative and political analysis are such different activities, and one must conclude that Solzhenitsyn is enormously gifted in the former and not in the latter.

The influence of *One Day*

Thirty years after the publication of *One Day*, it is evident that it was the novel's special qualities, in particular the apparent simplicity and limited scope of the story, which made it, on the one hand, so superficially attractive as a political weapon to Khrushchev and, on the other, capable of reaching such a vast audience in the Soviet Union. Once it had reached that audience, its productive force as a critique of the Soviet system past and present unfolded in dramatic fashion. Had it not been published in his own country and with acclaim from the nation's leadership, Solzhenitsyn would never have gained the public prominence and respect in the Soviet Union which then made it possible for him to increase the range and sharpness of his criticisms of the Soviet system with relative impunity for more than ten years. The authorized publication of *One Day* was the foundation on which the whole of his subsequent career and political influence was based. Indeed, it was because they had read *One Day* that hundreds of ex-prisoners wrote to him with the testimonies which constituted the raw material for *The Gulag Archipelago*. If now one feels disappointment that Solzhenitsyn's direct comments on world politics are of less value than those of a host of other commentators, it is essential not to underplay the long-term importance of the seventy-page story which "burst upon the Soviet reader like a shot in the night" in 1962. With *One Day in the Life of Ivan Denisovich* Solzhenitsyn opened a cupboard jam-packed with items which the Soviet authorities would rather have left unseen and, as happens with such cupboards, once the door has been opened, however briefly, and the objects start to tumble out, it can never be quite forced shut again.

NOTES TO CHAPTER 5

1. Recorded by Ilya Zilberberg, "A Necessary Talk with Solzhenitsyn," published in Russian in England in 1976, quoted by Michael Scammell, *Solzhenitsyn: A Biography* (London, Melbourne, Sydney, Auckland, Johannesburg: Hutchinson, 1985): 400. Scammell's monumental work is a fundamental source for any study of Solzhenitsyn.
2. Scammell, *Solzhenitsyn*: 450.
3. *Solzhenitsyn: A Documentary Record*, ed. Leopold Labedz (London: Allen Lane, 1970): 15-16.
4. David Burg and George Feifer, *Solzhenitsyn* (New York: Stein and Day, 1972): 218.
5. Quoted in, for instance, Kochan and Abraham, *The Making of Modern Russia*: 447.
6. I have used the current Penguin edition of the text in English translation by Ralph Parker (first published, London: Gollancz, 1963) throughout. A second translation, by Max Hayward and Ronald Hingley, was published at just about the same time (New York: Praeger, 1963) and has achieved comparable circulation. While some Russian specialists prefer the translation by Hayward and Hingley as conveying better the strong, sometimes crude, flavor of the original (see, for instance, Leonard Schapiro's review "Bent Backs," *New Statesman*, 1 February 1963: 158), others, including Scammell, see little to choose between them. The most recent English version, translated by Harry Willetts (London: Harvill, 1991), includes a number of harsher passages and phrases which Solzhenitsyn removed before publication in 1962, either of his own volition or at the request of Tvardovsky. While it is the version now authorized by Solzhenitsyn, it did not seem appropriate to use it for my purpose, since it is not the form in which *One Day* actually engaged with public reality in the 1960s.
7. For detailed discussion of the work's narrative strategies, see Vladimir J. Rus, "*One Day in the Life of Ivan Denisovich*: A Point of View Analysis," *Canadian Slavonic Papers* 13, no. 2-3 (1971): 165-178; and Richard Luplow, "Narrative Style and Structure in *One Day in the Life of Ivan Denisovich*," *Russian Literature Triquarterly* 1, (Fall 1971): 339-412.
8. Scammell, *Solzhenitsyn*: 406.
9. Scammell, *Solzhenitsyn*: 407.
10. Zhores Medvedev, *Ten Years after Ivan Denisovich*, trans. Hilary Sternberg (London: Macmillan, 1973): 9.

11. Scammell, *Solzhenitsyn*: 435.
12. Peter Benno, "The Political Aspect," in *Soviet Literature in the Sixties*, ed. Max Hayward and Edward L. Crowley (London: Methuen, 1965): 191.
13. Benno, "The Political Aspect": 191.
14. Philip Rahv's review, "House of the Dead?" *New York Review of Books* 1, no. 1 (1963): 4.
15. Priscilla Johnson, *Khrushchev and the Arts: The Politics of Soviet Culture, 1962-1964* (Cambridge, Mass.: M.I.T. Press): 6.
16. See Scammell, *Solzhenitsyn*: 436 and Medvedev, *Ten Years after Ivan Denisovich*: 17.
17. Johnson, *Khrushchev and the Arts*: 8 and Scammell, *Solzhenitsyn*: 460.
18. Johnson, *Khrushchev and the Arts*: 102-3.
19. Solzhenitsyn, *One Word of Truth*: 15.
20. Heer, *Politics and History in the Soviet Union*: 138.
21. Heer, *Politics and History in the Soviet Union*: vii.
22. Quoted by David Remnick, *New York Review of Books*, 19 December 1991.
23. The full text, in a translation by George Reavey, is to be found in Johnson, *Khrushchev and the Arts*: 93-95.
24. Heer, *Politics and History in the Soviet Union*: 141.
25. György Lukács, *Solzhenitsyn*, trans. William David Graf (London: Merlin Press, 1970): 33.
26. Solzhenitsyn, *The Oak and the Calf: Sketches of Literary Life in the Soviet Union*, trans. Harry Willetts (New York: Harper and Row, 1980): 11.
27. Scammell, *Solzhenitsyn*: 452.
28. Lukács, *Solzhenitsyn*: 13. See also Abraham Rothberg, *Alekzandr Solzhenitsyn: The Major Novels* (Ithaca and London, Cornell University Press, 1971): 57.
29. Peter Viereck makes the important point that Khrushchev's initiative in authorizing publication takes its place in a long history of "pendularity" in Soviet cultural policy ("The Mob within the Heart" in *Soviet Policy-Making: Studies of Communism in Transition*, ed. Peter H. Juviler and Henry W. Morton (New York: Praeger, 1967): 83-120. He and the editors of the volume in which his essay appears distinguish *eleven* phases between 1917 and 1965 in which permissiveness and oppression in the handling of cultural works alternated.
30. An account of how this story, by Georgi Shelest, came to be published is to be found in Scammell, *Solzhenitsyn*: 441.
31. For a translation of the text of this Preface see Labedz, *Solzhenitsyn*: 9-10.
32. *Trud*, 12 December 1962. See Christopher Moody, *Solzhenitsyn* (Edinburgh: Oliver and Boyd, 1973): 12.
33. *Pravda*, 23 November 1962. See Labedz, *Solzhenitsyn*: 12.
34. *Izvestia*, 18 November 1962. See Labedz, *Solzhenitsyn*: 11.
35. Labedz, *Solzhenitsyn*: 10.
36. Scammell, *Solzhenitsyn*: 448.
37. Labedz, *Solzhenitsyn*: 11.

38. Heer, *Politics and History in the Soviet Union*: 139.
39. See Paul N. Siegel, "The Political Implications of Solzhenitsyn's Novels," *Clio* 112, no. 3 (1983): 211-232 for a discussion of the shift of political position visible even between *The First Circle* and *August 1914*.
40. Max Hayward, *Writers in Russia: 1917-1978* (San Diego, New York, London: Harcourt Brace Jovanovich, 1983): 71.
41. Scammell, *Solzhenitsyn*: 430.
42. Solzhenitsyn, *The Oak and the Calf*: 50-51.
43. George Gibian, "The Russian Theme in Solzhenitsyn," in *Russian Literature and American Critics*, ed. Kenneth N. Brostrom (Michigan: Ann Arbor, 1984): 55-73.
44. The Parker translation suffers more from this kind of flatness than the Hayward and Hingley translation. For discussion of the richness and inventiveness of Solzhenitsyn's language see F. D. Reeve, "The House of the Living," *Kenyon Review* 25 (1963): 356-360 and, for detailed illustration of the point, see Vera V. Carpovich, *Solzhenitsyn's Peculiar Vocabulary: Russian-English Glossary* (New York: Technical Dictionaries, 1976).
45. James M. Curtis, *Solzhenitsyn's Traditional Imagination* (Athens, Georgia: University of Georgia Press, 1984): 42-46.
46. Labedz, *Solzhenitsyn*: 17.
47. Labedz, *Solzhenitsyn*: 16.
48. Kochan and Abraham, *The Making of Modern Russia*: 449.
49. Labedz, *Solzhenitsyn*: 17.
50. Scammell, *Solzhenitsyn*: 466.
51. Labedz, *Solzhenitsyn*: 18.
52. Labedz, *Solzhenitsyn*: 19.
53. Labedz, *Solzhenitsyn*: 16.
54. Labedz, *Solzhenitsyn*: 17.
55. Solzhenitsyn, *The Oak and the Calf*: 86-87.
56. Labedz, *Solzhenitsyn*: 21.
57. Labedz, *Solzhenitsyn*: 21.
58. Scammell, *Solzhenitsyn*: 467.
59. Scammell, *Solzhenitsyn*: 494. For documentation of the process by which exclusion from *One Day* from the short list was engineered, see Johnson, *Khrushchev and the Arts*: 70-78, 271-288.
60. Scammell refers to interviews with workers on the streets of Moscow carried by Soviet television which demonstrate as much, *Solzhenitsyn*: 860.
61. Solzhenitsyn, *The Oak and the Calf*: 149.
62. Solzhenitsyn, *The Oak and the Calf*: 128.
63. Solzhenitsyn, *The Oak and the Calf*: 196-197.
64. *Time*, 27 September 1968.
65. Solzhenitsyn, *The Oak and the Calf*: 204.
66. Scammell, *Solzhenitsyn*: 626.

67. Solzhenitsyn, "As Breathing and Consciousness Return," in Solzhenitsyn et al., *From Under the Rubble*, trans. A. M. Brock et al. (London: Collins and Harvill, 1975): 3-25.
68. Solzhenitsyn, *The Oak and the Calf*: 134.
69. Scammell, *Solzhenitsyn*: 570; for an example of the semi-official accusations levelled against him that "cancer" was a metaphor with a wider significance, see the speech by M. V. Zimyanin (Editor-in-chief of *Pravda*), reproduced in Labedz, *Solzhenitsyn*: 102.
70. Lukács, *Solzhenitsyn*: 87.
71. Lukács, *Solzhenitsyn*: 33.
72. Lukács, *Solzhenitsyn*: 79-80.
73. Solzhenitsyn, *The Oak and the Calf*: 119.
74. Solzhenitsyn, *The Oak and the Calf*: 484.
75. Scammell, *Solzhenitsyn*: 551.
76. Solzhenitsyn's letter is reproduced in *The Oak and the Calf*: 497; for an account of the Nobel banquet, see Scammell, *Solzhenitsyn*: 717-718.
77. *Washington Post*, 15 February 1974.
78. Scammell, *Solzhenitsyn*: 936.
79. Deming Brown, *Soviet Literature since Stalin* (Cambridge: Cambridge University Press, 1978): 310-311.
80. Solzhenitsyn, *Letter to the Soviet Leaders*, trans. Hilary Sternberg (London: Writers and Scholars International, 1974).
81. Deming Brown, *Soviet Literature since Stalin*: 312.
82. See his commencement address at Harvard University in 1978, published as *A World Split Apart*, trans. Irina Alberti (New York: Harper and Row, 1978).
83. *Le Monde*, 12th April 1975.
84. Scammell: *Solzhenitsyn*: 971.
85. Scammell: *Solzhenitsyn*: 929.

6. SALMAN RUSHDIE:
"*The Satanic Verses*" (1988)

▼ ▼ ▼

History imitating fiction?

It is sometimes difficult to decide which has the more bizarre plot: Rushdie's novel, *The Satanic Verses*, or any version a historian might set down of the spectacular series of events on a national and international level, linked to the publication of the novel, which has unfolded in front of us over the last five years and which has come to be known as "the Rushdie affair."[1]

In the novel, two Indian-born actors fall out of an exploding jumbo jet over the English Channel, unaccountably surviving to land on the south coast of England. Pursued by the police as supposed illegal immigrants, one of them, Saladin Chamcha, increasingly takes on goatlike physical characteristics, is granted refuge over a Bangladeshi restaurant in London and eventually, having recovered his human form, returns to Bombay to be reconciled with his dying father; the other, Gibreel Farishta, undergoes a psychotic breakdown, during which, amongst other things, he imagines himself to be the Archangel Gibreel dictating a Qur'an-like sacred scripture to the founder of a new religion in seventh-century Arabia, and eventually commits suicide.

Moments in the development of "the Rushdie affair" include: public demonstrations of anger by many thousands of Muslims from the various immigrant communities in Britain (and Canada) shortly after its publication; demands by governments of several Islamic countries that the book be banned; riots in India and Pakistan in which a total of twenty people were killed; the issuing of a *fatwah* (a formal religious pronouncement) against Rushdie and his novel by the Ayatollah Khomeini; repeated offers from organizations in Iran of a bounty for any Muslim to kill Rushdie, and his going into hiding under police protection; the withdrawal for several months by all the countries of the European Community of their ambassadors to Iran; the killing in Brussels of two imams who spoke out against the *fatwah*; the murder of one translator of the novel and life-threatening attacks on two others; Rushdie's declaration after a meeting with some senior Islamic clerics that he was, after all his assertions to the contrary, now a Muslim; requests from the relatives of British hostages in Beirut that the paperback version of the novel not be published; the burning down of a hotel in Turkey by Muslim fundamentalists because people associated with publication of the novel in that country were staying there, and so on.[2]

When the Rushdie affair was at its height in 1989 and 1990, a number of European commentators made a dramatic analogy with the assassination of Archduke Ferdinand in Sarajevo in 1914, as it seemed that it might be the spark which could start the conflagration, the all-out conflict which appeared to be shaping up between Iran and Western nations — but that was before, in a metamorphosis entirely worthy of a Rushdie novel, the monster that the United States and Britain saw lurking in the Middle East was miraculously transformed. It no longer had the elderly, ascetic face of the Islamic cleric, the Ayatollah Khomeini, but the swarthy, mustachioed face of his archenemy, the secular, pragmatic Saddam Hussein.

The problem of teasing out the causal connections between these two narratives and of describing the associated issues of power is made all the greater not only by our closeness to them in time but the fact that we have all, whether Muslim or not, whatever our cultural or national origins, been participants of some sort in the affair, having, at the very least, made moral and political judgements about actions of the various parties as they have taken place, on the basis of the information available to us at the time. In bringing this account of the affair together it has been hard, too, not to be overwhelmed by the combination of passion and intellectual brilliance which has been focused on the Rushdie case from all sides by thinkers of the stature of Ali Masrui, Gayatri Spivak, and Tzvetan Todorov.

A match tossed into a powder keg?

A number of commmentators in the West have been tempted to interpret the causal relationship between the publication of *The Satanic Verses* and this extraordinary series of events as being analogous to what happens when a spark is accidentally struck in the vicinity of a powder keg (or a munitions factory). According to this view, the force of the "explosions" which have occurred is related hardly at all to the intrinsic significance of the novel itself, but rather to the extreme explosive potential of the various intercommunal and international situations into which it dropped. Almost any other slightly provocative act would have been enough to produce a similar chain of events (just as any of a great number of possible events, quite small in themselves, might have triggered the First World War). Moreover (it is said), the whole affair is an appalling mistake, with the provocation which so many Muslims have detected in the novel deriving from their disasastrously misreading it. Rushdie, himself, asks how he could possibly have predicted the response since "nothing on the scale of this controversy has, to my knowledge, ever happened in the history of literature. If I had told anyone before publication that such events would occur as a result of my book, I would instantly have proved the truth of the accusations of egomania ... "[3] Two weeks before publication he gave an interview to an Indian newspaper in which, among other things, he said: "it would be absurd to think that a book can cause riots."[4] Indeed, a major theoretical plank in his repeated justifications of himself and his book is that literature does not have that kind of direct power. As he said in the same interview, "the way in which art changes society is never in a broad sweep — you write a book and governments fall — that never happens." (And if there is no power, there can be no responsibility.) Muslims offended by the novel, writes Rushdie, have read its fictions as if they were being offered as fact: "The case of *The Satanic Verses* may be one of the biggest category mistakes in literary history."[5]

To his Muslim antagonists, such an argument is entirely unacceptable. *The Satanic Verses* is not just offensive, it was *designed* to offend; the causal relationship between its publication and the events that have followed is direct and strong. To many Muslim commmentators, the novel is one or another type of *weapon* designed to wound Islam and its believers, its publication an act of "literary terrorism."[6] On the international level, they depict it as some kind of parcel bomb which its author mailed to the Islamic community, killing twenty or so people and wounding millions. "Even without being published in India *The Satanic Verses* has already killed more than a dozen people in Rushdie's country of birth. It has also caused deaths in Pakistan."[7] It was, in addition, a propaganda weapon which he offered to Zionism and the West in their ongoing war with the Islamic East.[8] As the Editors of *The Black Scholar* wrote in April

1989: "For some Third World thinkers, the publication of *The Satanic Verses*, with its parody of Islam, was yet another salvo in the ideological warfare that rages between the West and Middle Eastern and Asian countries, as devastating in its way as the U.S. downing of the Iranian jet-liner on July 3, 1988, in the Persian Gulf or the Union Carbide explosion in Bhopal, India."[9]

Rushdie, it has been suggested, committed, not just blasphemy, but "treason in a special sense," betraying the faith and the religious community he grew up in by turning it into a laughing stock for its great enemy, the secular, materialist, imperialist West.[10] Objections to *The Satanic Verses* have especially focussed on three major episodes, though several Muslim commentators (partly to combat the claim by defenders of Rushdie that they object *only* to those passages and have wrenched them out of their proper context) have written detailed critiques of the whole novel which I shall refer to later. The first episode (which occurs in Chapter 2) centers on a Muhammad-like prophet in ancient Arabia, named Mahound. The main grounds for offence in this chapter are not only that "Mahound" is the abusive name that medieval Christians gave the Prophet, with its associations of false god, even devil, but that he is shown as first admitting three local goddesses to the role of intermediate divinities between humanity and Allah, in order to gain support for the new religion among the people of Jahilia, and then cancelling this pragmatic move from the "true recitation" (as Rushdie calls the Qur'an-like document in which Mahound's words are recorded) on the grounds that it was dictated to him by Satan (hence the title of the novel). Given that the Qur'an is regarded by most Muslims as, in every particular, the product of divine revelation, and Muhammad's role in the reception of the revelation as being "that of a robot,"[11] this episode is seen by his Muslim antagonists as seeking to undermine both the integrity of the Prophet and the validity of the sacred text. The second episode is to be found in Chapters 4 and 8, where a young Muslim holy woman, Ayesha, from a village in modern India, sets out, clothed only in a swarm of butterflies, to lead her devoted followers through the sea on a pilgrimage to Mecca. Almost all are drowned. This episode is interpreted as a ridiculing of religious devotion. The third (in Chapter 6) "Return to Jahilia," depicts a brothel in the period of Mahound where the prostitutes take on the names and identities of the Prophet's wives — and so increase business by 300 percent. This is interpreted as the crudest kind of insult to the wives of Muhammad with the comment frequently being heard among Muslim protesters on the streets of Bradford and

London that "Rushdie calls the Prophet's wives whores," which is particularly offensive since many Muslims feel a personal devotion to them.

There is an intimate, almost domestic, character to some of the imagery used by Muslims to convey the nature of Rushdie's offense. Ali Masrui, an African Muslim scholar, describes the novel as "poisoned food for thought" which Rushdie was trying to feed to Muslims.[12] And, "it is as if Rushdie had composed a brilliant poem about the private parts of his parents, and then recited the poem in the market place to the cheers and laughter of strangers."[13] Imagery of sexual violence and betrayal is especially prevalent: "What he has written is far worse to Muslims than if he had raped one's daughter," Dr Zaki Badawi, a liberal Muslim leader in Britain, told a British newspaper.[14] The comparison has been made with the American-born William Joyce (known as Lord Haw-Haw) who was hanged by the British after the Second World War for broadcasting Nazi propaganda in English from Germany.[15] In the statement with which it broke diplomatic relations with Britain on 7 March 1989, the Iranian government declared that, having been "in the front line of plots and treachery against Islam and Muslims" for two centuries, the British government had suffered reverses at the hands of Islamic movements in recent times and had switched from military tactics to more sophisticated political and cultural weapons such as sponsoring *The Satanic Verses*.[16]

One of the many ironies of the whole Rushdie affair is that, as the above passages illustrate, his supporters and his most prominent opponents have made more or less equal use of a form of argument, concerning the author's intention, which has been largely discredited in literary critical discourse for nearly fifty years. Whether for the reasons given by W. K. Wimsatt in "The Intentional Fallacy" ("the design or intention of the author is neither available nor desirable as a standard for judging the success of a work of literary art")[17] or for those given by Roland Barthes in "The Death of the Author" ("a text is made of multiple writings, drawn from many cultures and entering into mutual relations of dialogue, parody, contestation, but there is one place where this multiplicity is focused and that place is the reader, not, as has hitherto been said, the author")[18] the concept of authorial intention has been widely argued to be either empty or irrelevant.

One of the most articulate and informed Muslim critics of *The Satanic Verses* has been Shabbir Akhtar, a Pakistan-born community leader with a doctorate on the philosophy of religion. He lives and works in the northern English city of Bradford, and in 1989 wrote a book entitled *Be Careful with Muhammad: The Salman Rushdie Affair*. After a detailed consideration of the passages which Muslims have found most offensive, he concludes: "Rushdie leaves too many clues in *The Satanic Verses* to show that unprincipled abuse rather than disciplined critique was his dominant intention."[19] An American Muslim, T. B. Irving, describes it as "a dirty book and worse; it mocks sacred matters deliberately."[20] The principal accusation against Rushdie is that he wrote his novel with the conscious intention of vilifying Islam, in order to ingratiate himself with Westerners and earn a lot of money. To quote the Indian Muslim member of Parliament, Syed Shahabuddin, "your act is not unintentional or a careless slip of the pen. It was deliberately and consciously planned and with devilish forethought, with an eye to your market."[21]

Rushdie's position is that, whatever the hostile interpretations that have been made of his book, its *real* meaning is to be found in his, very different, intentions for it. "*The Satanic Verses* is, I profoundly hope, a work of radical dissent and questioning and reimagining. It is not, however, the book it has been made out to be, that book containing 'nothing but filth and insults and abuse' that has brought people out on to the streets across the world. That book simply does not exist ... There are times when I feel that the original intentions of *The Satanic Verses* have been so thoroughly scrambled by events as to be lost forever."[22] In the simplest terms, while he cheerfully admits that his novel constituted an attack on fanaticism, bigotry, and fundamentalism of all kinds (Thatcherite as much as Islamic) he absolutely denies that it was intended as an attack on Islam itself.

Rushdie's account of the meaning of the three episodes which have caused most offense starts from the point that they are all to be understood as the dreams or fantasies of an increasingly psychotic Gibreel Farishta as he struggles with his loss of faith. So the episodes centering on the life of Muhammad are not to be read, says Rushdie, as slyly claiming precedence *as history* over the account of the same events to be found in the Qur'an. They are rather "a key moment of doubt in dreams which persecute a dreamer by making vivid the doubts he loathes but can no longer escape."[23] In any case, he argues, to suggest the hesitant humanity of Muhammad is not to insult the Prophet but to make him more approachable. Of the brothel sequence, he writes: "That men should be so aroused by the great ladies' whorish counterfeits says something about *them*, not the great ladies, and about the extent to which sexual relations have to do with possession."[24] Nor is the Ayesha episode to be read as humorously mocking Islamic tradition or faith. Indeed, Rushdie reminds us, the nonbelieving landowner who witnessed the drowning of his wife along with the other believers "experiences the truth of a miracle at the moment of his own death, when he opens his heart to God, and 'sees' the waters part." Of all these dreams, he writes, "they are *agonizingly painful to the dreamer.* They are a 'nocturnal retribution, a punishment' for his loss of faith. This man, desperate to regain belief, is haunted, possessed, by visions of doubt, visions of scepticism and questions and faith-shaking allegations that grow more and more extreme as they go on."[25] In other words, these episodes are not, in themselves blasphemous, they are *about* the circumstances in which a wavering believer may commit blasphemy. "*The Satanic Verses* is, in part, a secular man's reckoning with the religious spirit. It is by no means always hostile to faith."[26]

While any idea that interpretations of a literary text should or could be limited to the supposed intentions of its author is clearly invalid, the Rushdie affair is a very useful reminder that, as soon as the question of authorial power and responsibility is to be discussed, it is inevitable and right that authorial intention should also be referred to. The issue of authorial intention is not, after all, dead! And yet how on earth is it to be handled? To quote Wimsatt: "One must ask how a critic expects to get an answer to the question about intention. How is he [*sic*] to find out what the poet tried to do? If the poet succeeded in doing it, then the poem itself shows what he was trying to do. And if the poet did not succeed, then the poem is not adequate evidence, and the critic must go outside the poem — for evidence of an intention that did not become effective in the poem."[27] While Western critics have been quick to spot the fallacy of the claim made by most of Rushdie's opponents — that, because they find his novel blasphemous and offensive, its author necessarily intended it to be so — they have been less scrupulous in noticing the fallacy in Rushdie's own argument — that, because (as he claims) he did not intend his book to be "filth and insults and abuse" his Muslim readers somehow should not have read it as such. Rushdie's own statements somewhat confuse intention and outcome: "*He did it on purpose* is one of the strangest accusations ever levelled at a writer. Of course I did it it on purpose. The question is, and it is what I have tried to answer: what is the 'it' that I did? What I did not do was conspire against Islam; or write — after years and years of antiracist work and writing — a text of incitement to racial hatred; or anything of the sort."[28] Yet, when Rushdie is accused by Muslims of causing "*fasad* or corruption in the world"[29] and, especially, with a death threat hanging over him, if his (conscious) intention had indeed been to hold Muhammad and all of Islam up to ridicule, you could hardly expect him to admit it! (Behind the question of a conscious authorial intention lies the even more heavily loaded issue of what *unconscious* intentions the author may have had.)

The question which must still be asked is: whatever Rushdie's own understanding of the meaning of his own book, to what extent could he or should he (and his publishers) have foreseen the depth and breadth of the offense it would engender and the political reverberations, including deaths, that would follow from the publication of *The Satanic Verses*? The ability to foresee the outcome of an action you are contemplating (such as dropping a match in the vicinity of a powder keg) gives you a very significant power — a power which is manifested in deciding whether or not to carry the action through or modify it. In discussion with the British writer, James Fenton, Rushdie uttered this characteristically acute oxymoron: "If the work is capable of being misread or misunderstood, it is the artist's fault ... [nevertheless] it's useless to try and predict what will happen to a book. All you can do is write the books which will come to you." In the same interview, he acknowledged "a sense of absolutely overwhelming failure ... what I tried to do was to bring two worlds which happened to be present inside me — more than two worlds actually — India, Islam, the West — these three worlds all of which are present inside me in a very vivid way — I tried to bring them together. I tried to describe each in terms of the other. Well, it didn't work. Whatever one may feel about *The Satanic Verses* as a novel, if you look at the *event* of *The Satanic Verses* it pushed those worlds further apart." (Is Rushdie's novel the most spectacular *failure* in all of literary history?) Reflecting more generally on the process of creation, he adds: "In the moment of doing it, I feel — I always have done — I feel alone. You make this thing by yourself and you send it out."[30]

Nevertheless, writers are not quite as isolated in the production of a book as these statements might suggest. The publishers of *The Satanic Verses* sought advice on the likely impact of the novel on Muslim religious sensibilities from sources both in Britain and in the Indian subcontinent in the months preceding its publication. The answers they received should have rung alarm bells. I have seen no indication of how fully they conveyed these warnings back to Rushdie himself. One of Viking Penguin's own editorial advisors in India, Khushwant Singh (a distinguished historian and a Sikh, not a Muslim), phoned Peter Mayer, Chair of the Penguin Group, several times to warn against publication on the grounds that he was "positive it would cause a lot of trouble ... There are several derogatory references to the Prophet and the Qur'an. Muhammad is made out to be a small-time impostor."[31] At the same time, the publishers are supposed also to have submitted the manuscript to nine British religious scholars, Muslim, Christian and Jewish, a majority of whom concluded that "the book could not be considered a work of fiction because it used historical figures and would therefore cause a lot of offence. We told Viking Penguin that if the book was released it would unleash terror beyond the control of one person or even one country."[32] It is arguable, too, that the large advance Rushdie received for the novel (whether it was $800,000 or, as some sources indicate, £800,000) suggests that both author and publishers expected the level of sales which only a *succès de scandale* could guarantee for a novel whose dense style and elusive structure would otherwise attract a relatively limited audience. In particular, there is widespread agreement amongst Indian and western commmentators, with expertise on Indian affairs, that, given the extreme sensitivity of intercommunal relations in India, it was entirely predictable that violence would follow its publication there. Malise Ruthven recalls several instances where books and articles (even a careless headline) published in India have been followed by fatal conflicts between Hindus and the minority Muslims. "What, in retrospect, seems absurd, is not the all too obvious, if unpalatable, fact that an item of fiction can cause rioting and death in India, but that a novelist whose reputation has been built on his grasp of the Indian psyche appeared to think otherwise."[33] In this respect, Rushdie's action has been characterized by some commentators as "carelessness" if not "callousness."[34] (An analogy to events which occurred as I was writing this book might be useful here. In early September 1992, the secretary-general of the African National Congress, Cyril Ramaphosa, led 70,000 South African ANC supporters into the so-called black homeland of Ciskei to demonstrate against the puppet regime of its ruler, Brigadier Joshua Gqozo. Ciskei troops opened fire and at least thirty demonstrators were killed and two hundred injured. An independent inquiry afterwards blamed not only the Ciskei authorities and the South African government but also the ANC leadership which, it said, *should have foreseen the risk it was exposing its members to.*)

Unwillingness to listen to advice was also a feature of the publishers' response to the first, moderate, direct protests which reached them from leaders of several of the Muslim community groupings in Britain within a few days of the novel's first publication in Britain and Canada in late

September 1988. Typical is a letter from Hesham El Essawi, chair of the Islamic Society for the Promotion of Religious Tolerance in London (a dentist by profession) which stated that the novel was an insult to Islam: "I would like to invite you to take some kind of corrective stand before the monster that you have so heedlessly created grows, as it will do worldwide, into something uncontrollable."[35] One can speculate now about whether, if Viking Penguin, and the British government, had taken these concerns more seriously at the time, they might have been able to defuse some of the anger that was to build in the following months. In not responding to them, the publishers surrendered any power they might have had to maintain control over the fate of the book. Important, too, was the failure of the British media to give appropriate coverage to the first expressions of mass disapproval from Muslim communities in Britain. In early December 1989, 7000 people gathered in the northern English city of Bolton to demonstrate against the book. There was a mass book-burning. This remarkable event was ignored by all but the local press. Only when the procedure was repeated, under the leadership of more prominent individual Muslims (though on a much smaller scale) in Bradford over a month later, did the national media start to take notice. The nature of the coverage, however, was almost uniformly dismissive and accurately described by a Muslim magazine as "gratuitous advice, part patronising, part intimidating."[36] There were countless challenges in the tabloid press to British-born Muslims who spoke out against the novel to "shut up or go home." Another factor in the escalation of feeling among Muslims in (and outside) Britain was the discovery that the British legal system discriminates against religions other than Christianity in not according them the protection against blasphemy toward their sacred figures, which, theoretically at least, it accords to the Christian god. When lawyers for a Muslim group attempted to bring a prosecution on grounds of blasphemy, their plea was refused. This blatant constitutional discrimination, alongside the unwillingness of the publishers and the British press to take the protests seriously, explains the sense of powerlessness to obtain redress experienced by those Muslims in Britain who objected to the novel.

Even this cursory survey of the circumstances surrounding the publication of *The Satanic Verses* reveals that, while Rushdie may well not have sought to cause widespread offense, he could have anticipated that it would have occurred. It also shows the fire being fanned by the arrogance of the publishers and the press who seem to have assumed that those who objected to the novel were not important or powerful enough to have their objections treated with any seriousness. The significance of the role of the Western media generally in setting up the binary oppositions between *our* tolerance and *their* fanaticism, *our* modernity and *their* archaic beliefs and practices, *our* generosity in allowing migrants to live among us and *their* ungratefulness, can hardly be underestimated.

A weapon for many struggles

A thesis advanced by Rushdie's more aggressive supporters (mostly, but not exclusively, Westerners) is that, rather than being intrinsically a weapon, *The Satanic Verses* was rather an innocent cultural artifact which was *appropriated as a weapon* (picked up as a chair or ornament might be to strike a perceived enemy) first by Islamic leaders in Britain and India, then by the Iranian leadership, in the context of ongoing struggles and the political agenda of Islamic fundamentalism. It was grabbed by the mullahs in Muslim immigrant communities in Britain to strike out at the secular materialist forces by which they perceived their communities to be besieged; by Muslim politicians in India to strengthen their hand in communal struggles; and, most dramatically of course, by the Ayatollah Khomeini and the Shi'ite leadership in Iran, as both a missile in their ideological war with the West and a device to enable them to assert supreme authority over all Muslims. In the words of Tzvetan Todorov: "If there were deaths in the streets of Islamabad or Bombay, they should not be attributed to the book, but to fanaticism and to the hate of the instigators of these demonstrations."[37] Similarly, Bhikhu Parek wrote that parts of the novel had been irresponsibly thrown around like "polemical hand grenades" by Muslim commentators.[38] Certainly Rushdie portrays himself as having gotten innocently caught up in a number of ongoing conflicts and power struggles. Far from being the villain of the piece, he sees himself as the "tarred and feathered victim" of the Muslim community and "the scapegoat for all its discontents," and his novel as a "burned, spurned child."[39]

What is certainly true is that these first tentative anti-Rushdie protests by British Muslims were very quickly amplified by rapid communications backwards and forwards between Britain and the Indian subcontinent. In early October 1988, just before the novel was due to be launched in India, the Muslim M.P., Syed Shahabuddin (not himself a fundamentalist), belonging to the opposition Janata party, saw interviews with Rushdie in two Indian magazines and, without reading the book, demanded of Rajiv Gandhi, the prime minister, that it be banned. In the political context of the moment, in the lead-up to a general election in which Gandhi was anxious to attract the Muslim vote, he acceded to Shahabuddin's wishes. Rushdie, in the letter he wrote at the time to Rajiv Gandhi, said: "I deeply resent my book being used as a political football, and what should matter to you more than my resentment is that you come out of this looking not only philistine and anti-democratic but opportunistic and that's bad" and he was supported on this by a number of Indian commentators.[40] Other commmentators, as I have already mentioned, believe Rushdie's attitude to have been ingenuous. Rukmini Bhaya Nair and Rimli Bhattacharya wrote that his response "seems an exceedingly naive assesssment of the pre-electoral scenario in India."[41]

Within only a few more days, in early October 1988, Aslam Ejaz of the Islamic Foundation in Madras wrote to Faiyazuddin Ahmad, a friend and director of the Islamic Foundation in Leicester, England, telling him of the success of the brief campaign against *The Satanic Verses* in India, recommending that a similar campaign be mounted to have the book banned in England. Ahmad obtained a copy of the book and, after reading it, had the passages he found most offensive photocopied and distributed to the ten or so major Islamic organisations in Britain and to the forty-five embassies in Britain of the countries belonging to the Islamic Conference Organisation. Dr Syed Pasha, secretary of the Union of Muslim Organisations in Britain, called a meeting of the council of the Union on 15 October to discuss the problems posed by the book. Among those attending was Sher Azam from Bradford, where the 50,000-strong Muslim community was subsequently to become a major force in protests.

To understand just how the reactions of Muslims in Britain and Muslims in India to the book reinforced each other, it is essential to appreciate several features of the context for their outrage. In the first place, there is the long history of prejudice and discrimination suffered by Asian migrants who have settled in, and joined the workforce of, the old industrial cities of Britain. Whether in terms of harassment by police and immigration officials, attacks by skinheads or the antipathy of white neighbors, the Asian communities, which are predominantly working class and concentrated in areas of economic decline, have tended to see themselves as being under siege. In the sympathetic words of Michael Wood, professor of English at a British university: "We should ask not what Rushdie has done to the Muslims in Britain. We should wonder, rather, what Britain has done to them, to make them so eager to turn their (admittedly mischievous) friend into their scapegoat."[42] Asian Muslims have been involved in particularly bitter struggles over their right to maintain certain religious and cultural practices, especially in the context of State-run schools.[43] Migrants of other religions, Hindu and Sikh especially, have had their battles with British officialdom, too, but there is an edge to the treatment of the Muslim communities in Britain which derives from prejudices against Islam which run long and deep in British (and more generally European) attitudes, having their origin in the intense rivalry existing between Islam and Christendom for centuries around the Mediterranean.[44] As Akeel Bilgrami has pointed out, in earlier centuries "there was a robustness in this exchange and there was a perverse form of respect that was shown by more or less equal foes. There was a genuine appreciation of and instruction in the achievement of the other in the wide span of culture, science, philosophy, and literature. It was only with the rise of Western colonial domination that the health of hostility eroded into a feeling of defensiveness bred upon the loss of autonomy and upon colonial attitudes of superiority and condescension."[45] (Edward Said, in his books *Orientalism* and *Covering Islam*, underlines the way in which the West's condescension has been sharpened into aggression by its interest in asserting that the vital resource discovered and exploited in the Muslim countries of the Middle East during this century should properly be regarded as "our oil.")[46]

The point has been well made by a number of commentators, however, that, while the siege mentality of Muslim communities in Britain derives to a considerable degree from concrete experience of deeply held British prejudices, it is also something which they have brought with them, a relic of communal conflicts on the Indian subcontinent, where Muslims have for centuries been a minority. In the words of Malise Ruthven, an Islamic specialist, "the temper of Indian Islam is, compared with Arab Islam, harsh, neurotic and insecure."[47] It should therefore not be surprising, argues Theodore P. Wright, that sensitivity about *The Satanic Verses* has been stronger among Muslims on the Indian/British axis than among Arab Muslims (nor, he adds, that Iran should subsequently have taken the issue up since "the historic minority position of Shias in the Islamic world is comparable to that of Muslims in South Asia.")[48] A specific contributing factor has been the tendency of the various Asian Muslim communities in Britain to import directly from India or Pakistan mullahs with little or no knowledge of English and a hostility to the dominant values of British society.

From the point at which Faiyazuddin Ahmad started to distribute photocopies of selected passages of *The Satanic Verses* from Leicester, England, responses to its publication split in a very obvious way. Among those commenting on the novel, or responding to it in other ways, there were now three groups: those who had read all or most of it (and it must be said that it is, by any standard, a difficult novel to read); those who had read only extracts selected by someone else (whether in English or in translation); and, finally, there was that vast number of people, Muslim and non-Muslim, in Britain and elsewhere, who only knew the work secondhand, on the basis of what they had been told about it, whether through their mosque or Islamic cultural center or through the mass media (if they were British Muslims, they received unsympathetic messages from television and the tabloid newspapers which conflicted distressingly with the messages they received from their own religious leaders).

Many of Rushdie's supporters have suggested that, since only a tiny number of those who have protested over the book (and, in some cases, died in the process) have (or could have) read the book, those protests are necessarily and entirely absurd, product of the machinations of political and religious leaders with ulterior motives. While there is, of course, some validity to this argument, it needs to be qualified in several important ways. In the era of the photocopier, instant electronic communication, and near-global television coverage, it would be naive in the extreme to suppose that Muslims in India and Pakistan, let alone Bradford or Toronto, would somehow not hear about a work as provocative as *The Satanic Verses*, written by a writer as prominent as Rushdie, even if, because they were not literate in English, or not used to reading postmodern fiction, they could not read it. More importantly, to know (or at least believe) that you, your culture, and your religion have been written about in a derogatory and insulting way, even if you can't read what has been written, is a legitimate cause for offense. There is a hint of the patronizing arrogance of the Western colonizer in the words of Tzvetan Todorov: "If they had only read the book ... ; but no: I will say by way of shortcut that those who are capable of reading *The Satanic Verses* from cover to cover are not capable of calling for death on the city streets."[49]

Muslims might well respond by asking how many Westerners who publicly dismiss Islam and the document on which it is founded as medieval, barbaric, and so on, have read all of the Qur'an (in translation, let alone in the Arabic that Muslims believe it should be read in)! In any case, as citizens of English-speaking countries in the West we must acknowledge that texts we regard as fundamental to our own culture (let alone that of another group) — the Bible, Shakespeare's plays, Dickens' novels — are only known to the very great majority of people, even literate people, through the filters provided by such intermediaries as priests, televised adaptations, professional educators, and critics writing in newspapers. (The mutilated, dramatized versions of *Uncle Tom's Cabin* which circulated in the northern states from the time of its first publication also reached vast numbers of people who could not, or would not, have read the novel itself.) It might be added that many non-Muslims have, likewise, been willing to make judgements about the novel and about Muslim anger over it without having read it! Moreover, postmodern ideology itself emphasises the degree to which texts will always be subject to selective quotation, adaptation, reuse for new purposes. The kind of power this gives creative writers, and the responsibility it places on them to anticipate the ways in which their work will be so processed, is a rather different matter. Nevertheless it must be emphasized that there is a considerable number of Muslims, ranging from so-called fundamentalists, to "moderate" believers, to secular individuals of Muslim origin and culture who have read Rushdie's novel from cover to cover and have written or spoken persuasively about why they find it deeply offensive, hurtful, or, at the very least, unwise — and that they have played a leading role in shaping the mass reaction of Muslims who have not read the novel (or who have not read all of it). Very few such commentators, to be sure, state unequivocally that, given the chance, they would kill, or assist in the killing of, Rushdie.[50]

If *The Satanic Verses* proved to be a text capable of furthering the intercommunal agendas of Muslim leaders in India and Britain, it was also soon to prove its utility to various interest groups on the level of international relations. The chronology of the affair makes clear that there had already been widespread expressions of anger for nearly four months among Muslim migrants in Britain and Canada, as well as among protesters in India, Pakistan, and the Middle East before Khomeini issued his *fatwah* in February 1989. Khomeini did not stir up the initial mass response but exacerbated, amplified and focused it by suggesting that there was an action which those who were angry about the novel might take to express their anger: the killing of the book's author. His appallingly brilliant insight was that he could translate communal anger in several countries into a coordinated international movement. The specific force of the *fatwah* derives from three related points: the difficulty for Rushdie and those protecting him to guard against assassination attempts, since any of several million people might feel inspired to carry them out; the power of the threat to haunt the author throughout his natural life without anyone actually making an attempt on his life; and lastly the *fatwah*'s appeal to the many Muslims who, though they would never themselves even contemplate killing him, must take great pleasure in Rushdie's torment. To quote Shabbir Akhtar: "Khomeini probably reasoned that an individual keenly threatened with death probably suffers far more than one who is killed without warning."[51]

The *fatwah* must also be seen as a moment in Khomeini's wider strategy for the Islamic world. It was an extraordinarily effective device for unifying Muslims across the deep Sunni-Shia divide, as it allowed them to oppose a common enemy. It brought the strongest pressure on the Saudi Arabian authorities, who are guardians of the most holy places of Islam, but also regarded by fundamentalists as decadent pawns in the hands of Western secularizers. And it was, most importantly of all perhaps, a signal to Muslims scattered through Europe and North America of the grip which his Islamic Republic was capable of exercising on their lives.[52] This last point was brutally reinforced by the murder, in Brussels at the end of March 1989, of two imams who questioned the validity and appropriateness of the *fatwah*. There is no question, in the British context, that, as Rushdie himself has observed, "where secular and religious leaders had been vying for power in the community for over a decade, and where for a long time, largely secular organizations such as the Indian Workers Association (IWA) had been in the ascendant, the 'affair' swung the balance of power back towards the mosques."[53] Moreover, Pakistani and Bangladeshi groups in Britain have come together in a way which would previously have seemed out of the question: in early 1992, a so-called "Islamic Parliament" was formed to express Muslim community demands to the *other* British parliament. As far as Iranian influence in the host of Islamic nations is concerned, Khomeini's successors can count some wins and some losses. When, in March 1989, the forty-six nations of the Islamic Conference Organization were asked by Iran to support the *fatwah*, they called for the book to be withdrawn, recommended that member states boycott books published by Penguin, but finally refused to back the threat of death on Rushdie. There has been heated debate, too, in the various Islamic religious centers, as to whether the *fatwah* was a legitimate act in terms of Islamic law, with senior clerics in Egypt and elsewhere concluding that it was not. Nevertheless, it is noticeable that the influence of fundamentalist groups linked to Iran has grown since 1989 in several countries such as Algeria, Egypt and even Turkey (whose tradition of secular government had hitherto seemed very strong), and there is no question that the *fatwah* has played its part in that development. Finding themselves in particular difficulty is that relatively large number of secular, or at least non-fundamentalist, writers in such countries as Egypt and Syria, like Nobel laureate Naguib Mahfouz, who, as Barbara Nimri Aziz predicted in May 1989, "more than anyone else will be crippled by the violent responses to *The Satanic Verses*."[54] Some responsibility for the deterioration of their situation may well be attributed to Rushdie and his publishers, as well as, of course, to the Iranian authorities.

The point that has been consistently ignored by most Western commentators is that, if *The Satanic Verses* has been appropriated by a variety of Muslim leaders to their particular ends, the novel, and the Muslim response to it, have equally been exploited by those in the West with an interest in depicting Islam as, by its very nature, fanatical and barbarically inhumane. Islamic fundamentalism of the Iranian type is, it can be argued, in large part a creation of the arrogance and stupidity of the West in its relations with Islamic peoples. The greatest blunder was, of course, setting up and defending the corrupt regime of the Shah in order to assert Western control over the oil reserves of the region. By this and other means, Western governments and business interests have driven the Muslim masses into the arms of the fundamentalist clerics. ("Fundamentalists are the illegitimate children of the colonial West," said Ashis Nandy, though in a rather wider context.[55]) To Palestinian-born Edward Said, who writes of Rushdie as "the same distinguished writer and intellectual who has spoken out for immigrant, black and Palestinian rights, against imperialism, racism and censorship," it is a source of enormous distress that Rushdie should have written a work which so readily lent itself to reinforcing the preconceptions of a Western "audience already primed to excoriate our traditions, reality, history, religious language and origins."[56] On the crudest level, this process was vividly exemplified by the attacks, explicitly linked to the Rushdie affair, by white racists on Muslims and Muslim-owned shops in Britain during 1989.

An arm in the tiger's cage

The central issue of this chapter, then, is: to what extent are the intensity and multiplicity of the reverberations which have followed the publication of *The Satanic Verses* to be attributed to specific characteristics of the novel, and to what extent are the novel and its author merely instruments used by others in ongoing struggles. In other words, and to put it more crudely, did they just happen to be in the wrong place at the wrong time?

Salman Rushdie, it must be conceded, was no innocent in the business of provoking major political figures to public response through attacks in his fictional writing. *Midnight's Children* (1981) and *Shame* (1983) had made him the object of the fury of a string of political leaders in India and Pakistan. Indeed he seems to have long been fascinated by the question of just how far he could press criticism and satirical mockery of them in his fiction without provoking retaliation.

In *Midnight's Children*, it is not only that a minor, historically real figure such as L. N. Mishra, "minister for railways and bribery,"[57] is unambiguously referred to as responsible for poll fixing in Kashmir, but that Indira Gandhi is pilloried for her reliance on astrology, her involvement in massive political corruption, and her megalomania, "the Widow, who was not only Prime Minister of India but also aspired to be the Devi, the Mother Goddess in her most terrible aspect, possessor of the shakti of the gods, a multi-limbed divinity with a centre-parting and schizophrenic hair"[58] and that the whole Gandhi family is referred to as "these Nehrus [who] will not be happy until they have made themselves hereditary kings."[59] Such references resulted in an action for defamation by the Gandhi family and a public apology from Rushdie.

In *Shame* his fierce mockery shifted from India to Pakistan and its leaders, Ayub Khan and Mujibur Rahman, the Bhutto family and Zia ul-Haq, and brought down on him the wrath of those who who were still alive or their representatives. Rushdie's attack on the role played by the fundamentalist party, Jamaat-i-Islam founded by Maulana Abu'l Ala Maududi (who died in 1979) was equally unsparing: "So-called Islamic 'fundamentalism' does not spring, in Pakistan, from the people. It is imposed on them from above. Autocratic regimes find it useful to espouse the rhetoric of the faith, because the people respect that language, are reluctant to oppose it. This is how religions shore up dictators; by encircling them with words of power, words which the people are reluctant to see discredited, disenfranchised, mocked."[60] *Shame* was banned in Pakistan.

So when, in *The Satanic Verses*, he satirized, on the one hand, Margaret Thatcher ("Maggie Torture") and, on the other, the Ayatollah Khomeini (transparently referred to in the various manifestations of "the Imam," comically depicted as living in exile in London, and most notably dreamed of by Gibreel Farishta as having returned to his homeland and "grown monstrous, lying in the palace forecourt with his mouth yawning open at the gates; as the people march through the gates he swallows them whole" [*The Satanic Verses*: 215]),[61] but also Yusuf Islam, the former Cat Stevens, British rock singer and convert to Islam (in the character of Bilal X, follower of the Imam, whose voice "in its previous incarnation succeeded in climbing the Everest of the hit parade, not once but a dozen times, to the very top" [*The Satanic Verses*: 211]), he would have known from experience how fierce their personal fury might be. Not only mischievousness but a sense of wonder about whether he does not, after all, have some magical power over the political figures he has pilloried in his fiction is evident in an interview he gave to an Indian correspondent: "There have been unbelievable coincidences. In my novels there are five political figures. All have come to a violent end. Mujibur Rahman in Bangladesh, Indira Gandhi and Sanjay Gandhi in India, Bhutto and Zia in Pakistan. This whole generation either falls out of planes, or gets shot or hanged. None of these people has had a quiet end."[62] There is a memorable episode in *The Satanic Verses*, where angry Asian and Caribbean immigrants in the Club Hot Wax in London melt a wax effigy of Margaret Thatcher in the microwave oven of a ceremonial Hell's Kitchen (*The Satanic Verses*: 293). It is as if he secretly wondered whether the "roasting" he had given all these political figures in his novels might actually contribute to their demise. He appears to see himself himself as locked in a duel with certain political leaders. Note the grandeur (if not arrogance) in the challenge he issued to Rajiv Gandhi after the banning of *The Satanic Verses* in India, but before the *fatwah*: "Mr Prime Minister, *The Satanic Verses* may just, in the eyes of the world, be the unmaking of you. Worse still is the judgement of the eye of eternity ... and, Mr Gandhi, has it struck you that I may be your posterity? Perhaps you feel that by banning my fourth novel you are taking long-overdue revenge for the treatment of your mother in my second; but can you be sure that Indira Gandhi's reputation will endure better and longer than *Midnight's Children*? Are you certain that the cultural history of India will deal kindly with the enemies of *The Satanic Verses*? You own the present, Mr Gandhi; but the centuries belong to art."[63] Before long, Rajiv Gandhi was to join the list of those who "have come to a violent end" after being written about in derogatory fashion by Rushdie.

Near the end of *Shame*, the narrative voice asks: "How does a dictator fall?" After a few sentences on the extreme durability of tyranny, it concludes: "My dictator will be toppled by goblinish, faery means. 'Makes it pretty easy for you,' is the obvious criticism; and I agree, I agree. But add, even if it does sound a little peeevish: '*You* try and get rid of a dictator some time.'"[64] He poses the question — it is difficult to know how seriously: can literature can work "by goblinish means" on history? What he did not foresee was the goblinish means which the Ayatollah Khomeini would use in retaliation against him! As Daniel Pipes has put it, Khomeini was "a man who does not play by the usual rules."[65] (Pipes mentions a fact not referred to by other commentators, as far as I can see: that, as far back as 1942, Khomeini wrote a polemic against an influential, anticlerical, Iranian writer, Ahmed Kasravi, which inspired a zealous follower to murder him.)[66]

In *Midnight's Children*, Rushdie explores in a dozen comic forms, but eventually with serious intent, the theme of the part played in history by the individual who is not a politician. The protagonist, Saleem Sinai, is preoccupied with the problem of what responsibility attaches to him for the constant conjunction of certain events in his life with major political events. So, for instance, Saleem is convinced that his use of a children's rhyme at the age of nine brought about language riots in which fifteen people were killed and over three hundred wounded. "In this way I became directly reponsible for triggering off the violence which ended with the partition of the state of Bombay, as a result of which the city became the capital of Maharashtra."[67] He is also convinced that wider events are focused on him and his family, "it is my firm conviction that the hidden purpose of the Indo-Pakistani war of 1965 was nothing more nor less than the elimination of my benighted family from the face of the earth."[68] Believing himself perhaps to have been responsible even for the death of Nehru, Saleem nevertheless declares with relief at one point: "And (without any assistance from me) relations between India and Pakistan grew worse; entirely without my help, India conquered Goa — 'the Portuguese pimple on the face of Mother India'." He lists several other political events and issues of the period, insisting, in each case, on his own lack of involvement in it. He concludes: " ... and in the election of 1962, the All-India Congress won 361 out of 494 seats in the Lokh Sabha, and over 61 per cent of all State Assembly seats. Not even in this could my hand be said to have moved; *except perhaps metaphorically*" (my italics).[69] Later in the same novel, he asks plaintively: "Why, alone of all the more-than-five-hundred million, should I have to bear the burden of history?"[70] Bearing the burden of history as a consequence of playing a dangerous kind of game with metaphor is precisely what

Salman Rushdie is doing, and may always, to a greater or lesser degree, be forced to do.

I picture Rushdie, through all his major novels, as a small boy at the zoo extending his arm further and further into the tigers' cage, never quite believing that he could cause the mighty beasts to leap, and unwisely convinced of the supposed (short-term) powerlessness of literature. Rushdie, of course, describes what has happened rather differently: he asks whether he can be said to have *provoked* the threat of assassination any more than the poet Osip Mandelstam provoked his own execution by writing a poem about Stalin or the students who filled Tiananmen Square to ask for freedom were "knowingly asking for the murderous repression that resulted." Or, and here he changes the analogy again: "Is any provocation a justification for rape?"[71] (The recurrence of imagery of sexual attack on both sides of the debate is something I shall return to later.)

The novelty of *The Satanic Verses*, in the context of Rushdie's work, is not that it has caused offense to a few political and religious leaders, but that it has been perceived by whole communities of Muslim believers in several countries to be insulting to them and their beliefs, and that some leaders have subsequently been able to exploit this mass anger.

Rushdie has always claimed that he intended his novel to dissent not from "people's right to faith" but from "imposed orthodoxies *of all types*."[72] He has also argued at certain moments that it is not (or not primarily) a novel about religion, but rather about migration: "*The Satanic Verses* is not an antireligious novel. It is ... an attempt to write about migration, its stresses and transformations from the point of view of migrants from the Indian subcontinent to Britain."[73] It depicts not only the pains associated with settling in another country (the traumas of being taken away from one's native soil, of prejudice and discrimination) but also the enrichment which can come from new experience. "*The Satanic Verses* celebrates hybridity, impurity, intermingling, the transformation that comes of new and unexpected combinations of human beings, cultures, ideas, politics, movies, songs. It rejoices in mongrelization and fears the absolutism of the Pure ... It is a love-song to our mongrel selves."[74] Rushdie can point to the fact that the twin protagonists are both, in their different ways, migrants. Both are faced by the problem of how to maintain, or gain, wholeness in their new state. "*The Satanic Verses* is the story of two painfully divided selves. In the case of one, Saladin Chamcha, the division is secular and societal: he is torn, to put it plainly, between Bombay and London, between East and West." Chamcha is the Anglophile Indian, long resident in Britain, successful as a voice-over actor in television commercials and children's programs, who has become dismissive of his country of origin and its people, but who is forced to confront the indignities suffered by newer and less successful migrants. At one point, alone in his attic room above the Shaandaar Café, he exclaims: "'I'm not your kind ... You're not my people. I've spent half my life trying to get away from you'" (*The Satanic Verses* : 253). (His first name, Saladin, links him to the medieval Christian type of the honorable Muslim warrior, suggesting that he is an example of the "acceptable" alien.) "For the other, Gibreel Farishta, the division is spiritual, a rift in the soul. He has lost his faith and is strung out between his immense need to believe and his new inability to do so." The episodes which have been regarded as most offensive by Muslims are products of his breakdown. "The novel," insists Rushdie "is 'about' their quest for wholeness."[75] The respective fates of the two protagonists must also be seen as significant, according to Rushdie: "Chamcha survives. He makes himself whole by returning to his roots and, more importantly, by facing up to, and learning to deal with, the great verities of love and death. [He goes back to his birthplace to be reunited with his dying father.] Gibreel does not survive. He can neither return to the love of God, nor succeed in replacing it by earthly love. In the end he kills himself, unable to bear his torment any longer."[76]

One of the greatest ironies about the *The Satanic Verses* is the fact that it has been so violently rejected and attacked by just that group, Asian migrants to Britain, whose situation Rushdie intended it sympathetically to represent. The action of *The Satanic Verses* is, as neither *Midnight's Children* nor *Shame* was, located primarily in Britain and concerned with the variety of discomforts and humiliations suffered by migrants: not only in the direct terms of, for instance, the beating which Saladin Chamcha, long a British resident but mistakenly supposed to be an illegal immigrant, receives in the police van, but in the rather less direct representation of Saladin and other Asians transformed by their treatment as "aliens" into mythically grotesque animals in a kind of fantasy hospital. As one character in the novel says: "'They [racist white Britons] have the power of description, and we succumb to the pictures they construct'" (*The Satanic Verses*: 168). As Edward Said noted, Rushdie has long been an articulate and passionate writer and activist against racism. Nevertheless, he has been perceived by the great majority of British Muslims as writing a book against them and their interests:

"He is no longer the articulator of grievance; he's part of the problem — the object of communal wrath, not the translator of it."[77]

The simple point that must be made here is that, however much Salman Rushdie aimed and claimed, in the *Satanic Verses*, to speak about and for the Muslim population in Britain, he failed to speak *to* more than a tiny portion of it. As Rushdie himself has expressed it: "This is what I want to say to the great mass of ordinary, decent, fair-minded Muslims, of the sort I have known all my life, and who have provided much of the inspiration for my work: to be rejected and reviled by, so to speak, one's own characters is a shocking and painful experience for any writer."[78] This occurrence illustrates well the broad problem of "speaking for" a group, which, when it is fully authorized by close interaction with the group, may serve to wonderfully empower its members, but which, if not so authorized, may be an act of arrogance, and disempowering. One interpretation of the response to the novel by Muslim immigrants to Britain is that it involves Muslims reclaiming a voice from someone who has claimed inappropriately to speak for the group: "Rushdie himself could be seen as encroaching upon the freedom of other people to voice their own opinions, however 'medieval' certain of these opinions may sound to a sophisticated intelligence like his own."[79] (In so doing, he gave the fundamentalists an excuse, even more arrogantly, to claim to be the voice for all Muslims.)

Few commentators have acknowledged that the anger against Rushdie expressed by so many thousands of ordinary Muslim migrants to Britain is as much an antagonism founded on class difference as on religious difference. However much Rushdie may project an image of himself as the outsider in British literary and social life, to the Indian busdriver, metalworker or unemployed person living in the same country, he must seem, with his famous private-school and Cambridge education and his success and wealth as a writer, as well as his secular lifestyle, to have been wholly assimilated into the British elite.[80] The Western media have in this, as in many other aspects of the affair, a considerable responsibility, since it is they who suggested, in responding to Rushdie's earlier work, that he should be seen as somehow able to speak for all of the many hundreds of millions of people of India, Pakistan, and Bangladesh, making such crass claims as: "*Midnight's Children* sounds like a continent finding its voice"[81] — as if it did not already have myriad voices!

The other side of the same coin is that there did not exist a large enough core consituency of readers competent to read the novel in the sophisticated manner Rushdie intended and to give the lead to both Muslims and non-Muslims in so doing. To be understood on a complex, rather than simply flippant, level, his exploration and parodying of episodes from the Qur'an and the history of Islam required a nucleus of readers who were either Muslims, and familiar with playful, postmodern narrative strategies, or non-Muslims who were unusually knowledgeable about Islam. Very few of the first Muslims to come across it were close enough to the postmodern ideology required to make it a productive text for them. And very few of the non-Muslims who have read it have brought sufficient knowledge of Islam to their reading to be able to understand the intricacies of reference built into, for instance, the episode of the satanic verses. Marlena G. Corcoran makes the valid point that, for most non-Muslims, the novel would be their first and only source of information on the episode.[82] Several Muslim commentators have provided illustrations of the impossibility for readers without a background in Islam of making more than the most rudimentary sense of the novel. Feroza Jussawalla of the University of Texas takes the argument furthest, arguing that the more "steeped in the lore of Muslim cultures" readers are, the more they will be aware of "the culturally coded abuses and jokes" built into the novel. (One example he gives depends on the reader's recognition of a reference to a cheap Hindi film song in the butterflies which surround Ayesha, the Muslim holy woman.)[83]

In a more general sense *The Satanic Verses* may be said to have betrayed its author's intentions in that the debate it has engendered, far from undermining those pairs of false binary conceptual opposites whose adequacy Rushdie insists that it has always been his aim to cast doubt on (good/bad, East/West, black/white, religious/secular), has served to reinforce them. "I have never seen this controversy as a struggle between Western freedoms and Eastern unfreedom," writes Rushdie, yet these are just the terms in which the controversy has been framed by most Western commentators.[84]

Rushdie and those who have attempted to debate the problems associated with his book have found themselves trapped in the grip of nutcracker-like binary thinking from which escape seems almost impossible. This was most vividly demonstrated by the responses to his declaration, in December 1990, after a meeting with a group of Egyptian Islamic clerics, that, contrary to all his previous statements: "I am certainly not a good Muslim. But I am now able to say that I am a Muslim; it is a source of happiness to say that I am now inside, and a part of, the community whose values have been closest to my heart."[85] He found it rejected not only by most of his Muslim opponents but by many of his supposed "supporters" in the West who angrily declared that he had betrayed them![86] A British lawyer, Francis Bennion, resigned from the Salman Rushdie Defence Committee, declaring: "There are several reasons why Rushdie is not worth defending ... Worst of all, he has now confounded his supporters by embracing the bigoted creed that holds its followers entitled to murder a novelist for what he has written in a novel."[87] Rushdie's attempt to negotiate just a little more space for himself was resisted equally by both parties. (A different kind of foolish binary thinking has been manifested in the comments of a number of Western liberals who, in their haste not to subscribe to the anti-Islamic jingoism of the mass media, have uttered such simplistic judgements as "He got what he was asking for.") One of several aims for this essay is to escape the trap of such binary thinking. For this reason I deliberately give space to the arguments of many commentators whose views belong neither to the pro-Rushdie nor to the anti-Rushdie camps and whose voices have been almost drowned by the shouts of abuse between the two.

The terrible power of metaphor

One of the most curious aspects of the Rushdie affair is that so many of the statements by his critics and attackers on the one side and by the novelist and his defenders on the other are expressed in the form of vivid metaphors, similes, and analogies. The frequency and diversity of the imagery — the references to *The Satanic Verses* as an act of terrorism, poisoned food, an act of rape or, alternatively, an accidental spark, a burned child — are not fortuitous. *The Satanic Verses* is not only packed with rich and shifting imagery but has served as an extraordinary generator of metaphor in its readers, which is eventually perhaps the greatest intrinsic "power" of this particular novel.

Early in the novel, the narrative voice describes Gibreel Farishta as "not understanding the terrible power of metaphor" (*The Satanic Verses*: 15). The context for this phrase is an account of the suicide of Gibreel's lover in Bombay, Rekha Merchant, who, when he leaves her recommending that she take a flight, takes her children up to the roof of her house and leaps to her death. When, in 1991, Rushdie came to describe his own existence since the *fatwah*, he chose another flying metaphor: it was as if he were a passenger in the basket of a hot-air balloon which had developed a leak while drifting over a bottomless chasm. The power of

The Power of the Story
▼▼▼

the metaphor, in both cases, lies in its capacity to close off other possibilities. Rushdie continues: "Trapped inside a metaphor, I've often felt the need to redescribe it, to change the terms. This isn't so much a balloon, I've wanted to say, as a bubble, within which I'm simultaneously exposed and sealed off. The bubble floats above and through the world, depriving me of reality, reducing me to an abstraction."[88] Reliance on a single metaphor (and a single interpretation of that metaphor) may imply closure, in very much the same way as a unified narrative implies limitation and finality. It is characteristic of Rushdie's method as a thinker and writer, however, that he is constantly on the move, refusing to be trapped by singularity. "Fiction uses facts as a starting-place and then spirals away to explore its real concerns, which are only tangentially historical."[89] The generation of multiple metaphors in his fiction is the means by which he "spirals away" from history. As I hope to show, *The Satanic Verses* is the one work, of all those I have discussed in this book, in which issues of narrative and power are most intricately interwoven with the problem of the power of metaphor.

Some commentators have argued, indeed, that the whole affair is best understood as an illustration of the incompatibility of two styles for reading or interpretation: the one literary and, by its very nature, metaphorical, the other literalist and theological. I shall argue that it is somewhat more complicated than this. Certainly it is true that, to Muslims who have read (or been told about) only the passages from *The Satanic Verses* which were distributed in photocopy form, the main objection is that they appear to propose a scandalous, alternative historical narrative concerning Muhammad's role in the composition of the Qur'an. Offense is taken because those passages have been interpreted literally, as (false) history. By contrast, however, the anger of those scholarly Muslims who have read the entire novel derives rather from their perception of the generally metaphorical character of the work, which they read as profoundly subversive, *metaphorically subversive*, of the whole Islamic tradition.

What Masrui, Akhtar, and some other Muslim scholars have correctly observed, is that the whole book is "a five-hundred-page parody of Muhammad's life." Timothy Brennan points out that the table of contents alone, with chapter headings such as "Mahound" and "Ayesha," the name of the prophet's favorite wife, signals as much.[90] With its complex, confusing structure, adds Malise Ruthven, it "seems in ways to mirror the Muslim scripture ... it is a kind of 'anti-Qur'an' which challenges the original by substituting for the latter's absolutist certainties a theology of doubt."[91] Or, as Brennan again puts it, "it projects itself as a rival Qur'an with Rushdie as its prophet and the devil as its supernatural voice."[92]

The best evidence for this interpretation is a dramatic moment in Gibreel Farishta's progressive breakdown when "the boundaries of the earth broke" and he "saw God." The trouble with his vision of God is, not only that he is so unimpressive-looking that to Gibreel he might just as well be the Devil, "the Guy from Underneath," as the Almighty, "the Fellow Upstairs," not only that he has something in common with Gibreel himself ("sitting on the bed, a man of about the same age as himself") but that he bears a clear resemblance to Salman Rushdie: "of medium height, fairly heavily built, with salt-and-pepper beard cropped close to the line of the jaw. What struck him most was that the apparition was balding, seeming to suffer from dandruff and wore glasses" (*The Satanic Verses*: 318-19). In opening up the possibility of a loose equation: Rushdie=Gibreel Farishta=Allah=Satan, the author was writing something which was, in his own prophetic words, "about as risky as I could get."[93] His aim was "to create metaphors of the conflict between different sorts of 'author' and different sorts of 'text'."[94] (Arabic as a language implies the contiguity of the act of literary creation with that of devilish inspiration: a poet is said to be possessed by a "*shaitan*" [spirit or genius], whereas "*al-shaitan*" is the chief of the evil spirits, corresponding to the Satan of Judaism and Christianity.)[95]

In his essay "One Thousand Days in a Balloon," Rushdie states that "the row over *The Satanic Verses* was at bottom an argument about who should have power over the grand narrative, the Story of Islam."[96] It is not, as might be supposed, that Rushdie seeks to narrate a coherent, alternative grand narrative, rather that, in his use of constantly shifting metaphor, he breaks up the grand narrative. Muhammad, for instance, is mirrored in the novel not just by Mahound, but in a split image, by the two protagonists. The grotesque, comic/tragic adventures of Saladin Chamcha and Gibreel Farishta in Britain and elsewhere and the revelations they experience are set up in parallel with (as analogous to) the journeying and the spiritual revelations of the Prophet as he undertook the founding of Islam. The pairing of the two figures, one nominally angelic (Gibreel — Gabriel — the Bombay film star with the name of the archangel who is supposed to have dictated the revelations of the Qur'an to Muhammad), the other apparently satanic (Chamcha, the genteel Anglophile who is appalled to discover that he is acquiring the physical characteristics of a priapic goat) with the self-destruction of the former and the final salvation of the latter, was designed, according to Rushdie, to demonstrate that, "if devils are not necessarily devilish, angels may not necessarily be angelic ... From this premise, the novel's exploration of morality as internal and shifting (rather than external, divinely sanctioned, absolute) may be said to emerge."[97] Shabbir Akhtar objects strongly to this "ethic of impurity" (Rushdie's words), declaring: "There are two separate issues here: one is the purity and integrity of an ideal (such as Islam or humanism). The other is the purity of those who espouse it. The fact that we all fail to live up to our professed ideals — a part of the failings of our common humanity — is not a reason for diluting the ideal."[98]

Certainly there is a basis in Islamic theology for viewing literature as an enemy of the divinely revealed word. The section of the Qur'an entitled "The Poets" condemns poets precisely for their lack of literalness and equates fiction with lying:

> Shall I tell you on whom the Satans come down?
> They come down on every guilty impostor.
> They give ear, but most of them are liars.
> And the poets — the perverse follow them;
> hast thou not seen how they wander in every valley
> and how they say that which they do not?[99]

The rivalry between the Prophet and the poet is underlined by the saying, traditional among Muslims, that no line written by a poet could ever be more beautiful than a single line of the Qur'an and is picked up (almost prophetically one might now feel!) in *The Satanic Verses* by Bilal, spokesman for the Imam in London: "'Burn the books and trust the Book; shred the papers and hear the Word, as it was revealed by the Angel Gibreel to the Messenger Mahound and explicated by your interpreter and Imam'" (*The Satanic Verses*: 211).

Rushdie also argues that literature and religion are rivals but defines that rivalry in a rather different way: "Between religion and literature, as between politics and literature, there is a linguistically based dispute. But it is not a dispute of simple opposites. Because where religion seeks to privilege one language above all others, one text above all others, the novel has always been *about* the way in which different languages, values and narratives quarrel, and about the shifting relations between them, which are relations of power."[100]

This paragraph betrays something of the confusion in Rushdie's own handling of religious material which I suspect lies at the heart of his novel's failure to engage the support of more than a few Muslims. In the same article, "Is Nothing Sacred?," Rushdie claims that the question he has asked himself throughout his life as a writer is: "Can the religious mentality survive outside of religious dogma and hierarchy?"[101] Elsewhere, too, he regularly distinguishes faith from fundamentalist dogmatism. And yet, in referring here to religion seeking "to privilege one language above all others," he fails to maintain the distinction between the imaginative energy that is at the origin of so many beliefs and the straitjacket of fundamentalism. It was partly because he failed, in the novel, adequately to illuminate the gap between that imaginative energy and oppressive dogmatism that the mass of believers swung in to support the vicious anger of the fundamentalists.

The religious mentality and the literary mentality are so close to each other and in competition, I suggest, *because of the centrality that both accord to metaphor*. The Qur'an itself is highly metaphorical, but Shi'ite fundamentalists (very much like Christian fundamentalists) want to argue both that its metaphors are susceptible of only one interpretation and that other texts employing metaphor should be viewed with great suspicion. (Religious fundamentalism typically employs metaphors at the very heart of its doctrines, yet denies their metaphorical nature. In his message, broadcast on Tehran radio nine days after the *fatwah*, insisting on the role of the Shi'ite clergy in defending the people against such attacks, Khomeini piles one metaphor upon another: "For hundreds of years the Islamic clergy has been the *shelter* of the deprived people. The oppressed people have always *drunk their fill from the pure fountain* of the gnosis of illustrious jurisconsults ... The issue of the book *The Satanic Verses* is that it is a calculated move aimed at *rooting out* religion and religiousness, and above all, Islam and its clergy. Certainly, if *the world devourers* could, they would have *burnt the roots* and the title of the clergy ..."- my italics).[102] *The Satanic Verses*, writes Peter van der Veer, a Dutch anthropologist, aims to show that "that there is no clear boundary between religion and fiction as products of the imagination."[103] And in one of the most illuminating of all the many commentaries on the Rushdie affair by Muslims, Rustom Bharucha makes the point that "religion offers some of the greatest possibilities of fiction, involving colour, texture, sensation, fantasy and transcendence." He goes on to argue that Rushdie's "crime ... is directly linked to the very faculty of the imagination that he upholds as a writer. In his sharp, though evasive, rebuttals of the charges of 'blasphemy' and 'western arrogance' raised against him, Rushdie has constantly reiterated that his work is a piece of fiction, and that people don't know how to read it. I would say that it is precisely the *nature* of his fiction that is the cause of the problem, because in asserting his own, rather manic imagination, Rushdie has desecrated the imagination of others, more specifically the 'private space' in which faith resides."[104] James Piscatori, a Western scholar in the politics of Islam, makes the specific point that, if Rushdie had really wanted to reinforce the progressive thread within contemporary Islam, he should have been much more subtle in his use of metaphor. He explains:

> Though the use of metaphor is meant to push our thinking along new paths, it is most effective when it seems to be compatible with high tradition, that loose collection of ideas, norms and legendary stories that make up a community's official world-view. When this is done in the case of Islam, historical leaps are possible in one imaginative bound and the pious fiction of a seamless Islam — of Muslim essence and interconnectedness — is maintained. ... But when the intended audience finds the metaphors crudely constructed and the instrument of political language blunt, offence is bound to be taken.[105]

It is, I shall be suggesting, its very metaphorical productivity in the minds of its (Muslim) readers that has made *The Satanic Verses* such a serious threat.

The metaphor of territory and the insider/outsider problem

The Satanic Verses poses three closely related conceptual problems in metaphorical form: the problem of the concept of territory, the problem of the insider/outsider, and the problem of gender. These problems are posed both in the sense that the novel is about them and in the sense that the Rushdie affair illustrates them in action.

One of the themes Rushdie had explored so effectively in *Midnight's Children* was the degree to which Britain left traces of itself in India after independence which would prove to be indelible. So when, in *The Satanic Verses*, Saladin Chamcha left India for England, adopting tweeds, the Royal family, cricket, warm beer, mince pies, and common sense (*The Satanic Verses*: 175) there was an odd sense in which he was both migrating to a foreign land *and* going home. "The West is now everywhere, within the West and outside it; in structures and in minds," wrote Ashis Nandy in a book entitled *The Intimate Enemy*.[106] But *The Satanic Verses* is a reminder that the East is everywhere too, most obviously in the sense that a country like Britain contains enclaves of

Muslim migrant citizens from many countries, forming little Indias, Pakistans and Bangladeshs within its major cities. It is in just such an enclave, the Shaandaar Café in London, that the Sufyan family takes care of the afflicted Saladin Chamcha. Yet however much Haji Sufyan might want and believe it to be a pure part of his homeland, the sexual exploits of his daughter, Mishal, and the unscrupulous business dealings of his wife, Hind, mean that it is far from being so. As Cockney Mishal says, "'Bangladesh in't nothing to me. Just some place Dad and Mum keep banging on about'" (*The Satanic Verses*: 259). The old notion of clearly defined geographical boundaries corresponding to national, cultural, or religious territory is dead, or alive only in metaphorical form in people's minds. So Peter Nazareth refers perceptively to Rushdie as having "colonized" the English language from India.[107] In a discussion with Günter Grass, televised in 1985 when Rushdie was in the middle of writing *The Satanic Verses*, Rushdie suggested that there was an intimate association between metaphor (whose Greek etymology suggests "carrying across") and migration, that migrants, by the very fact that they had been uprooted from the place, the language, and the social conventions within which they had lived, "had so to speak entered the condition of metaphor and … their instinctive way of looking at the world was in that more metaphorical, imagistic manner," and that it was in terms of metaphor that they were "required to reinvent the sense of the self."[108]

One of the aspects of the novel most neglected by critics, Muslim and Western, is the extent to which it is not just about the interpenetration of Muslim and secular Western values in the experience of migrants, but the prior contamination of Indian Islam by Hinduism. It is no coincidence that the films in which Gibreel Farishta acts are the hugely popular Hindu "theologicals." This should have been evident to anyone who had read *Midnight's Children*, whose hero, Saleem, says at one moment, "'born and raised in the Muslim tradition, I find myself overwhelmed all of a sudden by an older learning'" and "'I was brought up in Bombay, where Shiva Vishnu Ganeg Ahuramazda Allah and countless others had their flocks.'"[109] The issue of the one Book or the many, the one God or the several, is at least as much a Muslim/Hindu issue as a Muslim/Western one. (There is, indeed, something extraordinarily postmodern about the combination, in Hinduism, of a preoccupation with a bewildering array of gods and demigods with the conviction that all the visible world and everything in it is illusion!) To quote from Rushdie's essay "In Good Faith": "My writing and thought have therefore been as deeply influenced by Hindu myths and attititudes as Muslim ones … Nor is the

West absent from Bombay. I was already a mongrel self, history's bastard, before London aggravated the condition."[110] The Hindu thread of the novel has featured little in the debate both because *The Satanic Verses* was permitted such limited circulation in India and because it pointed to a fact about their own culture which Muslims who had migrated from the subcontinent partly to escape Hindu domination had no wish to acknowledge.

One of the main sources of anger against the novel amongst leaders of the various Muslim communities in Britain derives from their resistance to these observations, since, in their view, it is only by keeping their social and religious practices pure and uncontaminated by Western values that those communities can survive, a form of "boundary maintenance."[111] Rushdie is telling them that battle was lost long ago. When Clark Blaise and Bharati Mukherjee visited a mosque in North London to gauge Muslim community opinion for themselves early in 1990, they found the vote on a renewal of the call for Rushdie's death unanimous. But their description of the voters and the dynamics of the community they were part of suggests something more complicated: "The faces are smiling, benign, anything but fanatical. These are the fathers, mechanics and shopkeepers, bus drivers and taxi drivers, of the boys and girls in fast cars and tight sweaters outside. They may have lost control of their children, but the Rushdie affair has given them a way to fight to get them back."[112]

Perhaps, in fact, the most satisfactory working metaphor for the way in which *The Satanic Verses* has functioned is that it is (or marks out) disputed "territory" between opposing groups, claimed on the Muslim side to be a scurrilous attack on their religion, their holy text, their prophet, by someone who grew up a Muslim, and so is subject to their jurisdiction; claimed on the Western side to be a complex, thoughtful, many-voiced literary work by a legal resident of a Western country, protected from attack by the laws supporting free expression in that country and, on a different level, by the seriousness and literary merit of the work itself. At one of the apparently least central or connected moments of the novel, Pamela, Chamcha's English wife, is recalling their attempts to define the nature of the Falklands War, "'if you must use these blasted cosy metaphors, then get them right. What it's *like* is if two people claim they own a house, and one of them is squatting the place, and *then* the other turns up with the shotgun'" (*The Satanic Verses*: 175). Much the same might be said of *The Satanic Verses* itself. (According to Rushdie, "literature and religion, like literature and politics, fight for the same territory.")[113]

Salman Rushdie: "The Satanic Verses"
▼ ▼ ▼

Gayatri C. Spivak uses the metaphor of territory, too, but in a somewhat different way in her "Reading *The Satanic Verses*" to define the nature of Khomeini's *fatwah*. The Ayatollah would probably never have issued that terrible edict if it had not been for Iran's political and military defeat in the war with Iraq. In her view, sacrificing "the heretic in a defence of the faith is a ruse to 'recover lost territory.'"[114] Khomeini's action thus, paradoxically, illustrates one of the major themes of the novel: that, in the modern world, traditional frontiers, whether national or cultural, no longer exist, they are rather constructs of the mind. There are many ways of gaining "territory" other than international treaty or military conquest.

The question of whether Rushdie wrote *The Satanic Verses* from inside or outside Islam is a metaphorical question, related closely to the issue of territory. It has several aspects to it. In his essay of mid-1990, "In Good Faith," he wrote: "To put it as simply as possible: *I am not a Muslim.*"[115] He argued that "after having lived my life as a secular, pluralist, eclectic man" he could not be decribed as a heretic or apostate. Nevertheless, from the perspective of many Muslims, his Muslim origins make him a member of the religious community of Islam, the *umma*, and his act in publishing the novel an act of both blasphemy and treachery to that community.[116] "*The Satanic Verses* is not simply blasphemous but a systematic attempt to unravel the religion *from within*" (my italics).[117] Paradoxically, however, he is also accused of writing about issues of Islamic history and doctrine with which he became acquainted *from the outside*, as a Western orientalist (with the negative connotations Said has attached to the term), through his undergraduate studies at Cambridge and without the knowledge of Arabic deemed indispensable for the devout scholar within Islam.

The question of his role as an insider and/or outsider is most vividly illustrated by the episode of the "satanic verses" itself. A major difficulty for Muslims about this episode (apart from the simple fact that it could so readily be detached from its context and read, by believers, as a standalone piece of historical heresy) is that, far from being a simple invention of Rushdie himself, it reworks apocryphal material recorded by two early Islamic commentators, Tabari and Ibn Sa'd, and revives an old debate within Islam about a passage of the Qur'an. Rushdie picks away at the scab covering an old wound on the body of Islam, displaying that wound to believers and nonbelievers. The lines of the Qur'an (in LIII "The Star") to which the episode refers concern a matter of great significance: the question of whether three female divinities honored in

– 223 –

Mecca in pre-Islamic times, El-Lat, El-'Uzza, and Manat, should continue to be so honored. The Qur'an as it has been preserved has the Prophet being unequivocally instructed to dismiss such a proposal, but in Rushdie's version (following Tabari's story) he first calculates that, in order to gain the support of the rulers and people of Mecca, the revelation he brings back from the mountain should offer them an "intermediate, lesser status" between Allah and humankind (*The Satanic Verses*: 107). Subsequently, however, he repudiates these lines as satanically inspired and replaces them with those found in the Qur'an. In the same chapter, Rushdie adapts another story from Tabari, having his character, Salman al Farisi, losing his faith when, as one of Mahound's scribes, he discovers that the prophet does not correct him when he, first unintentionally, and then intentionally, alters some of the words Mahound dictates to him. It is hardly surprising that, even to many scholarly Muslims who have read the whole novel, the episode has been read as both exploiting an insider's knowledge of an in-house disagreement and casting doubt from a Western Christian perspective on the divine nature of the Qur'an's dictation.

Rushdie's own position on his Muslim status has shifted markedly. Whereas, in his early statements in his own defense he insisted, "I am not a Muslim ... I do not accept the charge of apostasy, because I have never in my adult life affirmed any belief, and what one has not affirmed one cannot be said to have apostasized from,"[118] after his meeting in late December of 1990 with the imams he declared that he now recognized that he was after all a Muslim. While many people, Muslim and non-Muslim, have expressed the greatest scepticism about Rushdie's sincerity in this "midnight's conversion," it seems to me that they have missed the very obvious point that, from Rushdie's own perspective, the one statement does not negate the other. He is uncomfortably but irremediably both inside *and* outside Islam — and that is, in large part, what his book is about!

While it has been in the interests of both Islamic fundamentalists and Western secularists to assert that *The Satanic Verses* emphatically takes the side of secularism against Islam, there is a small group of critics, several of Muslim origin, who argue that the novel focuses rather on the more difficult idea of what a coherent *Islamic secularism* might look like. *The Satanic Verses* is indeed blasphemous but, in its very blasphemy, it manifests a closeness to, and dependence on, belief. In the words of Sara Suleri, "blasphemy can be expressed only within the compass of belief." "Rushdie," she insists, "has written a deeply Islamic book ... *The*

Satanic Verses is, from a cultural point of view, a work of meticulous attentiveness to religion ... the term *blasphemy* itself must be reread as a gesture of reconciliation toward the idea of belief rather than as the insult that it is commonly deemed to be."[119] And, as Marlena G. Corcoran has written, the doctrine that the every word of the Qur'an came direct from God "is the governing narrative that Rushdie is working both with and against."[120]

The inside/outside problem also has an aesthetic dimension to it. Rushdie's "directions" for reading *The Satanic Verses* rely heavily on the argument that the adventures of the two Indian-born actors, Gibreel Farishta and Saladin Chamcha, constitute the principal level of the plot and should be viewed as "framing" the Mahound and Ayesha episodes which are to be understood as dream sequences in the mind of an increasingly distressed Gibreel Farishta. More specifically, he explains his choice of the name "Mahound" for the Prophet by saying that it involves "the process of reclaiming language from one's opponents."[121] He quotes from *The Satanic Verses* itself: "To turn insults into strengths, whigs, tories, Blacks all chose to wear with pride the names they were given in scorn; likewise, our mountain-climbing, prophet-motivated solitary is to be the medieval baby-frightener, the Devil's synonym: Mahound" (*The Satanic Verses*: 93). (This is surely only part of the story, even from Rushdie's perspective: he could well have added that a feature of the crumbling of Gibreel Farishta's faith and Muslim identity is their contamination with abusive Western names and imagery.) Similarly he explains the title of the novel thus: "You call us devils? It seems to ask. Very well, then, here is the devil's version of the world, of 'your' world, the version written *from the experience* of those who have been demonized [as immigrants] by virtue of their otherness."[122] The quotation from Defoe (neglected by almost all commentators, whether favorable or antagonistic) which he placed at the very beginning of the novel certainly supports this claim, suggesting, as it does, that to be a migrant is a kind of devilish torment: "Satan, being thus confined to a vagabond, wandering, unsettled condition, is without any certain abode; for though he has, in consequence of his angelic nature, a kind of empire in the liquid waste or air, yet this is certainly part of his punishment, that he is ... without any fixed place, or space, allowed him to rest the sole of his foot upon."[123] The novel thus represents the outpourings of such a vagabond.

On the other hand, several Muslim critics make the valid point that Farishta, a glossy Bombay film star who has made his name acting in films about the adventures of characters from the Hindu epics, would hardly have had the scholarly Islamic background from which to extract materials for such fantasies. The most sophisticatedly antagonistic Muslim commentators on *The Satanic Verses*, such as Masrui and Akhtar, argue that it is a work which purports to express innocent doubt yet, once the reader is seduced into its narrative enclosure, reveals itself to be wholly subversive of Islamic tradition and belief. Ali Masrui reminds us that there is a well-established tradition in Western literature of the play-within-a-play and the dream-within-a fiction being used to convey what is claimed to be a truth denied by those in power: *Hamlet* offers prime examples of both. Similarly, there is a long tradition (and not only in Western culture) of the Fool (in *King Lear*, for instance) whose role it is to display painful truths about the actions of those in power through jokes, wordplay, mockery — and who is (or hopes to be) protected from their wrath by apparently making no claims for the serious validity of his words. Rushdie, it is suggested, has been caught out "playing the fool" in that sense. Shabbir Akhtar declares that Rushdie dressed up the Mahound and Ayesha episodes as dream or fantasy merely in order to avoid taking responsibility for the damage they would do: "Though much of *The Satanic Verses* is incoherent and apparently unmotivated, the dream sequences, in which the tenets of Islam are ridiculed, retain complexity, motivation and coherence. Here Rushdie freely adds to the existing stock of Western prejudices against the religion of the Arabian Prophet."[124] The dreams and the wordplay are mere devices by which a vicious traitor seeks to conceal his treachery. In the words of Rustom Bharucha, there is an "inadequately disguised realism underlying the fiction,"[125] or, according to Feroza Jussawalla, "his chosen technique of the novel — imitative Joycean wordplay and choppy stream-of-consciousness narrative — is less an exploration of artistic techniques than a cover for his political or racial attitudes."[126]

This is a reminder that what we call the "structure" of a literary work is a matter of perception rather than of objective fact. Like the diagrammatic staircases drawn by gestalt psychologists, it may with equal legitimacy be interpreted this way *or* that! Indeed, *The Satanic Verses* has a good deal in common with the surreal architectural drawings of the Dutch artist M. C. Escher, whose columns, windows, arches, and staircases always resist the viewer's attempts to bring them together into a coherent whole. The "outside" of the building is constantly merging with its "inside."

Rushdie has, on many occasions, expounded his belief that moral and intellectual boundaries (like national and aesthetic ones) are far less clear than is generally supposed. The origins of good are not entirely distinct from the origins of evil, just as revelation can never be quite distinguished from calculation, or faith from reason.[127] This is why, according to the author, not only do the two protagonists, from the moment of their first "angelicdevilish fall" from the exploding aircraft (*The Satanic Verses*: 5) find it impossible, however much they try, to detach themselves entirely each from the other, but the whole novel undergoes constant metamorphosis. Conventional boundaries of time and space are continually blurred or broken down. So the city of London (already referred to in the first few pages of the novel as "Mahagonny, Babylon, Alphaville") merges progressively with the two other main cities of the book, ancient Jahilia in the Arabian Desert (obviously referring to Mecca) and modern Bombay. What this merging *means* varies from one group of readers to another. Most British critics see it as suggestive, in general terms, of the ways in which, for the migrant moving from a city in his or her own country to live in a city in an alien land, impressions of the new and the old slide across each other and, more specifically, of the way in which a religion having its origins in one country (Arabia) comes to be appropriated, made familiar by believers in another country (India or Britain). So, it is not surprising that the Indian Muslim, Gibreel, should conceive of ancient Mecca in ways which curiously recall modern Bombay (just as northern European Christians have for generations visualized Christ and the Virgin Mary as blond!) Yet to Muslim readers concerned with emphasizing distance and difference, this merging is, at best, absurd, at worst, deeply offensive. They read *analogy* as signifying *identity*. So Shabbir Akhtar asks: "Is it indeed a coherent assumption that cities as historically and geographically diverse as Bombay, London and Jahilia are really the same place?"[128] (There is a sense, too, in which this blurring of historical distinctions works quite against Rushdie's implied intentions for his novel. He refers to the Imam as viewing History as the enemy of belief, "the blood-wine that must no longer be drunk ... History is a deviation from the Path, knowledge is a delusion, because the sum of knowledge was complete on the day Al-Lah finished his revelation to Mahound" [*The Satanic Verses*: 210]. Yet Rushdie's narrative strategy might be said to unravel "the veil of history," disrupt the notion of historical sequence and difference, almost as completely as the Imam could wish!) Akhtar is hostile, on much the same grounds, to Rushdie's intertwining of the angelic with the satanic: "Our failure to attain either pure good or pure evil in our lives does not imply that there is no distinction between good and evil. As for Rushdie's obscure metaphysical claim that good and evil have a common origin, it is difficult even to grasp its meaning. In any case, having a common origin need not entail any subsequent lack of distinction: the fact that men and women have a common origin in their mother's womb does not entail that there is no real distinction between the sexes."[129] This last comment, with its association of a binary distinction between good and evil with a similar distinction between man and woman, leaps out at the reader familiar with contemporary Western feminist argument and the notion that binary thinking consistently establishes woman as the alien, the other, and, eventually, as the moral inferior to man. It also offers access to a feature of the novel, its representation of women, which has perhaps been the most unsettling for traditional Muslim men and, partly for this very reason, least discussed by any of the parties. "What is certain," writes Malise Ruthven, "is that the Muslim psyche was bruised at a tender spot: relations between the sexes."[130]

The feminization of prophecy

Traditional Muslim views of the place of women in their religious and civil life are remarkably similar, as many feminists have sarcastically observed, to the traditional Jewish and Christian views: the divinity is single and male, women are accorded a "special" place within a strictly domestic sphere and are not permitted a public voice. The critics of Rushdie claiming to speak on behalf of all Muslims have for this reason all been men. It has been extraordinarily difficult for British Muslim women to have an independent voice on this, as on so many issues: it is not just Muslim men who speak for them, but, in some cases, non-Muslim men and women. "Women's voices have been largely silent in the debate where battle lines have been drawn between liberalism and fundamentalism," states a resolution adopted by Southall Black Sisters and Southall women's section of the British Labour Party. "Often it's been assumed that the views of local community leaders are our views and their demands are our demands. We regret this absolutely. We have struggled for many years in this country and across the world to express ourselves as we choose within and outside our communities."[131] The honor of women in traditional Muslim societies reflects on the men of the family, who have an obligation to defend it against any slur from outside and the right to punish any tendency by women themselves to undervalue it, either by sexual activity outside marriage or by religious deviation. In immigrant society, women's honor is seen as continually under threat, at school, at work, and in public places, as it would not be in India or Pakistan.[132] While the punishment of Muslim women by their men has been most evident to Westerners in reports from Iran of women being chastised for not wearing the *chador* or for appearing as announcers on television, and reports from Saudi Arabia of women being dragged from cars which they were presuming to drive, it is also a continuing fact of life within migrant groups in Britain, as became clear when a group of Asian women attending the big anti-Rushdie demonstration in London on 27 January 1989 under the dissenting banner of "Women Against Fundamentalism," were attacked by Muslim men who tried to assault them physically and silence them.[133] Women are "other" to a male-centered norm, to be "protected" and, above all, controlled.

While (male) Muslim critics have, of course, expressed their displeasure at the brothel episode in *The Satanic Verses*, they have made little reference to the fact that the two other episodes at which they take the greatest offense, the Ayesha story and the story of the satanic verses, also, in their different ways, center on the question of the role of women in Islam.

The simple, popular reaction to the sequence in the brothel (called "the Curtain") in Jahilia in the later years of Mahound has been that "Rushdie calls the Prophet's wives whores." Muslim critics who have read the whole work concede that "it is true that Rushdie does not say it was the prophet's real wives who were prostitutes. He creates prostitutes who adopt the names of the Prophet's wives, whores who play at being the spouses of Mahound."[134] The disturbing feature of this episode is, not only that the prostitutes' customers get additional (blasphemous) excitement from pretending to make love to the prophet's wives, but that, in their own minds, the prostitutes lose their old identities and begin to think of themselves as in fact his wives. To quote from the novel: "The Madam then married them all off herself, and in that den of degeneracy, that anti-mosque, that labyrinth of profanity, Baal became the husband of the wives of the former businessman, Mahound" (*The Satanic Verses*: 383). (Baal is a cynical, decrepit poet, who in his younger years was required by the Grandee of Jahilia, Abu Simbel, to write satirical verses against Mahound. He is one of several characters in the novel suggesting Rushdie himself.) Baal then falls in love with the youngest prostitute who has taken the name of Mahound's (but actually, too, Muhammad's) favorite wife, Ayesha, having, as the narrative voice comments, "fallen prey to the seductions of becoming the secret, profane mirror of Mahound" (*The Satanic Verses*: 384).

The drawing of an analogy between Muhammad's household arrangements and a brothel is read, not surprisingly, by most Muslims as acutely disrespectful of the prophet and his wives. Several Muslim commentators have referred also to the way in which the episode reinforces crude Western stereotypes about the life of the Muslim "harem." To quote Shabbir Akhtar:

> The Muslim anger at the brothel scenes is not properly explicable as being due to mere prudery ... Islam is not an antisensual faith; and sexual appetite has always been regarded as wholesome and good within certain limits. But Muslims are rightly troubled by Rushdie's speculations because these reinforce a stereotypical and false picture of Muslim sexuality. The West has produced its own fantastic and romanticised portrait of the sexual dimension of Islamic civilisation, a portrait that in turn feeds the very fantasies that helped to create it. Rushdie is merely exploiting the Western image of Muslim sexuality as exotic and untamed.[135]

Most subversive, and for this reason, no doubt, not referred to at all by Muslim critics, is surely the role of fantasy among the characters themselves, both the representation of blasphemous male sexual fantasy (in the minds of the clients and of Baal, the "possession" of the Prophet's wives) and the acknowledgement that women indulge in sexual fantasy at all. As one Western commentator has observed, though in a wider context: "the immigrant defends himself against his own desires. It is easy to understand why immigrants feel threatened."[136] It is acutely uncomfortable for the believer to be reminded by an outsider of those images he finds most seductively tempting.

If the analogy between Muhammad's household arrangements and a brothel were not unsettling enough, the role of the goddesses in the episode of the satanic verses themselves is unsettling in a rather different direction. The subject on which Rushdie chose to have his Prophet prevaricate also concerns the role accorded to women by Islam. Mahound first contemplates, then discards, the idea that three goddesses worshipped according to one of the old religions might be "kept on" as subordinate divinities to Allah under the new regime. Rushdie did not invent this episode but rather, as has already been mentioned, borrowed and adapted it from an apocryphal story in the work of two early Islamic scholars. The phrase which his Mahound first inserts into his recitation to indicate approval of their role, "'They are the exalted birds, and their intercession is desired indeed'" (*The Satanic Verses*: 114), is borrowed from Tabari. The phrase used by Mahound to replace these verses is the one to be found in the Qur'an: "Shall He [Allah] have daughters while you have sons? That would be an unjust division."[137] It is not that the text suggests that, with the founding of Islam, a genuinely matrifocal culture was replaced with a patriarchal culture: in the same chapter, the narrative voice (referring, in fact, to Mahound's first wife in the period before his revelations) underlines the contradictions in the old order: "It isn't easy to be a brilliant, successful woman in a city where the gods are female but the females are merely goods" (*The Satanic Verses*: 383). What seems to be suggested is that one kind of injustice and hypocrisy came to be replaced with another. As Rushdie concedes, though with unusual vagueness, in the essay "In Good Faith," "I thought it was at least worth pointing out that one of the reasons for rejecting these goddesses was that *they were female*. The rejection has implications that are worth thinking about."[138] The episode attaches a question mark to both the singleness and the maleness of the Islamic conception of divinity.

Criticism of the Ayesha episode centers on the juxtaposition of what many educated Muslims regard as an instance of ignorant (modern) popular superstition with episodes which parody the life of the Prophet. They may have no objection to what they see as its dismissal of superstition. Shabbir Akhtar, for instance, comments: "Rushdie ably uses the incident to condemn the impotence of religion in an age in which experimental science yields techniques independent of transcendent miracle and supernatural aid. It is also a powerfully relevant comment on the prostitution of religion, particularly in cult form, which can lead to social catastrophe." It seems highly likely that one of the reasons for its relative acceptability is that Ayesha is an uneducated *woman*. Akhtar's concern is rather that "though Rushdie's exploration here is largely fair, one still needs to take exception to the possible implication that *all* religion is essentially superstition."[139] He sees it as implying that no distinction can be made between a serious religious belief deriving from a sacred text and superstitious gullibility. (There is also the fact that this holy woman is given the same name as that taken by the youngest prostitute, which is also the name of Muhammad's favourite wife.)

But just how completely *does* Rushdie dismiss this example of popular devotion? Even Shabbir Akhtar refers to it as one of the novel's "rare tender moments."[140] The simple young woman, dressed only in butterflies, sustaining herself on her faith and by eating butterflies is genuinely charismatic, considerably more attractive in many ways than the calculating businesssman-prophet, Mahound. While the satanic verses episode leaves the reader with a sense that the secret of the conjurer's trick has been explained, the Ayesha episode suggests that beyond the failure of her enterprise lies a magnificent mystery. With only one exception, the survivors agree, without having had the opportunity to confer, that they saw the waters of the Arabian Sea open (*The Satanic Verses*: 504-5). Their accounts give even the CID men investigating the case goose pimples. While the male Muslim critics who attack the novel don't refer to this, it may well be that they sense it and are angry also over the subversive quality of this moment.

"We've only been allowed one reading of the book, because of the Muslim reaction. It would be interesting to see a feminist reaction," Rana Kabbani, a Syrian-born Muslim woman, educated in Britain and America and living in London is reported as saying. Her answer is that *The Satanic Verses* is "a cry of rage against women, Britain, and Islam."[141] (Other commentators, for instance Daniel Pipes, argue indeed that *every* group comes almost equally under attack in the novel: Western capitalists, Jews, fundamentalist Christians, etc.) It is certainly arguable that at the heart of the novel is always the relationship between two *men* and that women are depicted as unknowable "other" to those men. When, at the beginning of the novel, the prim Saladin sees the extravagant Gibreel, whom he loathes, floating through the air toward him he "would have shouted, 'Keep away, get away from me,' except that something prevented him, the beginning of a little fluttery screamy thing in his intestines, so instead of uttering words of rejection he opened his arms and Farishta swam into them until they were embracing head-to-tail" (*The Satanic Verses*: 6). The whole novel might be said to involve a working out of the love-hate relationship between these two men who have chosen such different solutions to the question of how to live as postcolonial Muslim Indians. There is a second, highly significant embrace between them in the middle of the novel when Gibreel rescues Saladin from the burning Café Shandaar. The novel ends, to be sure, with the suicide of Gibreel Farishta in Saladin's presence in Bombay, but this act is associated with Saladin's embrace of another man, his father, on his deathbed, and his "falling in love" with him.

Both Saladin and Gibreel are obsessed with women who are depicted as desirable but unknowable, "other" to them. In Saladin's case, she is his English wife, Pamela Lovelace, who epitomizes, for him, every aspect of the England he vainly aspires to be part of. In Gibreel's, it is the blonde, icy, Jewish-Polish Alleluia Cone, climber of Everest. Nevertheless, the very ending of the book, after the death of Gibreel and of Saladin's father, has Saladin reconciled with, and taken off to bed by, the Bombay woman, Zeenat Vakil, who has so persistently and brutally pointed out to him the foolishness of his desire to suppress his own Indianness. If there is a lesson in this happy ending, it could be said that complete "otherness" is not what a man should aspire to in a heterosexual relationship.

While Gayatri Spivak acknowledges Rushdie's "anxiety to write woman into the narrative of history," and that the satanic verses episode is "a story of negotiation in the name of woman," she concludes that "here again we have to record a failure." She goes on: "All through, the text is written on the register of male bonding and unbonding, the most important being, of course, the double subject of migrancy. Gibreel Farishta and Saladin Chamcha. The two are tortured by obsession with women, go through them, even destroy them, within a gender code that is never opened up, never questioned, in this book where so much is called into question, so much is reinscribed."[142]

That is not the view of Sara Suleri in her illuminating and provocative essay, "Contraband Histories: Salman Rushdie and the Embodiment of Blasphemy." She treats the Ayesha episode as a key to the whole work, viewing it as a retelling of "the tale of the satanic verses in a contemporary cultural context," a daring attempt to restate the monolithic, nationalist, masculine dogma of Mahound in a more ambiguous, postcolonial feminine form. It is not just that this religious leader happens to be a woman: her gender, indeed her sexuality, are central to the episode. "Her extraordinary desirability is matched only by her chastity, which is expressed by her insistence on feeding herself solely on butterflies." Suleri underlines the imagery built into the tale of division, the opening of the sea and its explicit association with both the partition of the Indian subcontinent ("a parting of the waters that both cannot, and can always, occur") and female sexuality. Not only do the survivors of the pilgrimage affirm that a parting of the waters did miraculously occur: "'Just when my strength failed and I thought I would surely die there in the water, I saw it with my own eyes; I saw the sea divide, like hair being combed; and they were all there, far away, walking away from me,'" but the most sceptical of them all undergoes a form of feminizing conversion on his deathbed. He experiences death as a kind of drowning. He finds himself in the water beside Ayesha who commands him to "'Open,'" but he closes: "Then something within him refused that, made a different choice, and at the instant that his heart broke, he opened. His body split apart from his adam's apple to his groin, so that she could reach deep within him, and now she was open, they all were, and at the moment of their opening the waters parted, and they walked to Mecca across the bed of the Arabian Sea" (*The Satanic Verses*: 507).

Suleri describes the whole process in terms of metaphor profoundly disrupting the linearity of masculine narrative and as "the feminization of prophecy": "In this extraordinary rendering of a limpid and free-floating devotion, the feminized prophet enters the body of dubiety, and the figurative miracle of their union points less to Mecca than to Rushdie's need to find openings in the structure of male desire."[143]

While it seems highly unlikely that male Muslim commentators would have been capable of formulating this illuminating interpretation on a conscious level (since the vast majority of Western critics, male and female, have not done so), Suleri's reading may, nevertheless, provide further clues as to why, on an unconscious level, they found the episode so acutely disturbing. (Nor is it necessary to pose the question about the extent to which Rushdie fully and consciously intended the passage to be read in such a way, since it was evidently "open" to being so interpreted.)

The novel as trap

In the short term *The Satanic Verses* has turned out to be a kind of gigantic trap, into which almost all those who have been closely involved with it have disastrously fallen. Its author set himself a cluster of objectives, in many of which, on his own admission, he utterly failed. Far from writing a book which would offer readers within the Muslim communities in Britain the opportunity to take "pleasure in finding their reality given pride of place,"[144] far from bringing his three worlds, India, Islam, and the West, together, far from contributing to the opening of the gap between moderate Islam and monolithic fundamentalism, far from revealing the potential for a "humanized, historicized, secularized way of being a Muslim,"[145] Rushdie has contributed, by a lack of foresight and control over his exuberant imagination, to exactly the opposite tendencies. (Most ironically of all, perhaps, he gave one of the figures he had pilloried so mercilessly in the novel, Margaret Thatcher, no option but to offer him armed protection against another of the novel's characters, "the Imam," which gained her some undeserved credit from liberals in the West!) As for moderate Muslims in the immigrant communities in Britain, they showed a lack of confidence in the durability of their own religious and cultural tradition by allowing their entirely justifiable distress and anger to be instrumentally appropriated by the fundamentalist leadership in Iran, and, as Rushdie himself has written, "let Muslim leaders make Muslims seem less tolerant than they are."[146] Rushdie's defenders have, meanwhile, only too often fallen into a self-righteous insensitivity to the feelings of those who had been offended, and a kind of "free speech fundamentalism" which they would have strenuously avoided (as several Muslims have pointed out) if the issue had been a text which had been found offensive and degrading by women or by Jews. There is a weird sense, too, in which the Ayatollah Khomeini, whose *fatwah* looked at the time like the most tremendous coup, may be said to have fallen into the trap the novel set for him, since all of his words and actions now look, to anyone who has read the novel, as if Rushdie had scripted them. (As Rushdie himself has said, "some passages in *The Satanic Verses* have now acquired a prophetic quality that alarms even me.")[147] For the moment, at least, it seems that the publication of Rushdie's novel has pushed intercommunal and international relations involving Islam even deeper into the mire than they were before.

Yet perhaps, in the long run, it will be possible to agree with Tzvetan Todorov's statement that "the affair is an illustration and a test of what the book itself tells us; [and] *the fact that the two, the book and the affair, have become inseparable is not necessarily a bad thing* (my italics)."[148] In *The Satanic Verses*, Rushdie identified and touched a whole series of "tender spots" and, in so doing, offered a series of challenges, by no means all of them directed at Islam. Certainly the novel poses the question: can moderate Islam renew itself, reassert the richness of its cultural heritage without succumbing to the oppression of monolithic, patriarchal fundamentalism? Central to such a renewal would have to be new thinking about the role of women in Islam. Rushdie asks: "Are all the rules laid down at a religion's origin immutable for ever? How about the penalties for prostitution (stoning to death) or thieving (mutilation)? How about the prohibition of homosexuality? How about the Islamic law of inheritance, which allows a widow to inherit only an eighth share, and which gives to sons twice as much as to daughters? What of the Islamic law of evidence, which makes a woman's testimony worth only half that of a man?"[149]

At the same time it offers a challenge to Western liberalism: to back away from its own tendency to denigrate Islam, which it treats as a relic left over from "our" Middle Ages, denying the diversity of Islam and the threads of scepticism woven into its fabric, driving decent Muslim people into the arms of the Iranian fundamentalists. As for Britain (and other European countries with large Muslim populations), the very immediate challenge remains as to whether it can work through the difficult problem of building a genuinely multicultural society, in which diversity of language and tradition will be fully respected both in law and in practice, but which will be quite uncompromising in its insistence on basic human rights for all its citizens. That requires post-Thatcherian Britain to follow Rushdie (as Thatcherian Britain certainly did not) in celebrating "hybridity, impurity, intermingling, the transformation that comes of new and unexpected combinations of human beings, cultures, ideas, politics, movies, songs." But it also requires that the rights of Muslim women in the immigrant communities to express themselves independently and determine their own future role be guaranteed. (Rushdie accuses the opposition British Labour Party of not, for instance, consulting Muslim girls about whether they want to be educated in segregated schools; he says that it "plans to deliver them into the hands of the mullahs.")[150] The more general insight to be found in Rushdie's fiction, and which is as relevant in the 1990s to the peoples of the former Jugoslavia, of Azerbaijan, of Fiji, and of several African countries as it is to the Indian subcontinent and Britain, is that when people in mixed populations try to turn their internal, metaphorical sense of territory into geographical reality, the consequences are, almost without exception, disastrous.

How will the story end?

The ending of *The Satanic Verses* is remarkably positive, showing Saladin Chamcha reconciled with his dying father and so with himself and his roots in Muslim India. It is an ending which most commentators find uncharacteristic of Rushdie and many quite unconvincing. The Rushdie affair is not yet concluded: on the one hand, Rushdie is showing himself more often in public, having made appearances in the United States and Germany in recent months; on the other, some Iranian clerics have renewed the *fatwah*, and the bounty offered for his murder has been further increased. The recent hotel bombing in Turkey shows people still dying in connection with Rushdie's novel. (To my mind, Rushdie's subsequent declaration that the Turkish publisher and associated secularists must bear some responsibility for having provoked the fundamentalists in Turkey is quite inconsistent with the arguments he used when, for instance, attacking Rajiv Gandhi for prohibiting publication in India.) While there is probably more reason to hope that Rushdie will live out the whole of his natural life, it is impossible to imagine a scenario in which any real reconciliation will occur.

As to future developments within Islam, let alone on the intercommunal and international level around Islam, it is difficult to make any kind of prediction, let alone a positive one. It is nevertheless worth observing perhaps that, if one had examined the "wound" probed by each of the other works of narrative that I have discussed — serfdom, slavery, fascism, the Russian labor camps — just four years after their first publication, one would probably have concluded that, if anything, those wounds had festered and, in each case, the condition of the body politic had deteriorated. In none of the four cases would the observer have had much cause for optimism. In the longer historical perspective, however, it is possible to take a much more positive view of the role each has played in the removal of a specific ill. Perhaps, by analogy with the earlier cases, a degree of optimism in the Rushdie affair is therefore not entirely misplaced. On the other hand it may well be that fictional works make their most *visible*, constructive contribution to world affairs when they treat a topic that, however large, can be readily defined and labeled as a problem (such as "serfdom", or "Italian Fascism") and whose removal can therefore be dated and applauded. Despite what many Westerners would like to believe, Islam is not, itself, the problem! Rather the "sores" touched by the Rushdie affair are many, complex, and located both within the body of Islam itself and in the relations between Islamic and non-Islamic peoples, nationally and internationally. While *The Satanic Verses* has had the subtlety and complexity to touch and inflame all those sores, it is difficult to see how, even in the medium term, it could contribute to their healing.

Let us hope, nevertheless, that healing does take place and that Salman Rushdie survives to have the pleasure of seeing it occur.

NOTES FOR CHAPTER 6

1. This chapter was completed in the last months of 1993.
2. The imams were shot in Brussels in March 1989, after they refused to call for the novel to be banned. In February 1990, the relatives of British hostages held in Beirut pressed Viking Penguin not to issue a paperback edition of *The Satanic Verses* since this could be expected to prolong the hostages' incarceration. Diplomatic relations between the United Kingdom and Iran were broken off soon after the issuing of the *fatwah* in early 1989 and renewed in September 1990. Rushdie's so-called "conversion" to Islam

occurred in December 1990. The Japanese translator of *The Satanic Verses* was murdered in July 1991, the Italian translator was stabbed in April of the same year, and the Norwegian translator was seriously injured in mid-1993. The diplomatic reverberations of the affair have continued throughout 1993, with Rushdie's claim that assassins backed by Iran were intercepted by the British secret service the previous year, the formal renewal by the Iranian religious authorities of the death threat, followed by a denial from the Iranian government that it intended to send killers to carry out that threat. John Major, the British Prime Minister, held a widely publicized meeting with Rushdie in May 1993, expressing his support for the writer.

3. Salman Rushdie, "In Good Faith," in his *Imaginary Homelands: Essays and Criticism, 1981-1991* (London: Granta Books, 1991): 407. This essay was first published in 1990.

4. Interview with Shrabani Basu, *Sunday*, India, 18-24 September 1988.

5. Rushdie, "In Good Faith": 409.

6. Shabbir Akhtar, *Be Careful With Muhammad! The Salman Rushdie Affair* (London: Bellew Publishing, 1989): 13.

7. Ali Masrui, "Is *The Satanic Verses* a Satanic Novel? Moral Dilemmas of the Rushdie Affair," in *Michigan Quarterly Review* 28, no. 3 (Summer 1989): 363.

8. The argument for the Zionist connection is specifically based on the flimsy ground that Peter Mayer, who chairs Viking Penguin, is an American Jew.

9. Editorial, *The Black Scholar* 20 (March/April 1989): 14.

10. See, for instance, Masrui, "Is *The Satanic Verses* a Satanic Novel?": 347-371.

11. Akhtar, *Be Careful With Muhammad!*: 20.

12. Ali Masrui, "Witness for the Prosecution: A Cross-Examination on *The Satanic Verses*," in *Third Text* 11 (Summer 1990): 35.

13. Masrui, "Is *The Satanic Verses* a Satanic Novel?": 347.

14. *Guardian* 27 February 1989.

15. Masrui, "Is *The Satanic Verses* a Satanic Novel?": 349.

16. Quoted in Daniel Pipes, "The Ayatollah, the Novelist and the West," *Commentary* 87 (June 1989): 14.

17. W. K. Wimsatt, *The Verbal Icon: Studies in the Meaning of Poetry* (Lexington: University of Kentucky Press, 1967): 3.

18. Roland Barthes, "The Death of the Author, in his *Image-Music-Text* translated by Stephen Heath (Glasgow: Fontana/Collins, 1977): 148.

19. Akhtar, *Be Careful with Muhammad*: 35.

20. T. B. Irving, "The Rushdie Confrontation: a Clash in Values," in *The Iowa Review* 20, no. 1 (Winter 1990): 176.

21. *The Times of India*, 13 October 1988.

22. Rushdie, "In Good Faith": 395 and 403.

23. Rushdie, "In Good Faith": 399.

24. Rushdie, "In Good Faith": 402.

25. Rushdie, "In Good Faith": 398.

26. Rushdie, "In Good Faith": 396.

27. Wimsatt, *The Verbal Icon*: 4.
28. Rushdie, "In Good Faith": 410.
29. Akhtar, *Be Careful with Muhammad*: 77.
30. James Fenton, "Keeping Up With Salman Rushdie," *The New York Review of Books*, 28 March 1991: 31-33.
31. See his account of these conversations in the Indian magazine *Sunday*, 2 October 1989: 78.
32. Dr Zahid Hussain as reported by Tim Kelsey and David Lister, in "Rushdie Publishers Told Book Would Unleash Terror," *The Independent*, 16 March 1989.
33. Malise Ruthven, *A Satanic Affair: Salman Rushdie and the Rage of Islam* (London: Chatto and Windus, 1990): 89.
34. Rukmini Bhaya Nair and Rimli Bhattacharya, "Salman Rushdie: The Migrant in the Metropolis," *Third Text* 11 (Summer 1990): 29.
35. Reported in the *Observer*, 19 February 1989.
36. *Impact International* (a Muslim news magazine published in London), 27 January 1989.
37. Tzvetan Todorov, "*The Satanic Verses* in Paris," in *Dissent* 37 (Winter 1990): 98.
38. Bhikhu Parek, "Between Holy Text and Moral Void," *New Statesman and Society*, 23 March 1989: 30.
39. Rushdie, "One Thousand Days in a Balloon," in his *Imaginary Homelands: Essays and Criticism, 1981-1991* (London: Granta Books, 1991): 431-32.
40. Reprinted in Lisa Appignanesi and Sara Maitland, eds., *The Rushdie File* (London: Fourth Estate, 1989): 42-45. This is a very important source of information and documents from the first year of the Rushdie affair.
41. Nair and Bhattacharya, "Salman Rushdie: The Migrant in the Metropolis": 23.
42. Michael Wood, "The Prophet Motive," *The New Republic*, 6 March 1989: 30.
43. For informed and sympathetic treatment of these issues in relation to *The Satanic Verses*, see Ruthven, *A Satanic Affair*, especially Chapter Three, "Islam in Britain"; Clark Blaise and Bharati Mukherjee, "After the Fatwah," *Mother Jones* 15 (April-May 1990): 28-31, 61-65.
44. For a review of Western images of Muhammad, see Norman Daniel, *Islam and the West: the Making of an Image* (Edinburgh: Edinburgh University Press, 1960), usefully summarized in James Piscatori, "The Rushdie Affair and the Politics of Ambiguity," *International Affairs* 66, no. 4 (1990): 767-89.
45. Akeel Bilgrami, "Rushdie, Islam and Postcolonial Defensiveness," *The Yale Journal of Criticism* 4, no. 1 (1990): 303.
46. See both his *Orientalism* (New York: Pantheon, 1978) and *Covering Islam: How the Media and the Experts Determine How We See the Rest of the World* (New York: Pantheon, 1981).
47. Ruthven, *A Satanic Affair*: 55.
48. Theodore P. Wright,"The Rushdie Controversy: the Spread of Communalism from South Asia to the West," *Plural Societies* 20, no. 3, (December 1990): 32.
49. Todorov, "The Satanic Verses in Paris": 98.

The Power of the Story
▼▼▼

50. In mid-1990, a lawyer, Geoffrey Robertson, brought together leading figures resident in Britain, from both sides of the struggle over the novel, for a television program entitled "Satanic Scenario," in the series "Hypotheticals," during which he cross-examined them on how they would behave if they found themselves in certain situations with Rushdie. In particular he asked some of Rushdie's fiercest opponents whether, if the opportunity arose, they would personally kill him. Not surprisingly, given the legal position in which they would have placed themselves if they had said "Yes," none said they would.

51. Akhtar, *Be Careful with Muhammad*: 67.

52. See especially Gayatri C. Spivak, "Reading *The Satanic Verses*," in *Third Text* 11 (Summer 1990): 53.

53. Rushdie, "In Good Faith": 410-11.

54. Barbara Nimri Azis, "Arab Writers Ride Out the Storm," *The Christian Science Monitor*, Thursday 11 May 1989: 19.

55. Ashis Nandy, "Dialogue and the Diaspora," *Third Text* 11 (Summer 1990): 101.

56. Edward W. Said, "*The Satanic Verses* and Democratic Freedoms," *The Black Scholar* 20 (March/April 1989): 17-18.

57. Salman Rushdie, *Midnight's Children* (London: Picador, 1982): 414.

58. Rushdie, *Midnight's Children*: 438.

59. Rushdie, *Midnight's Children*: 275.

60. Salman Rushdie, *Shame* (London: Picador, 1984). For a discussion of the references to fundamentalism in Pakistan, see Ruthven, *A Satanic Affair*: 63-66.

61. Salman Rushdie, *The Satanic Verses* (London: Viking Penguin, 1988).

62. Interview with Madhu Jain, *India Today*, 15 September 1988.

63. *Illustrated Weekly of India*, 7 October 1988: 12.

64. Rushdie, *Shame*: 257.

65. Pipes, "The Ayatollah, the Novelist and the West": 12.

66. Pipes, "The Ayatollah, the Novelist and the West": 15.

67. Rushdie, *Midnight's Children*: 192.

68. Rushdie, *Midnight's Children*: 338.

69. Rushdie, *Midnight's Children*: 292-3.

70. Rushdie, *Midnight's Children*: 382.

71. Rushdie, "In Good Faith": 407.

72. Rushdie, "In Good Faith": 396.

73. *The Times of India*, 27 January 1989.

74. Rushdie, "In Good Faith": 394.

75. Rushdie, "In Good Faith": 397.

76. Rushdie, "In Good Faith": 398.

77. Blaise and Mukherjee, "After the Fatwah": 61.

78. Rushdie, "In Good Faith": 395.

79. Nair and Bhattacharya, "Salman Rushdie: The Migrant in the Metropolis": 28, though they, in turn, refer to the article by Bhikhu Parek.
80. But see Timothy Brennan, *Salman Rushdie and the Third World: Myths of the Nation* (Basingstoke: Macmillan, 1989): 145; and Nair and Battacharya, "The Migrant in the Metropolis": 23.
81. *New York Times* review, quoted on cover of paperback edition.
82. Marlena G. Corcoran, "Salman Rushdie's Satanic Narration," in *The Iowa Review* 20, no. 1 (Winter 1990): 155-167.
83. Feroza Jussawalla, "Resurrecting the prophet: the Case of Salman, the Otherwise," *Public Culture* 2, no. 1 (Fall 1989): 106.
84. Rushdie, "In Good Faith": 396.
85. Reported in *The New York Times*, early January 1991, quoted in an editorial, "Midnight's Conversion," in *The New Republic* 21 January 1991: 9.
86. See, for instance, "Midnight's Conversion": 9-10.
87. Quoted in James Fenton, "Keeping Up With Salman Rushdie": 26.
88. Rushdie, "One Thousand Days in a Balloon": 430.
89. Rushdie, "In Good Faith": 409.
90. Brennan, *Salman Rushdie and the Third World*: 144.
91. Ruthven, *A Satanic Affair*: 17.
92. Brennan, *Salman Rushdie and the Third World*: 152.
93. Interview with Sean French, *Observer*, 25 September 1988.
94. Rushdie, "In Good Faith": 408.
95. Corcoran, "Salman Rushdie's Satanic Narration": 159.
96. Rushdie, "One Thousand Days in a Balloon": 432.
97. Rushdie, "In Good Faith": 402-3.
98. Akhtar, *Be Careful with Muhammad*: 18.
99. Qur'an, Chapter 26, verses 221-26, in *The Koran Interpreted*, 2 vols., trans. Arthur J. Arberry (London: Allen and Unwin, 1955).
100. Rushdie, "Is Nothing Sacred?" in his *Imaginary Homelands: Essays and Criticism, 1981-1991* (London: Granta Books, 1991): 420.
101. Rushdie, "Is Nothing Sacred?": 420.
102. BBC Summary of World Broadcasts, quoted in Appignanesi and Maitland, *The Rushdie File*: 90.
103. Peter van der Veer, "Satanic or Angelic? The Politics of Religious and Literary Inspiration," *Public Culture* 2, no. 1 (Fall 1989): 101.
104. Rustom Bharucha, "The Rushdie Affair: Secular Bigotry and the Ambivalence of Faith," *Third Text* 11 (Summer 1990): 62.
105. Piscatori, "The Rushdie Affair and the Politics of Ambiguity": 776.
106. Ashis Nandy, *The Intimate Enemy* (New Delhi: Oxford University Press, 1984) quoted in Ashis Nandy, "Dialogue and the Diaspora: Conversation with Nikos Papastergiadis" in *Third Text* 11 (Summer 1990): 99

107. Peter Nazareth, "Rushdie's Wo/manichean Novel," *The Iowa Review* 20, no. 1 (Winter 1990): 168.
108. In ed. Bill Bourne, Udi Eichler, and David Herman, *Voices: Writers and Politics* (Nottingham: Spokesman, 1987): 63.
109. Rushdie, *Midnight's Children*: 194.
110. Rushdie, "In Good Faith": 404.
111. Wright, "The Rushdie Controversy": 34.
112. Blaise and Mukherjee, "After the Fatwah": 61.
113. Rushdie, "In Good Faith": 408.
114. Spivak, "Reading *The Satanic Verses*": 54.
115. Rushdie, "In Good Faith": 405.
116. See for instance Masrui, "Moral Dilemmas of *The Satanic Verses*": 20-21.
117. Brennan, *Salman Rushdie and the Third World*: 144.
118. Rushdie, "In Good Faith": 405.
119. Sara Suleri, "Contraband Histories: Salman Rushdie and the Embodiment of Blasphemy," *The Yale Review* 78, no. 4 (1989): 606-7.
120. Corcoran, "Salman Rushdie's Satanic Narration": 157.
121. Rushdie, "In Good Faith": 402.
122. Rushdie, "In Good Faith": 403.
123. The quotation is from Defoe's *The History of the Devil*.
124. Akhtar, *Be Careful with Muhammad*: 27.
125. Bharucha, "The Rushdie Affair: Secular Bigotry and the Ambivalence of Faith": 63.
126. Jussawalla, "Resurrecting the Prophet: the Case of Salman, the Otherwise": 108.
127. See, for instance, the interview with Sean French, in the London *Observer*, 25 September 1988.
128. Akhtar, *Be Careful with Muhammad*: 15.
129. Akhtar, *Be Careful with Muhammad*: 19.
130. Ruthven, *A Satanic Affair*: 5.
131. Resolution of March 9 1989, quoted by John La Rose in "'Writers Have Their Right to Write," *The Black Scholar* 20 (March/April 1989): 15.
132. Ruthven, *A Satanic Affair*: 73.
133. Ruthven, *A Satanic Affair*: 5.
134. Masrui, "Is *The Satanic Verses* a Satanic Novel?": 354.
135. Akhtar, *Be Careful with Muhammad*: 28.
136. Editorial, "Two Cheers for Blasphemy," *The New Republic* 200, no. 11 (1989): 8.
137. Qur'an, chapter 53, verses 19-20.
138. Rushdie, "In Good Faith": 399-400.
139. Akhtar, *Be Careful with Muhammad*: 29.
140. Akhtar, *Be Careful with Muhammad*: 28.

141. Quoted in Blaise and Mukherjee, "After the Fatwah": 62-63.
142. Spivak, "Reading *The Satanic Verses*": 46-47.
143. Suleri, "Contraband Histories": 622-3.
144. Rushdie, "In Good Faith": 414.
145. Rushdie, "One Thousand Days in a Balloon": 436.
146. Rushdie, "In Good Faith": 413.
147. Rushdie, "In Good Faith": 407.
148. Todorov, "*The Satanic Verses* in Paris": 97.
149. Rushdie, "In Good Faith": 400.
150. Rushdie, "In Good Faith": 400.

BIBLIOGRAPHY

▼ ▼ ▼

Adams, John R. *Harriet Beecher Stowe.* New York: Twayne, 1963.

Akhtar, Shabbir. *Be Careful With Muhammad! The Salman Rushdie Affair.* London: Bellew Publishing, 1989.

Aksakov, Konstantin S. "On the Internal State of Russia." *Russian Intellectual History: An Anthology.* Edited by Marc Raeff. New York, Chicago, San Francisco, Atlanta: Harcourt, Brace and World, 1966: 230-251.

Albertazzi, Silvia. *Il tempio e il villaggio.* Bologna: Patron, 1978.

Almedingen, E. M. *The Emperor Alexander II.* London: Bodley Head, 1962.

Amiconi, Nando. *Il comunista e il capomanipolo.* Milan: Vangelista, 1977.

Ammons, Elizabeth. "Stowe's Dream of the Mother-Savior: *Uncle Tom's Cabin* and American Women Writers before the 1920s." *New Essays on "Uncle Tom's Cabin."* Edited by Eric J. Sundquist. Cambridge: Cambridge University Press, 1986: 155-195.

Anchor, Robert. "Narrativity and the Transformation of Historical Consciousness." *Clio* 16, no. 2 (1987): 121-137.

Appignanesi, Lisa and Maitland, Sara, eds. *The Rushdie File.* London: Fourth Estate, 1989.

Arendt, Hannah. *On Violence.* London: The Penguin Press, 1970.

Azis, Barbara Nimri. "Arab Writers Ride Out the Storm." *The Christian Science Monitor,* Thursday 11 May 1989: 19.

Bakhtin, Mikhail. "Discourse in the Novel." *The Dialogic Imagination: Four Essays by M. M. Bakhtin.* Edited by Michael Holquist, translated by Caryl Emerson and Michael Holmquist. Austin, Texas: University of Texas Press, 1981.

Baldwin, James. "Everybody's Protest Novel" (1949). *The Price of the Ticket: Collected Nonfiction, 1948-1985.* London: Michael Joseph, 1985: 27-33.

Bandler, Richard and Grinder, John. *The Structure of Magic I: A Book about Language and Therapy.* Palo Alto: Science and Behavior Books, 1975.

Barthes, Roland. "The Death of the Author." *Image-Music-Text.* Translated by Stephen Heath. Glasgow: Fontana/Collins, 1977: 142-48.

———. "Introduction to the Structural Analysis of Narratives." *Image — Music — Text.* Translated by Stephen Heath. Glasgow: Fontana/Collins, 1977: 79-124.

———. "Lecture in Inauguration of the Chair of Literary Semiology, Collège de France, January 7, 1977." Translated by R. Howard. *October* 8 (Spring 1977): 3-16.

———. *S/Z.* New York: Hill and Wang, 1970.

Bibliography
▼▼▼

——. "Theory of the Text." Translated by Ian McLeod. *Untying the Text: A Post-Structuralist Reader*. Edited by Robert Young. Boston, London and Henley: Routledge and Kegan Paul, 1981: 31-47.

Bass, Ellen, and Thornton, Louise, eds. *I Never Told Anyone: Writings by Women Survivors of Child Sexual Abuse*. New York: Harper and Row, 1983.

Battaglia, Roberto and Garritano, Giuseppe. *La resistenza italiana: lineamenti di storia*. Rome: Editori Riuniti, 1974.

Bauer, Werner, et al. *Text und Rezeption: Wirkungsanalyse Zeitgenössischer Lyrik am Beispiel des Gedichtes "Fadensonnen" von Paul Celan*. Frankfurt: Athenäum, 1972.

Belinsky, Vissarion. *Selected Philosophical Works*. Moscow: Foreign Languages Publishing House, 1956.

Benno, Peter. "The Political Aspect." *Soviet Literature in the Sixties*. Edited by Max Hayward and Edward L. Crowley. London: Methuen, 1965: 178-202.

Berry, Mary Frances. *Long Memory: The Black Experience in America*. New York: Oxford University Press, 1982.

Berryman, Philip. *Liberation Theology*. Philadelphia: Temple University Press: 1987.

Bharucha, Rustom. "The Rushdie Affair: Secular Bigotry and the Ambivalence of Faith." *Third Text* 11 (Summer 1990): 61-69.

Bilgrami, Akeel. "Rushdie, Islam and Postcolonial Defensiveness." *The Yale Journal of Criticism* 4, no. 1 (1990): 301-11.

Blaise, Clark and Mukherjee, Bharati. "After the Fatwah." *Mother Jones* 15 (April-May 1990): 28-31, 61-65.

Bourne, Bill, Eichler, Udi and Herman David, eds. *Voices: Writers and Politics*. Nottingham: Spokesman, 1987.

Brecht, Bertolt. *Brecht on Theater: The Development of an Aesthetic*. Edited by J. Willett. New York: Hill and Wang, 1964.

Brennan, Timothy. *Salman Rushdie and the Third World: Myths of the Nation*. Basingstoke: Macmillan, 1989.

Brown, Deming. *Soviet Literature since Stalin*. Cambridge: Cambridge University Press, 1978.

Burg, David and Feifer, George. *Solzhenitsyn*. New York: Stein and Day, 1972.

Carpovich, Vera V. *Solzhenitsyn's Peculiar Vocabulary: Russian-English Glossary*. New York: Technical Dictionaries, 1976.

Caute, David. *The Illusion: an Essay on Politics, Theater and the Novel*. London: André Deutsch, 1971.

Cecchi, Emilio. *Di giorno in giorno*. Milan: Garzanti, 1954.

Chaadaev, Peter. *The Major Works of Peter Chaadaev*. Translated by Raymond T. McNally. Notre Dame and London: 1969.

Chambers, Ross. *Story and Situation: Narrative Seduction and the Power of Fiction*. Minneapolis: Manchester and Minneapolis University Presses, 1984.

Cixous, Hélène. "Entretien avec Françoise van Rossum-Guyon." *Revue des Sciences Humaines* 168 (1977): 479-93.

Cohen, S. and Young, J. eds. *The Manufacture of News*. London: Constable, 1973.

Bibliography
▼ ▼ ▼

Conti, Flavio. *I prigionieri di guerra italiani, 1940-1945*. Bologna: Il Mulino, 1986.

Corcoran, Marlena G. "Salman Rushdie's Satanic Narration." *The Iowa Review* 20, no. 1 (Winter 1990): 155-67.

Craven, Avery O. *The Coming of the Civil War*, 2nd ed. Chicago: University of Chicago Press, 1957.

Crozier, Alice. *The Novels of Harriet Beecher Stowe*. New York: Oxford University Press, 1969.

Culler, Jonathan. "Story and Discourse in the Analysis of Narrative." *The Pursuit of Signs: Semiotics, Literature, Deconstruction*. Ithaca: Cornell University Press, 1981: 169-187.

Curry, Richard O., ed. *The Abolitionists*. Hinsdale, Illinois: Dryden Press, 1973.

Curtis, James M. *Solzhenitsyn's Traditional Imagination*. Athens, Georgia: University of Georgia Press, 1984.

Dal Pont, Adriano, Leonetti, Alfonso, and Massara, Massimo. *Giornali fuori legge: la stampa clandestina antifascista 1922-43*. Rome: Associazione Nazionale Perseguitati Politici Italiani Antifascisti, 1964.

Daniel, Norman. *Islam and the West: the Making of an Image*. Edinburgh: Edinburgh University Press, 1960.

De Certeau, Michel. "On the Oppositional Practices of Everyday Life." *Social Text* 3 (Fall 1980): 3-43.

D'Eramo, Luce. *L'opera di Ignazio Silone: saggio critico e guida bibliografica*. Milan: Mondadori, 1971.

De Felice, Renzo. *Mussolini il fascista: l'organizzazione dello Stato fascista 1925-1929*. Turin: Einaudi, 1968.

De Robertis, Giuseppe. Review of *Fontamara*. *Tempo*, 11 June 1949: 14.

Deutscher, Isaac. "*1984* — The Mysticism of Cruelty." *Heretics and Renegades*. London: Hamish Hamilton, 1956: 35-51.

Dexter, L. A. and White, D. M., eds. *People, Society and Mass Communications*. Glencoe, Illinois: Free Press of Glencoe, 1964.

Durzak, Manfred. "Plädoyer für eine Rezeptionsästhetik: Anmerkungen zur Deutschen und Amerikanischen Literarturkritik am Beispiel von Günter Grass *Örtlich Betaübt*." *Akzente* 6 (1959): 487-504.

Eco, Umberto. *The Role of the Reader: Explorations in the Semiotics of Texts*. London: Hutchinson, 1981.

Eichler, Willy. "Silone: Poet, Socialist and Political Thinker." *Socialist Commentary* (October 1943): 87-91.

Elwin, William. *Fascism at Work*. London: Martin Hopkinson, 1934.

Emmons, Terence, ed. *Emancipation of the Russian Serfs*. New York: Holt, Rinehart and Winston, 1970.

____. *The Russian Landed Gentry and the Peasant Emancipation of 1861*. Cambridge: Cambridge University Press, 1968.

Erickson, Milton H. *The Nature of Hypnosis and Suggestion*. New York: Irvington Publishers, 1980.

Falconi, Carlo. "La letteratura ispirata al Marxismo." *Humanitas* 5 (May 1950).

Bibliography

Farinelli, Giuseppe. "*Fontamara* di Silone nella prospettiva delle varianti." *Testo* 5, no. 6-7 (1984): 33-48.

Farrell, James T. "Ignazio Silone." *Southern Review* 4, no. 4 (Spring 1939): 771-783.

Fellman, Michael. "Rehearsal for the Civil War: Antislavery and Proslavery at the Fighting Point in Kansas, 1854-1856." *Antislavery Reconsidered: New Perspectives on the Abolitionists*. Edited by Lewis Perry and Michael Fellman. Baton Rouge and London: Louisiana State University Press, 1979.

Fenton, James. "Keeping Up With Salman Rushdie." *The New York Review of Books*, 28 March 1991: 26-34.

Fokkema, D. W. and Kunne-Ibsch, Elrud. *Theories of Literature in the Twentieth Century: Structuralism, Marxism, Aesthetics of Reception, Semiotics*. London: C. Hurst and Co, 1977.

Forgacs, David, ed. *Rethinking Italian Fascism: Capitalism, Populism and Culture*. London: Lawrence and Wishart, 1986.

Foucault, Michel. *Power/Knowledge: Selected Interviews and Other Writings, 1972-1977*. Edited by Colin Gordon. Brighton: Harvester Press, 1980.

Francovich, C., ed. *Non mollare (1925): Riproduzione fotografica dei numeri usciti. Tre saggi storici di Ernesto Rossi, Piero Calamandrei, Gaetano Salvemini*. Florence: Nuova Italia, 1955, 2nd ed. 1968.

French, Marilyn. *The Women's Room*. London: André Deutsch, 1977.

Gibian, George. "The Russian Theme in Solzhenitsyn." *Russian Literature and American Critics*. Edited by Kenneth N. Brostrom. Michigan: Ann Arbor, 1984: 55-73.

Gilbert, Sandra M. and Gubar, Susan. *The Madwoman in the Attic: The Woman Writer and the Nineteenth-Century Literary Imagination*. New Haven: Yale University Press, 1979.

Gilbert, Martin. *Winston Churchill: 1922-1939*. London: Heinemann, 1976.

Glickstein, Jonathan A. "'Poverty Is Not Slavery': American Abolitionists and the Competitive Slave Market." *Antislavery Reconsidered: New Perspectives on the Abolitionists*. Edited by Lewis Perry and Michael Fellman. Baton Rouge and London: Louisiana State University Press, 1979.

Goldmann, Lucien. *The Hidden God: a Study of Tragic Vision in the 'Pensées' of Pascal and the Tragedies of Racine*. Translated by P. Thody. London: Routledge and Kegan Paul, 1964.

———. *Towards a Sociology of the Novel*. Translated by Alan Sheridan. London: Tavistock Publications, 1975.

Gossett, Thomas F. *'Uncle Tom's Cabin' and American Culture*. Dallas: Southern Methodist University Press, 1985.

Granjard, Henri. *Ivan Tourguénev et les courants politiques et sociaux de son temps*, 2nd ed. Paris: Institut d'études slaves, 1966.

Greene, Graham. "Fontamara." *Spectator*, 2 November 1934: 692.

Griswold, Wendy. "The Fabrication of Meaning: Literary Interpretation in the United States, Great Britain, and the West Indies." *American Journal of Sociology* 92, no. 5 (March 1987): 1077-1117.

Guerriero, Elio. *L'inquietudine e l'utopia: il racconto umano e cristiano di Ignazio Silone*. Milan: Jaca, 1979.

Bibliography
▼▼▼

Guevara, Che. *Guerrilla Warfare*. Lincoln and London: University of Nebraska Press, 1985.

——. *Reminiscences of the Cuban Revolutionary War*. Translated by Victoria Ortiz. London: Allen and Unwin, 1968.

Guimaraes, Ney. "Ignacio Silone — Escritor social." *Cla, revista de cultura* (Fortalezar Ceará, Brazil) (August 1948) 4: 58-61.

Hanne, Michael. "Peasant Storytelling Meets Literary Theory: The Case of *La finta nonna*." *The Italianist* 12 (1992): 42-58.

Hayward, Max. *Writers in Russia: 1917-1978*. San Diego, New York, London: Harcourt Brace Jovanovich, 1983.

—— and Crowley, Edward L. *Soviet Literature in the Sixties*. London: Methuen, 1965.

Heer, Nancy Whittier. *Politics and History in the Soviet Union*. Cambridge, Mass. and London: M.I.T. Press, 1971.

Hillman, James. "A Note on Story." *Loose Ends: Primary Papers in Archetypal Psychology*. Dallas: Spring Publications, 1975: 1-4.

Holub, Robert C. *Reception Theory*. New York and London: Methuen, 1984.

Howe, Irving. *Politics and the Novel*. New York: Horizon, 1957.

Irving, T. B. "The Rushdie Confrontation: a Clash in Values." *The Iowa Review* 20, no. 1 (Winter 1990): 175-184.

Iser, Wolfgang. *The Implied Reader: Patterns of Communication in Prose Fiction from Bunyan to Beckett*. Baltimore and London: Johns Hopkins University Press, 1974.

Jameson, Fredric. *The Political Unconscious: Narrative as a Socially Symbolic Act*. Ithaca: Cornell University Press, 1981.

Jauss, Hans Robert. "Literary History as a Challenge to Literary Theory." *New Directions in Literary History*. Edited by Ralph Cohen. London: Routledge and Kegan Paul, 1974: 11-41.

Johnson, Priscilla. *Khrushchev and the Arts: The Politics of Soviet Culture, 1962-1964*. Cambridge, Mass.: M.I.T. Press, 1965.

Jussawalla, Feroza. "Resurrecting the Prophet: the Case of Salman, the Otherwise." *Public Culture* 2, no. 1 (Fall 1989): 106-117.

Kagan-Kans, Eva. *Hamlet and Don Quixote: Turgenev's Ambivalent Vision*. The Hague and Paris: Mouton, 1975.

Knowles, Anthony V. *Ivan Turgenev*. Boston: Twayne, 1988.

Kochan, Lionel and Abraham, Richard. *The Making of Modern Russia*, 2nd ed. New York: St. Martin's Press, 1983.

The Koran Interpreted, 2 vols. Translated by Arthur J. Arberry. London: Allen and Unwin, 1955.

Kristeva, Julia. *Desire in Language: A Semiotic Approach to Literature and Art*. Translated by Alice Jardine, Thomas Gora, Léon Roudiez. Oxford: Blackwell, 1980.

Kuhn, Thomas S. *The Structure of Scientific Revolutions*. London: University of Chicago Press, 1962.

Labedz, Leopold, ed. *Solzhenitsyn: A Documentary Record*. London: Allen Lane, 1970.

Labov, William and Waletzky, Joshua. "Narrative Analysis: Oral Versions of Personal Experience." *Essays on the Verbal and Visual Arts: Proceedings of the 1966 Annual Spring Meeting of the American Ethnological Society.* Edited by June Helm. Seattle and London: University of Washington Press, 1967: 12-44.

Lankton, Stephen R. *Enchantment and Intervention in Family Therapy: Training in Ericksonian Approaches.* New York: Brunner/Mazel, 1986.

La Rose, John. "'Writers Have Their Right to Write." *The Black Scholar* 20 (March/April 1989): 15-16.

Leitch, Thomas M. *What Stories Are: Narrative Theory and Interpretation.* University Park and London: Pennsylvania State University, 1986.

Liebermann, Marcia. "Some Day My Prince Will Come: Female Acculturation through the Fairy Tale." *College English* 34 (December 1972): 383-395.

Lukács, György. *Solzhenitsyn.* Translated by William David Graf. London: Merlin Press, 1970.

Lukes, Stephen. "Power and Authority." *A History of Sociological Analysis,* Edited by T. Bottomore and R. Nisbet. New York: Basic Books, 1978: 633-676.

Luplow, Richard. "Narrative Style and Structure in *One Day in the Life of Ivan Denisovich.*" *Russian Literature Triquarterly* 1, (Fall 1971): 339-412.

Lyotard, Jean-François. *The Postmodern Condition.* Translated by G. Bennington and B. Massumi. Minneapolis: University of Minnesota Press, 1984.

Macherey, Pierre. *A Theory of Literary Production.* Translated by G. Wall. London and Boston: Routledge and Kegan Paul, 1978.

Mack Smith, Denis. *A History of Sicily: Modern Sicily.* London: Chatto and Windus, 1968.

_____. *Italy: a Modern History.* Ann Arbor: University of Michigan Press, 1969.

Maclean, Marie. "Oppositional Practices in Women's Traditional Narrative." *New Literary History* 19 (1987-8): 37-55.

Magarshack, David. *Turgenev: A Life.* London: Faber, 1954.

Marani, Alma Novella. *Narrativa y testimonio: Ignazio Silone.* Buenos Aires: Nova, 1967.

Marx, Karl. *Grundrisse.* Harmondsworth: Penguin, 1973.

_____ and Engels, Friedrich. *The German Ideology.* London: Lawrence and Wishart, 1963.

_____. *Marx and Engels on Literature and Art.* Edited by Lee Baxandall and Stefan Morawski. New York: International General, 1974.

Masrui, Ali. "Is *The Satanic Verses* a Satanic Novel? Moral Dilemmas of the Rushdie Affair." *Michigan Quarterly Review* 28, no. 3 (Summer 1989): 347-371. For another version of the same essay see his "Moral Dilemmas of *The Satanic Verses.*" *The Black Scholar* 20 (March/April 1989): 19-32.

_____. "Witness for the Prosecution: A Cross-Examination on *The Satanic Verses.*" *Third Text* 11 (Summer 1990): 31-40.

Medawar, P. B. *The Art of the Soluble,* 6th ed. London: Methuen, 1967.

Medvedev, Zhores. *Ten Years after Ivan Denisovich.* Translated by Hilary Sternberg. London: Macmillan, 1973.

Miliband, Ralph. *Marxism and Politics.* Oxford: Oxford University Press, 1977.

Bibliography

Millett, Kate. *Sexual Politics.* Garden City, New York: Doubleday, 1970.

Mills, C. Wright. "The Structure of Power in American Society." *Power, Politics and People: The Collected Essays of C. Wright Mills.* Edited by I. L. Horowitz. New York and London: Oxford University Press, 1963: 23-38.

Mink, Louis O. "Narrative Form as a Cognitive Instrument." *The Writing of History. Literary Form and Historical Understanding.* Edited by Robert H. Canary and Henry Kozicki. Madison: University of Wisconsin Press, 1978: 129-49.

———. "History and Fiction as Modes of Comprehension." *New Literary History* 1 (1969-70): 541-558.

Moers, Ellen. *Literary Women.* Garden City, New York: Anchor Press/Doubleday, 1977.

Moi, Toril. *Sexual/Textual Politics: Feminist Literary Theory.* London: Methuen, 1986.

Moody, Christopher. *Solzhenitsyn.* Edinburgh: Oliver and Boyd, 1973.

Moser, Charles A. *Ivan Turgenev.* New York and London: Columbia University Press, 1972.

Mosse, W. E. *Alexander II and the Modernization of Russia.* London: English Universities Press, 1958.

Naik, M. K. *Raja Rao.* New York: Twayne, 1972.

Nair, Rukmini Bhaya and Bhattacharya, Rimli. "Salman Rushdie: The Migrant in the Metropolis." *Third Text* 11 (Summer 1990): 17-30.

Nandy, Ashis. "Dialogue and the Diaspora: Conversation with Nikos Papastergiadis," *Third Text* 11 (Summer 1990): 99-108.

———. *The Intimate Enemy.* New Delhi: Oxford University Press, 1984.

Nazareth, Peter. "Rushdie's Wo/manichean Novel." *The Iowa Review* 20, no. 1 (Winter 1990): 168-174.

Nelson, Lowry. "The Fictive Reader: Aesthetic and Social Aspects of Literary Performance." *Comparative Literature Studies* 15, no. 2 (1978): 203-210.

Niranjan, Shiva. "Philosophy into Fiction: A Study of the Thematic Aspects of Raja Rao's Novels." *Response: Recent Revelations of Indian Fiction in English.* Edited by Hari Mohan Prasad. Bareilly: Prakash Book Depot, 1983: 94-111.

Nye, R. B. and Morpurgo, J. E. *A History of the United States*, 2 vols. Harmondsworth: Penguin, 1965.

Origo, Iris. *Bisogno di testimoniare. Quattro vite: Lauro de Bosis, Ruth Draper, Gaetano Salvemini, Ignazio Silone e un saggio sulla biografia.* Milan: Longanesi, 1985.

———. "Ignazio Silone: A Study in Integrity." *Atlantic Monthly* 219 (1967): 86-93.

Pampaloni, Geno. "L'opera narrativa di Ignazio Silone." *Il ponte* 5 (January 1949): 49-58.

Parek, Bikhu. "Between Holy Text and Moral Void." *New Statesman and Society*, 23 March 1989: 29-33.

Parkin, Frank. *Class, Inequality and Political Order.* London: MacGibbon Kee, 1971.

Passerini, Luisa. "Oral Memory of Fascism." *Rethinking Italian Fascism: Capitalism, Populism and Culture*, ed. David Forgacs. London: Lawrence and Wishart, 1986: 185-196.

Pipes, Daniel. "The Ayatollah, the Novelist and the West." *Commentary* 87 (June 1989): 9-17.

Piscatori, James. "The Rushdie Affair and the Politics of Ambiguity." *International Affairs* 66, no. 4 (1990): 767-89.

Ponziani, Luigi. "Dopoguerra e fascismo in Abruzzo. Orientamenti storiografici." *Italia contemporanea* 164 (September 1986): 93-103.

Poulantzas, Nicos. *Political Power and Social Classes*. Translated by T. O'Hagan. London: New Left Books and Sheed and Ward, 1973.

Poulet, Georges. "Phenomenology of Reading." *New Literary History* 1 (1969): 53-68.

Rahv, Philip. "House of the Dead?" *New York Review of Books* 1 no.1 (1963): 4.

Rao, Raja. *Kanthapura*. Delhi: Hind Pocket Books, 1971.

Rawson, Judy. "'Che fare?': Silone and the Russian 'Chto Delat'?' Tradition." *The Modern Language Review* 76, no. 3 (July 1981): 556-565.

Reeve, F. D. "The House of the Living." *Kenyon Review* 25 (1963): 356-60.

Rhodes, James Ford. *The History of the United States from the Compromise of 1850 to the Final Restoration of Home Rule at the South in 1877*, 8 vols. New York: Harper, 1892.

Ripp, Victor. *Turgenev's Russia: From "Notes of a Hunter" to "Fathers and Sons."* Ithaca and London: Cornell University Press, 1980.

Rothberg, Abraham. *Alekzandr Solzhenitsyn: The Major Novels*. Ithaca and London, Cornell University Press, 1971.

Rus, Vladimir J. "*One Day in the Life of Ivan Denisovich*: A Point of View Analysis." *Canadian Slavonic Papers* 13, no. 2-3 (1971): 165-78.

Rushdie, Salman. "In Good Faith." *Imaginary Homelands: Essays and Criticism, 1981-1991*. London: Granta Books, 1991: 393-414.

――――. "Is Nothing Sacred?" *Imaginary Homelands: Essays and Criticism, 1981-1991*. London: Granta Books, 1991: 415-429.

――――. *Midnight's Children*. London: Picador, 1982.

――――. "One Thousand Days in a Balloon." *Imaginary Homelands: Essays and Criticism, 1981-1991*. London: Granta Books, 1991: 430-39.

――――. *The Satanic Verses*. London: Viking Penguin, 1988.

――――. *Shame*. London: Picador, 1984.

Russi, Antonio. *Gli anni della antialienazione: 1943-1949*. Milan: Mursia, 1966.

Russo, Luigi. *I narratori: 1850-1950*. Milan: Principato, 1951.

Ruthven, Malise. *A Satanic Affair: Salman Rushdie and the Rage of Islam*. London: Chatto and Windus, 1990.

Said, Edward. *Covering Islam: How the Media and the Experts Determine How We See the Rest of the World*. New York: Pantheon, 1981.

――――. *Orientalism*. New York: Pantheon, 1978.

――――. "*The Satanic Verses* and Democratic Freedoms." *The Black Scholar* 20 (March/April 1989): 17-18.

Salvemini, Gaetano. *Under the Axe of Fascism*. London: Gollancz, 1936.

Sarkis Najjar, J. "La traduzione araba di *Fontamara*." *Levante*, Rome, January 1965.

Scammell, Michael. *Solzhenitsyn: A Biography*. London, Melbourne, Sydney, Auckland, Johannesburg: Hutchinson, 1985.

Bibliography
▼ ▼ ▼

Schafer, Roy. "Narration in the Psychoanalytic Dialogue." *Critical Inquiry* 7, no. 1 (Fall 1980): 29-53.

Schapiro, Leonard. "Bent Backs." *New Statesman*, 1 February 1963: 158-59.

_____. *Turgenev: His Life and Times.* New York: Random House, 1978.

Schmidt, Carl T. *The Corporate State in Action: Italy Under Fascism.* London: Gollancz, 1939.

Scholes, Robert. "Language, Narrative, and Anti-Narrative." *Critical Inquiry* 7, no. 1 (Fall 1980): 204-212.

Seeley, Frank Friedeberg. *Turgenev: a Reading of His Fiction.* Cambridge: Cambridge University Press, 1991.

Showalter, Elaine. *A Literature of Their Own: British Women Novelists from Brontë to Lessing*, revised edition. London: Virago, 1984.

Siegel, Paul N. "The Political Implications of Solzhenitsyn's Novels." *Clio* 112, no. 3 (1983): 211-32.

Silone, Ignazio. "Avezzano e la Marsica: un West italiano." *Tuttitalia: Enciclopedia dell'Italia Antica e Moderna*, volume on Abruzzo Molise. Florence: Sadea Sansoni, 1965: 231-34.

_____. *Fontamara.* Translated by Gwenda David and Eric Mosbacher. Harmondsworth: Penguin, 1938, first published 1934.

_____. *Fontamara.* Translated by Eric Mosbacher. London: J. M. Dent, 1985.

_____. *Uscita di sicurezza.* Milan: Mondadori, 1965.

Sinclair, Upton. *The Jungle.* New York: Viking Penguin, 1985.

Skerpan, Alfred A. "The Russian National Economy and Emancipation." *Essays in Russian History: A Collection Dedicated to George Vernadsky.* Edited by Alan D. Ferguson and Alfred Levin. Hamden, Connecticut: Archon Books, 1964: 161-229.

Smith, Barbara Herrnstein. "Narrative Versions, Narrative Theories." *Critical Inquiry* 7, no. 1 (Fall 1980): 213-236.

Solzhenitsyn, Alexander. *The First Circle.* Translated by Michael Guybon. London: Collins and Harvill, 1968.

_____. *Letter to the Soviet Leaders.* Translated by Hilary Sternberg. London: Writers and Scholars International, 1974.

_____. *The Oak and the Calf: Sketches of Literary Life in the Soviet Union.* Translated by Harry Willetts. New York: Harper and Row, 1980.

_____. *One Day in the Life of Ivan Denisovich.* Translated by Ralph Parker. Harmondsworth: Penguin, 1963.

_____. *One Word of Truth: The Nobel Speech on Literature 1970.* London: Bodley Head, 1972.

_____. *A World Split Apart.* Translated by Irina Alberti. New York: Harper and Row, 1978.

_____. et al. *From Under the Rubble.* Translated by A. M. Brock et al. London: Collins and Harvill, 1975: 3-25.

Spender, Dale. *Man Made Language*, 2nd edition. London, Boston, Melbourne and Henley: Routledge, 1985.

_____. *Women of Ideas and What Men Have Done to Them: From Aphra Behn to Adrienne Rich.* London and Boston: Routledge and Kegan Paul: 1982.

Spivak, Gayatri C. "Reading *The Satanic Verses.*" *Third Text* 11 (Summer 1990): 41-60. This essay was published in a first version in *Public Culture* 2, no. 1 (Fall, 1989): 79-99.

Srivastava, Ramesh K. "Raja Rao's *Kanthapura*: a Village Revitalised." *Six Indian Novelists in English*. Amritsar: Guru Nanak Dev University, 1987: 3-16.

Steiner, George. *After Babel: Aspects of Language and Translation*. London: Oxford University Press, 1975.

Stone, Kay F. "The Misuses of Enchantment: Controversies on the Significance of Fairy Tales." *Women's Folklore, Women's Culture*. Edited by R. Jordan and S. Kalcik. Philadelphia: University of Pennsylvania Press, 1985: 125-145.

Stowe, Harriet Beecher. *Dred: A Tale of the Great Dismal Swamp*. London: Sampson, Low, Marston, 1856.

_____. *A Key to 'Uncle Tom's Cabin': Presenting the Original Facts and Documents upon which the Story is Founded*. Boston: J. P. Jewett, 1853.

_____. *Uncle Tom's Cabin, or Life Among the Lowly*. Edited by Kenneth S. Lynn. Cambridge, Mass.: Harvard University Press, 1962.

_____. *Uncle Tom's Cabin*, with an Afterword by John William Ward. New York: New American Library, 1981.

Stowe, Lyman Beecher. *Saints, Sinners and Beechers*. Indianapolis: Bobbs-Merrill, 1934.

Suleiman, Susan. "Ideological Dissent from Works of Fiction: Toward a Rhetoric of the Roman a Thèse." *Neophilologus* 60 (April 1976): 162-177.

Suleri, Sara. "Contraband Histories: Salman Rushdie and the Embodiment of Blasphemy." *The Yale Review* 78, no. 4 (1989): 604-624.

Thompson, E. P. *The Making of the English Working Class*. London: Gollancz, 1963.

Thoreau, Henry David. *Walden and Civil Disobedience*. Edited by Owen Thomas. New York: W. W. Norton, 1966.

Todorov, Tzvetan. "*The Satanic Verses* in Paris." *Dissent* 37 (Winter 1990): 97-100.

Tompkins, Jane P. "Sentimental Power: *Uncle Tom's Cabin* and the Politics of Literary History." *Feminist Criticism: Essays on Women, Literature and Theory*. Edited by Elaine Showalter. London: Virago, 1986: 81-104.

Traldi, Alberto. *Fascism and Fiction: A Survey of Italian Fiction on Fascism*. Metuchen and London: Scarecrow Press, 1987.

_____. "Realism and Nonrealism in Ignazio Silone's *Fontamara*." Ph.D. dissertation, Columbia University, 1973.

Turgenev, Ivan. *A Sportsman's Notebook*. Translated by Charles and Natasha Hepburn. New York: The Ecco Press, 1986, first published New York: Viking, 1950.

_____. *Turgenev Letters*, 2 vols. Edited and translated by David Lowe. Ann Arbor: Ardis, 1983.

Van der Veer, Peter. "Satanic or Angelic? The Politics of Religious and Literary Inspiration." *Public Culture* 2, no. 1 (Fall 1989): 100-105.

Varese, Claudio. "Ignazio Silone." *Lo Spettatore italiano* 2 (1949): 169-174.

Venturi, Franco. *Roots of Revolution*. Chicago: University of Chicago Press, 1983.

Vicentini, Marzia Terenzi. "Silone sulle tracce di Celestino." *Revista de Letras* (Brazil) 12 (1969): 155-165.

Bibliography

Viereck, Peter. "The Mob within the Heart." *Soviet Policy-Making: Studies of Communism in Transition.* Edited by Peter H. Juviler and Henry W. Morton. New York: Praeger, 1967: 83-120.

Vittorini, Elio. *Le due tensioni: appunti per una ideologia della letteratura.* Edited by Dante Isella. Milan: Il Saggiatore, 1967.

Wachter, Oralee. *No More Secrets for Me.* Ringwood, Australia: Penguin, 1986.

Wagenknecht, Edward. *Harriet Beecher Stowe: The Known and the Unknown.* New York: Oxford University Press, 1965.

Walicki, Andrzey. *The Slavophile Controversy.* Oxford: Clarendon Press, 1975.

Walters, Ronald G. "The Boundaries of Abolitionism." *Antislavery Reconsidered: New Perspectives on the Abolitionists.* Edited by Lewis Perry and Michael Fellman. Baton Rouge and London: Louisiana State University Press, 1979: 3-23.

Watzlawick, Paul, Weakland, John H., and Fisch, Richard. *Change: Principles of Problem Formation and Problem Resolution.* New York: W.W. Norton, 1974.

Weber, Max. *Economy and Society.* Edited by G. Roth and C. Wittich. New York: Bedminster, 1968.

Whicher, George F. "Literature and Conflict." *Literary History of the United States.* Edited by Robert E. Spiller, Willard Thorp, Thomas H. Johnson, Henry Seidel Canby, Richard M. Ludwig, 3rd ed. New York: Macmillan, 1963: 563-586.

White, Hayden. *The Content of the Form: Narrative Discourse and Historical Representation.* Baltimore and London: Johns Hopkins University Press, 1987.

_____. "The Value of Narrativity in the Representation of Reality." *Critical Inquiry* 7, no. 1 (Fall 1980): 5-27.

Wiecek, William M. "Latimer: Lawyers, Abolitionists, and the Problem of Unjust Laws." *Antislavery Reconsidered: New Perspectives on the Abolitionists.* Edited by Lewis Perry and Michael Fellman. Baton Rouge and London: Louisiana State University Press, 1979: 219-237.

Williams, Raymond. "Introduction" to Charles Dickens. *Dombey and Son.* Harmondsworth: Penguin, 1970.

Wilson, Edmund. *Patriotic Gore: Studies in the Literature of the American Civil War.* New York: Oxford University Press, 1962.

Wolff, Janet. *The Social Production of Art.* London and Basingstoke: Macmillan, 1981.

Wimsatt, W. K. *The Verbal Icon: Studies in the Meaning of Poetry.* Lexington: University of Kentucky Press, 1967.

Wood, Michael. "The Prophet Motive." *The New Republic,* 6 March 1989: 28-30.

Woodcock, George. *The Writer and Politics.* London: Porcupine Press, 1948.

Wright, Theodore P. "The Rushdie Controversy: the Spread of Communalism from South Asia to the West." *Plural Societies* 20, no. 3 (December 1990): 31-40.

Wyatt-Brown, Bertram. "William Lloyd Garrison and Antislavery Unity: A Reappraisal." *Civil War History* 13 (1967): 5-24.

Yarborough, Richard. "Strategies of Black Characterization in *Uncle Tom's Cabin* and the Early Afro-American Novel." *New Essays on "Uncle Tom's Cabin."* Edited by Eric J. Sundquist. Cambridge: Cambridge University Press, 1986: 45-84.

Bibliography

Yarmolinsky, Avrahm. *Turgenev: The Man — His Art — His Age.* London: Hodder and Stoughton, 1926.

Yellin, Jean Fagan. "Doing it Herself: *Uncle Tom's Cabin* and Woman's Role in the Slavery Crisis." *New Essays on "Uncle Tom's Cabin."* Edited by Eric J. Sundquist. Cambridge: Cambridge University Press, 1986: 85-105.

Zipes, Jack. *Breaking the Magic Spell: Radical Theories of Folk and Fairy Tales.* Austin: University of Texas, 1979.

INDEX

▼ ▼ ▼

Abraham, Richard, 53, 185
Adams, John R., 86
Ahmad, Faiyazuddin, 200, 202
Akhtar, Shabbir, 193, 214, 216, 224, 225, 228, 229
Aksakov, Konstantin S., 60
Albertazzi, Silvia, 141
Alexander I, Tsar, 53
Alexander II, Tsar, 2, 28, 43, 44, 50, 52-56, 63, 65-70, 151
Allen, Walter, 143
Almedingen, E. M., 53, 54
Althusser, Louis, 22
Amiconi, Nino, 144
Ammons, Elizabeth, 77, 82
Anchor, Robert, 10
Annenkov, Pavel Vasilyevich, 45, 51
Appignanesi, Lisa, 237
Arendt, Hannah, 23
authors,
    intentions of, 5, 25, 44-45, 80-82, 193-94, 212
    responsibilities of, 5, 195-96, 203
Azam, Sher, 200
Aziz, Barbara Nimri, 205

Badawi, Zaki, 193
Bakhtin, Mikhail, 31
Baldwin, James, 79, 95
Balzac, Honoré de, 25, 35
Bandler, Richard, 16
Barthes, Roland, 7, 21, 23, 24, 29, 32-33, 139, 177-78, 193
Bass, Ellen, 39
Basu, Shrabani, 236
Battaglia, Roberto, 144
Bauer, Werner, 41
Beecher, Catharine, 80, 82, 87

Beecher, Henry Ward, 87
Beecher, Lyman, 83, 85, 86
Belinsky, Vissarion, 19, 20, 52
Benediktova, G., 163
Bennion, Francis, 213
Benno, Peter, 186
Bergin, Thomas G., 118
Berry, Mary Frances, 13
Berryman, Philip, 145
Berzer, Anna, 150, 151
Bharucha, Rustom, 217, 224
Bhattacharya, Rimli, 200
Bhutto, Zulfikar Ali, 206, 207
Bilgrami, Akeel, 200
Blaise, Clark, 220
Boccaccio, Giovanni, 15
Boff, Leonardo, 139
Bondarev, Iury, 154
Bottai, Giuseppe, 124
Brecht, Bertolt, 25, 26
Brennan, Timothy, 214, 215
Brown, Deming, 181, 183
Brown, George, 181
Brown, John, 87, 88
Brown, P. M., 117
Bulgakov, Mikhail, 170
Burg, David, 185
Burns, Anthony, 84

Carpovich, Vera V., 187
Caute, David, 38
Cecchi, Emilio, 129
censorship, 56, 57, 64, 151
Chaadaev, Peter, 60
Chagall, Marc, 132
Chamberlain, John, 143
Chambers, Ross, 9-10, 14, 27, 169
Chavchavadze, Olga, 164

Index

Choate, Rufus, 93
Churchill, Winston, 116
Cixous, Hélène, 24, 32, 107
Cohen, S., 38
Connolly, Cyril, 3
Conti, Flavio, 128
Corbi, Bruno, 127
Corcoran, Marlena G., 212, 223
Craven, Avery O., 77
Crozier, Alice, 91
Culler, Jonathan, 7
Curtis, James M., 162

D'Eramo, Luce, 33, 128, 143
Dal Pont, Adriano, 144
Daniel, Norman, 237
Daniel, Yuli, 167
De Beauvoir, Simone, 107
De Certeau, Michel, 39
De Felice, Renzo, 143
De Robertis, Giuseppe, 132
Defoe, Daniel, 223
Deutscher, Isaac, 5
Dexter, L. A., 38
Dickens, Charles, 35, 37, 58
Dobryak, I., 163
Dos Passos, John, 35
Dostoevsky, Fyodor, 52
Douglass, Frederick, 77
Dumond, Dwight L., 105
Durzak, Manfred, 30, 119

Eco, Umberto, 29
Eichler, Willy, 145
Ejaz, Aslam, 200
El Essawi, Hesham, 198
Eliot, George, 35
Elwin, William, 143
Emmons, Terence, 44
Engels, Friedrich, 22, 24, 25
Ercole, Francesco, 125
Erickson, Milton, 17-18
Ermilov, Vladimir, 158
Escher, M. C., 224

Fadiman, Clifton, 117
Falconi, Carlo, 129

Farinelli, Giuseppe, 144
Farrell, James T., 118
Feifer, George, 185
Fellman, Michael, 111
feminist theory and criticism, 13, 22-24, 28, 32-33, 78-80, 82, 108, 230
Fenton, James, 196
Feuer, Katherine, 172
fiction
    and disruption of traditional categories, 98-99, 107, 225
    and history, 4, 7, 34-37, 60-61, 114, 148, 153, 194, 214, 225
    and religion, 217
    and subversion, 20, 29, 134, 139, 152, 164, 170, 174, 177, 224
    and truth claims, 90-92, 114, 117-21, 154, 157-58, 177-78
    as a weapon, 3-5, 108, 191, 199
    as empowering, 25
    as territory, 5, 220-226
    as therapy, 16-18
    open and closed interpretations of, 4, 6, 29, 32, 70, 122, 166
    political appropriation of, 5, 123, 138, 151-52, 155, 159, 199, 203, 205
Fisch, Richard, 41
Fitzhugh, George, 102
Fo, Dario, 134
Fokkema, D.W., 41
Foot, Michael, 114
Foucault, Michel, 22
Freire, Paulo, 138
French, Marilyn, 37
French, Sean, 240

Gandhi, Indira, 206, 207
Gandhi, Rajiv, 200, 207, 234
Gandhi, Sanjay, 207
Garaudy, Roger, 3
García Márquez, Gabriel, 139
Garrison, William Lloyd, 85, 86, 88, 104, 105, 106
Garritano, Giuseppe, 144
Gibian, George, 162
Gilbert, Martin, 142

Index
▼▼▼

Gilbert, Sandra, 33
Ginzburg, Evgenia, 144
Glickstein, Jonathan A., 112
Goethe, Johann Wolfgang von, 37
Gogol, Nikolai, 35, 52, 64
Goldmann, Louis, 25
Gorbachev, Mikhail, 148, 153
Gorbanevskaya, Natalia, 175
Gossett, Thomas F., 91, 193
Gottesman, Ronald, 37
Gramsci, Antonio, 22
Granjard, Henri, 43, 53, 64
Granovsky, T.N., 52
Grass, Günter, 30, 219.]
Greene, Graham, 117, 118, 121
Grigorovich, D. V., 45, 51
Grimké, Angelina, 80, 97
Grimké, Sarah, 80, 85, 97
Grinder, John, 16
Griswold, Wendy, 41
Gubar, Susan, 33
Guerriero, Elio, 144
Guevara, Che, 138, 139
Guimaraes, Ney, 145
Gutiérrez, Gustavo, 139

Hanne, Michael, 145
Hayward, Max, 160, 185
Heer, Nancy Whittier, 11, 153, 155
Hillman, James, 9
Hingley, Ronald, 185
Holub, Robert C., 41
Howe, Samuel Gridley, 101
Hussain, Zahid, 237

Irving, T. B., 194
Iser, Wolfgang, 26-27, 90
Islam, Yusuf, 207

Jain, Madhu, 238
Jameson, Fredric, 8
Jauss, Hans Robert, 30, 128, 141
Johnson, Priscilla, 186
Joyce, William (Lord Haw-Haw), 193
Jussawalla, Feroza, 212, 224
Juviler, Peter H., 186

Kabbani, Rana, 230
Kagan-Kans, Eva, 47, 57
Kasravi, Ahmed, 208.
Kazakevich, Em., 154
Kennedy, John F., 146
Khan, Ayub, 206
Khomeini, Ayatollah, 2, 4, 189, 190, 199, 203, 204, 206, 208, 217, 221, 233
Khrushchev, Nikita, 2, 6, 123, 146-159, 161-68, 171
Kingsley, Charles, 37
Kissinger, Henry, 180
Knowles, Anthony V., 72
Kochan, Lionel, 53, 185
Koestler, Arthur, 37, 91
Kristeva, Julia, 24, 29
Kropotkin, Peter, 55
Kuhn, Thomas, 27
Kunne-Ibsch, Elrud, 41
Kuslov, Frol, 151

La Rose, John, 240
Labov, William, 15
Lambert, Yelizaveta, 45
Lamming, George, 41
Lankton, Stephen R., 39
Lawrence, D. H., 28
Lebedev, Vladimir, 151, 156
Leitch, Thomas M., 7
Lenin, Vladimir Ilich, 141
Levi, Carlo, 129
Liebermann, Marcia, 38
Lincoln, Abraham, 2, 75, 76, 79, 86
Litvinov, Pavel, 175
Lukács, György, 155, 157, 174
Lukes, Stephen, 40
Luplow, Richard, 185
Lvov, Prince V. V., 65
Lyotard, Jean-François, 8, 12

Macherey, Pierre, 26, 34
Maclean, Marie, 134
Magarshack, David, 73
Mahfouz, Naguib, 205
Mailer, Norman, 28
Maitland, Sara, 237
Mandelstam, Osip, 170, 209

Index
▼ ▼ ▼

Marani, Alma Novella, 145
Marie of Hesse, 53
Martynyuk, P. R., 162
Marx, Karl, 22, 24, 25, 26
Masrui, Ali, 190, 193, 214, 224
Mayer, Peter, 196, 236
Medawar, P. B., 19
Medvedev, Zhores, 151
metanarrative, 12, 17, 60
metaphor, 208, 211-12, 218-232
Miliband, Ralph, 21
Miliutin, D. A., 67
Miller, Henry, 28
Millett, Kate, 28
Mills, C. Wright, 21
Mink, Louis O., 10, 34-35, 91
Mishra, L. N., 206
Moers, Ellen, 13
Moi, Toril, 18, 23
Moody, Christopher, 186
Morpugo, J. E., 110
Morton, Henry W., 186
Mosbacher, Eric, 142
Moser, Charles A., 72
Mosse, W. E., 73
Mott, Lucretia, 79
Mukherjee, Bharati, 220
Mussolini, Benito, 2, 30, 114, 116, 117, 124, 128

Naik, M. K., 141
Nair, Rukmini Bhaya, 200
Najjar, J. Sarkis, 137
Nandy, Ashis, 205, 218
Naritsa, Mikhail, 170
narrative (or story)
    absences in, 26, 55-59
    and competition, 13-15
    and counternarrative, 15, 93, 168
    and forgetting, 8
    and gender, 13, 226
    and history, 11, 153, 231
    and ideology, 10-11
    and knowledge, 7, 9
    and mental disorders, 9
    and metaphor, 208
    and power, 8, 14
    and seduction, 10, 14, 169, 224, 232
    and subversion, 17
    as trigger, 15, 157
    grand, 12, 153, 215
    reductive force of, 11
    untold, 13-14, 51, 58, 90
Nazareth, Peter, 219
Nechkina, M.V., 73
Nelson, Lowry, 27
Nicholas I, Tsar, 43, 52, 53, 54, 65
Niranjan, Shiva, 145
Nixon, Richard, 180
Nye, Russell B., 110

Origo, Iris, 133, 143
Orwell, George, 5, 20, 37, 121

Pampaloni, Geno, 127
Parek, Bhikhu, 199
Parker, Ralph, 185
Parkin, Frank, 21
Pasha, Syed, 200
Passerini, Luisa, 39, 134, 135
Pasternak, Boris, 150, 177
Philaret, Orthodox Metropolitan of Moscow, 54
Pierce, Franklin, 84
Piovene, Guido, 138
Pipes, Daniel, 208, 230
Pisarev, I. G., 164
Piscatori, James, 218, 237
Ponziani, Luigi, 143
Poulantzas, Nicos, 21
Poulet, Georges, 41
power
    and literature, 18-19, 24-33
    concepts of, 20-24, 152

Radek, Karl, 115, 118
Raeff, Marc, 73
Rahman, Mujibur, 206, 207
Rahv, Philip, 152
Rao, Raja, 140, 141, 142
Rawson, Judy, 143
readers
    and nonreaders, 4, 93, 202
    constituencies of, 4, 63, 128, 130-134, 141, 160-62, 166-67
    power of, 21, 29, 166

Index

reading process, 26-30
Rees, Goronwy, 37
Reeve, F. D., 187
Remnick, David, 186
Reshetovskaya, Natalia, 150
Rhodes, James Ford, 77, 80
Rieber, Alfred J., 67
Ripp, Victor, 51, 58, 63
Robertson, Geoffrey, 238
Rothberg, Abraham, 186
Rus, Vladimir J., 185
Rushdie, Salman, 2, 3, 4, 5, 29, 189-241
Russi, Antonio, 144
Russo, Luigi, 129
Ruthven, Malise, 197, 201, 214, 226
Ryabinin, N. I., 163

Said, Edward, 5, 201, 205, 210
Sakharov, Andrei, 173, 176, 178
Salvemini, Gaetano, 117, 120, 121
Sapir, Edward, 12
Sartre, Jean-Paul, 171
Scammell, Michael, 172, 185
Schafer, Roy, 17
Schapiro, Leonard, 43, 51, 55, 185
Schmidt, Carl T., 120, 124, 125
Scholes, Robert, 10
Scott, Dick, 37
Seeley, Frank Friedeberg, 72
Shaftesbury, Earl of, 81
Shahabuddin, Syed, 194, 199
Shelest, Georgi, 186
Sholokhov, Mikhail, 176
Showalter, Elaine, 39
Siegel, Paul N., 187
Silone, Ignazio, 2, 4, 30, 114-145
Simms, Willian Gilmore, 97
Simonov, Konstantin, 158
Sinclair, Upton, 37, 91
Singh, Kushwant, 196
Sinyavsky, Andrei, 167, 171, 175
Skerpan, Alfred A., 73
Slavophiles, 60, 183
Smith, Barbara Herrnstein, 9
Smith, Denis Mack, 144, 145
Soldati, Mario, 129
Solzhenitsyn, Alexander, 2, 20, 29, 31, 35, 37, 91, 146-188
Solzhenitsyn, Ermolai, 183
Spender, Dale, 13, 22
Spiller, Robert E., 19
Spivak, Gayatri C., 190, 221, 231
Srivastava, Ramesh K., 145
Stalin, Joseph, 2, 19, 147, 154, 159, 170
Stanton, Elizabeth Cady, 79
Steinbeck, John, 35, 91
Steiner, George, 39
Stone, Kay F., 39
story (*see* narrative)
Stowe, Calvin, 86
Stowe, Frederick William, 108
Stowe, Harriet Beecher, 1, 2, 4, 5, 19, 75-113, 183
Suleiman, Susan, 41
Suleri, Sara, 222, 231
Sumner, Charles, 77, 88
Suslov, Mikhail, 151
Svetlova, Natalia, 177

Tarsis, Valeri, 173
Teush, Veniamin, 146
Thatcher, Margaret, 4, 206, 207
Thompson, E. P., 13
Thoreau, Henry David, 104
Todorov, Tzvetan, 190, 199, 202, 233
Tolstoy, Lev, 141, 162
Tompkins, Jane P., 82
Traldi, Alberto, 121
Trotsky, Leon, 115, 130
Turgenev, Ivan, 1, 4, 35, 43-74, 90
Tvardovsky, Alexander, 150, 151, 157, 160, 164, 173, 182

Ul-Haq, Zia, 206, 207

Van der Veer, Peter, 217
Varese, Claudio, 132
Venturi, Franco, 74
Vicentini, Marzia Terenzi, 145
Vierek, Peter, 186
Vittorini, Elio, 31
Voronskaya, Elizaveta, 178

Wachter, Oralee, 39
Wagenknecht, Edward, 111
Waletzky, Joshua, 39
Walicki, Andrzey, 73
Walters, Ronald G., 112
Washington, George, 103
Watzlawick, Paul, 27
Weakland, John H., 41
Weber, Max, 21
Weld, Theodore Dwight, 85, 92
Weldon, Fay, 37
Westernizers, 60-61
Whicher, George, 19, 20, 78
White, D. M., 38
White, Hayden, 9, 11, 13
Whorf, B. L., 12
Wiecek, William M., 112
Willetts, Harry, 185
Williams, Raymond, 99
Wilson, Edmund, 111, 113
Wimsatt, W. K., 193, 195
Wolff, Janet, 40
Wood, Michael, 200
Woodcock, George, 122
Wright, Theodore P., 201
Wyatt-Brown, Bertram, 105

Yarborough, Richard, 78
Yarmolinsky, Avrahm, 43
Yellin, Jean Fagan, 111
Yevtushenko, Yevgeni, 154
Young, J., 38

Zakharova, A. F., 166
Zhukovsky, Vassily, 53, 54
Zilberberg, Ilya, 184.
Zipes, Jack, 145
Zola, Émile, 25